Teaching and Researching Listening

Michael Rost

Longman

An imprint of **Pearson Education**

Harlow, England · London · New York · Reading, Massachusetts · San Francisco
Toronto · Don Mills, Ontario · Sydney · Tokyo · Singapore · Hong Kong · Seoul
Taipei · Cape Town · Madrid · Mexico City · Amsterdam · Munich · Paris · Milan

Pearson Education Limited
Edinburgh Gate
Harlow
Essex CM20 2JE,
England

and Associated Companies throughout the world

Visit us on the World Wide Web at:
www.pearsoned.co.uk

First published in Great Britain in 2002

© Pearson Education, 2002

The right of Michael Rost to be identified as Author
of this Work has been asserted by him in accordance
with the Copyright, Designs and Patents Act 1988.

ISBN 0 582 36930 4

British Library Cataloguing in Publication Data
A CIP catalogue record for this book can be obtained from the British Library

10 9 8 7 6 5 4 3 2
07   06   05   04

Set in 10.5/12pt Janson by Graphicraft Limited, Hong Kong
Printed in Malaysia, LSP

The Publishers' policy is to use paper manufactured from sustainable forests.

Teaching and Researching Listening

APPLIED LINGUISTICS IN ACTION

General Editors:

Christopher N. Candlin and David R. Hall

Books published in this series include:

Contents

General Editors' Preface

Applied Linguistics in Action, as its name suggests, is a Series which focuses on the issues and challenges to practitioners and researchers in a range of fields in Applied Linguistics and provides readers and users with the tools they need to carry out their own practice-related research.

The books in the Series provide readers with clear, up-to-date, accessible and authoritative accounts of their chosen field within Applied Linguistics. Using the metaphor of a map of the landscape of the field, each book provides information on its main ideas and concepts, its scope, its competing issues, solved and unsolved questions. Armed with this authoritative but critical account, readers can explore for themselves a range of exemplary practical applications of research into these issues and questions, before taking up the challenge of undertaking their own research, guided by the detailed and explicit research guides provided. Finally, each book has a section which is concurrently on the Series *web site* www.booksites.net/alia and which provides a rich array of chosen resources, information sources, further reading and commentary, as well as a key to the principal concepts of the field.

Questions that the books in this innovative Series ask are those familiar to all practitioners and researchers, whether very experienced, or new to the fields of Applied Linguistics.

- What does research tell us, what doesn't it tell us, and what should it tell us about the field? What is its geography? How is the field mapped and landscaped?
- How has research been carried out and applied and what interesting research possibilities does practice raise? What are the issues we need to explore and explain?
- What are the key researchable topics that practitioners can undertake? How can the research be turned into practical action?

- Where are the important resources that practitioners and researchers need? Who has the information? How can it be accessed?

Each book in the Series has been carefully designed to be as accessible as possible, with built-in features to enable readers to find what they want quickly and to home in on the key issues and themes that concern them. The structure is to move from practice to theory and research, and back to practice, in a cycle of development of understanding of the field in question. Books in the Series will be usable for the individual reader but also can serve as a basis for course design, or seminar discussion.

Each of the authors of books in the Series is an acknowledged authority, able to bring broad knowledge and experience to engage practitioners and researchers in following up their own ideas, working with them to build further on their own experience.

Applied Linguistics in Action is an **in action** Series. Its *web site* will keep you updated and regularly re-informed about the topics, fields and themes in which you are involved.

We hope that you will like and find useful the design, the content, and, above all, the support the books will give to your own practice and research!

Christopher N. Candlin & David R. Hall
General Editors

A Companion Web Site accompanies
Teaching and Researching Listening
by Michael Rost

Visit the *Teaching and Researching Motivation* Companion Web Site at www.booksites.net/Rost to find valuable teaching and learning material including:

www.booksites.net

- Links to valuable resources on the web
- Useful sources and resources relating to the study of Listening
- Search for specific information on the site

Acknowledgements

Due to the inclusive and ever-expanding nature of this project on listening, I have had the good fortune of reviewing the work of a range of researchers, language specialists and teachers. Through correspondence, interviews, conferences and reading, I have come in contact with many individuals who have made lasting contributions in areas that are relevant to this project. Without their willingness to share their ideas, this present volume would not be possible. In particular, I wish to thank: Susan Braidi, Gillian Brown, Gary Buck, Anne Cutler, Patricia Carpenter, Karen Carrier, Wallace Chafe, Craig Chaudron, Rod Ellis, John Flowerdew, Stephen Handel, Jonathan Harrington, Greg Kearsley, Walter Kintsch, Tony Lynch, Dominic Massaro, Lindsay Miller, David Nunan, Teresa Pica, Jill Robbins, Larry Vandergrift, Jef Verschueren. Although I have tried to do justice to their work in integrating, paraphrasing and synthesising selected portions of it, I accept responsibility for any oversimplifications or omissions.

I would like to thank my research assistants, Julie Winter and Ruth Desmond, for their high-spirited work at checking out references and sources. I also wish to thank the TESOL students at Temple University and University of California, Berkeley, and particularly Sakae Onoda and Sarah Jung, for their reviews of the teaching applications and research projects.

I especially wish to thank Chris Candlin, series editor and personal guru, for inviting me to undertake this project, for providing me with access to his broad knowledge of applied linguistic realms, and for patiently guiding me through the maze of developing this work.

I would also like to thank David Hall, the series co-editor, and the staff at Pearson Education, particularly Liz Mann, Casey Mein, Emily Pillars, Jacqueline Cassidy and Margaret Wallis, for shepherding this book through development and production.

Preface

Teaching and researching listening is designed to be a reference source and collaborative guide for teachers and researchers who have an interest in the role of listening in language education and other applied linguistics areas. In keeping with the intentions of the **Applied Linguistics in Action** Series, *Teaching and researching listening* outlines issues of ongoing relevance to teachers and researchers of both first and second languages and suggests concepts and principles, approaches and resources for exploring these issues.

Readers may use the book as a selective reference, using only those sections that may help clarify their current teaching or research goals. Or because of the wide range of issues introduced, the book may be used as an exploratory text that may impact the reader's work and interests in a broader sense and provide useful points of departure for further exploration.

A chief function of this title, and this series, is to provide an interactive means of revising and updating the content. Readers are encouraged to contact the author or publisher via www.booksites.net/rost to be informed of updates and commentary and to help maintain the currency of this volume.

Introduction: Interests, beliefs and metaphors

In my research of listening over the past several years, I have looked for definitions of listening in various fields, and have tried to see how these definitions have changed over time.

Not surprisingly, academics in the social sciences have defined listening in terms of their theoretical interests in the topic. In the early 1900s, when acoustic phonetics was seen as a major breakthrough in communications research, due to developments in recording technology, listening was defined in terms of reliably recording acoustic signals in the brain. In the 1920s and 1930s with advancing knowledge of the human brain, listening was defined as a largely unconscious process controlled by hidden cultural 'schemata'. In the 1940s, when advances in telecommunications were exploding, and information-processing was seen as the new scientific frontier, listening was defined in terms of successful transmission and recreation of 'messages'. In the 1950s when computer science began to dominate, listening was defined in terms of analysing and tagging input so that it could be stored and retrieved efficiently. In the 1960s, with the rise of transpersonal psychology, listening included heuristics for understanding the intent of the speaker. With the renewed interest in anthropology in the 1970s, definitions of listening as interpreting the cultural significance of 'speech behaviour' gained acceptance. In the 1980s and 1990s, with advances in computer software for dealing with vast quantities and types of data, listening came to be defined as parallel processing of input. There is no way around it: we tend to define things in terms of our current interests and beliefs. Particularly when we are defining a psychological construct such as listening, we tend to focus on those aspects of it that are most consistent with our way of looking at the world.

Over the past several years, I have also asked many individuals – applied linguists, psychologists, language teachers, language students – the same question: 'What is listening?' After hundreds of responses, I started to see different patterns. Because listening is an invisible mental process, we tend to use indirect analogies and metaphors to describe it. A common metaphor from language students is in terms of 'getting something': 'listening means "catching what the speaker says"'. Among applied linguists, there is the familiar 'shopping' allusion: 'negotiating meaning' is a frequent response. Anthropologists sometimes answer with 'tactic' metaphors: 'reframing a message in relevant terms'. Psychologists occasionally answer with 'sensitivity' imagery: 'being open to what is in the speaker'.

While virtually every definition I have heard has some unique aspect, personal definitions of listening typically draw upon one of four orientations or perspectives: receptive, constructive, collaborative, or transformative.

Orientation 1: Receptive

Listening = receiving what the speaker actually says.

- Listening means catching what the speaker has said.
- Listening means getting the speaker's idea.
- Listening means decoding the speaker's message.
- Listening means unpacking the speaker's content.
- Listening is receiving the transfer of images, impressions, thoughts, beliefs, attitudes and emotions from the speaker.

Orientation 2: Constructive

Listening = constructing and representing meaning.

- Listening means figuring out what is in the speaker's mind.
- Listening means finding something interesting in what the speaker is saying.
- Listening means finding out what is relevant for you.
- Listening means reframing the speaker's message in a way that's relevant to you.
- Listening means understanding why the speaker is talking to you.
- Listening means noticing what is not said.

Orientation 3: Collaborative

Listening = negotiating meaning with the speaker and responding.

- Listening is coordination with the speaker on the choice of a code and a context.
- Listening means responding to what the speaker has said.

- Listening is the process of negotiating shared information or values with the speaker.
- Listening means acting interested while the speaker is talking.
- Listening is signalling to the speaker which ideas are clear and acceptable to you.

Orientation 4: Transformative

Listening = creating meaning through involvement, imagination and empathy.

- Listening is involvement with the speaker, without judgement.
- Listening is creating a connection between the speaker and the listener.
- Listening is empathising with the speaker's motivation for speaking.
- Listening is imagining a possible world for the speaker's meaning.
- Listening is the process of creating meaning in the speaker.
- Listening is the completion of communication.
- Listening is feeling the flow of consciousness as you pay attention to things.
- Listening is the process of altering the cognitive environment of both the speaker and the listener.

Many people, in turn, have asked me my definition. The briefest and broadest definition I can think of is: listening = experiencing contextual effects. But this definition is not much better than any of the others. It merely defines listening as a neurological event (experiencing) overlaying a cognitive event (creating a change in a representation).

The purpose of this book is not to come up with the 'right' definition of listening, nor the single best way of teaching it, nor the most appropriate way to research it. One purpose, however, is to exhort the reader to consider each of these four perspectives – receptive, constructive, collaborative, transformative – in any teaching or researching endeavour. *All* of these perspectives contribute *fundamentally* to what listening is. Any sound instructional approach or research approach needs to account for all of these perspectives.

A key concern of many readers will be: What is the difference between first-language (L1) listening and second-language (L2) listening? The short answer is that there are *many* more similarities than differences, and that these similarities need to be fully appreciated before the differences are considered. The differences, however, are crucial and involve neurological, psycholinguistic, developmental and pragmatic processes, which are explored in the initial section of this book. Both the similarities and the differences must be taken into account in arriving at an appropriate approach to teaching and researching L2 listening, and these considerations are explored in detail in later sections.

The purpose of this book is to motivate informed teaching and research in listening, in either L1 or L2, by providing background concepts, reviewing teaching methodologies and tasks, reviewing exemplary research and introducing resources for researchers and teachers.

Organisation of *Teaching and researching listening*

Section I: Defining listening, introduces the conceptual background of listening, by highlighting a number of notions relevant to the teaching and researching of listening. **Section II: Teaching listening**, reviews principles of instructional design and methods of teaching listening, highlighting key features of various approaches and suggesting solutions to various pedagogic issues. **Section III: Researching listening**, provides a selective set of research areas involving listening that can be undertaken by teachers in the context of their own teaching, and provides action research frameworks for investigating these areas. **Section IV: Exploring listening**, provides a range of resources that can be used in pursuing questions related to defining, teaching and researching listening. Readers can use this book in a number of ways. The book has been partitioned into sections with particular orientations and chapters with particular content focuses. There is intentionally considerable overlap between the issues outlined in each section, so that readers will encounter the main concepts outlined in any of the three main sections of the book.

1 Defining listening

Chapter 1

Neurological processes

Listening is a process involving a continuum of active processes, which are under the control of the listener, and passive processes, which are not. Section I outlines concepts from psychology, linguistics, psycholinguistics, pragmatics, and education, that are relevant to understanding this complex process.

This chapter...

- differentiates 'hearing' from 'listening' and describes in detail the processes involved in 'audition';
- defines the properties of consciousness that are involved in listening;
- describes attention as the initiation of 'involvement'.

1.1   Hearing

A suitable starting point for an exploration of listening in language teaching and research is to consider the physical and cognitive systems and processes that are involved.

Hearing is the primary physiological system that allows for reception and conversion of sound waves that surround the listener. These converted electrical pulses are transmitted through the **inner ear** to the **auditory cortex** of the brain.

But beyond this passive conversion process, hearing is the sense that is often identified with our experience of participating in events. Hearing, unlike our other senses, has unique observational and monitoring characteristics that can be equated with perception of life's rhythms, with the 'real time' tempo of human interaction, and with the 'feel' of human contact and communication.

Hearing also plays an important role in animating the brain, what Tomatis (1991) calls 'cortical recharging', a kind of refuelling of the dynamism of the brain. In physiological terms, hearing is part of the vestibular system of the brain, which is responsible for both spatial orientation (balance), temporal orientation (timing), as well as what J. H. Austin (1998) calls 'interoception', the monitoring of sensate data for our internal bodily systems.

Of all our senses, hearing may be said to be the most 'grounded' because it occurs 'in real time', in a temporal continuum. Sound perception involves continually organising incoming sound into 'auditory events' which span a period of several seconds (Handel, 1993). Sound perception is always anticipating – 'hearing forward' – as well as retrospecting – 'hearing backward'.

How then is 'hearing' different from 'listening'? The terms **hearing** and **listening** are often used interchangeably, but there are important differences between them. Although both hearing and listening involve sound perception, the difference in terms reflects a *degree of intention*.

We often consider the active, intentional processes that we term 'listening' to begin after the electrical pulses of sound reach the auditory cortex of the brain. Because the processes of listening are inaccessible to objective measurements or descriptions, we necessarily use more subjective definitions and metaphors to describe them.

Hearing is a form of perception. Perception refers to the actual contact between 'distal objects' (objects that exist independently) and the perceiver. All objects in the world exist at some 'remove' from the perceiver and impart a pattern to an energy field. This energy field is what mediates the contact between the 'perceiver' and the 'perceived'. Our senses then transport the effects of the energy field.

In psychological terms, perception creates knowledge of these distal objects by detecting and differentiating properties in the energy field. In the case of audition, the energy field is the air surrounding the listener. The perceiver detects movements in the air, in the form of sound waves, and differentiates their patterns. The perceiver designates the patterns in the sound waves to various categories, which is the first stage of assigning some meaning to the sound (cf. Handel, 1993).

The human auditory system consists of the outer ear, the middle ear, the inner ear, and the auditory nerves connecting to the brain stem. The auditory system consists of several interdependent subsystems.

The outer ear consists of the pinna (this is the part of the ear we can see) and the auditory canal. The pinna modifies the incoming sound, in particular the higher frequencies, and allows us the ability to locate the source of the sound.

Sound waves travel down the canal and cause the eardrum to vibrate. The vibrations are passed along through the middle ear, which is a remarkable

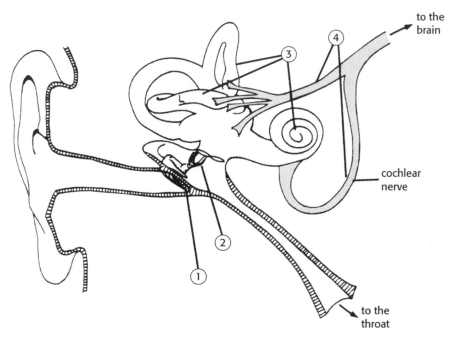

to the
brain

cochlear
nerve

to the
throat

The human auditory system is a series of stages for converting sound to neural stimuli. Hearing occurs when: (1) sound vibrations reach the eardrum; (2) causing the ossicles to vibrate and the stapes to move; (3) the vibrations pass through the oval window to the fluid-filled canals of the cochlea; and (4) are transmitted to the cochlear duct where they set off nerve impulses which are sent along the cochlear nerve to the brain.

Figure 1.1 The human auditory system (Gardner, 1990)

transformer consisting of three small bones (the ossicles) surrounding a small opening in the skull (the oval window). The major function of the middle ear is to ensure efficient transfer of sounds (which are in the form of air particles) to the fluids inside the cochlea.

In addition to this transmission function, the middle ear also has a protective function. The ossicles have tiny muscles which can contract (this is called the reflex action) to reduce the level of sound that will reach to the inner ear. This reflex action occurs when we are presented with loud sounds such as the roar of an airplane engine. This protects the delicate hearing mechanism from damage. Interestingly, the reflex action also occurs when we begin to speak. In this way the reflex protects us from too much feedback – it prevents us from hearing too much of our own speech and thus becoming distracted by it.

The cochlea is the most important part of the ear in terms of auditory perception. The cochlea is a small bony structure, about the size of your thumbnail, which is narrow at one end and wide at the other. It is filled with fluid. The membranes inside in the cochlea respond mechanically to movements of the fluid (this is called sinusoidal stimulation). Lower frequency sounds stimulate primarily the narrower end of the membrane and higher frequencies stimulate only the broader end. Each different sound, however, produces varying patterns of movement in the fluid and the membrane.

At the side of the cochlea nearest the brain stem are thousands of tiny hair cells, with ends both inside and outside the cochlea. The outer hair cells are connected to the auditory nerve fibres which lead to the auditory cortex of the brain. These hair cells respond to minute movements of the fluid in the membrane, and transduce the mechanical movements of the fluid into nerve (neural) activity.

As with other neural networks in the human body, these nerves have evolved to a high degree of specialisation. Different auditory nerve fibres have different characteristic frequencies (CF) that they respond to. Fibres with high CFs are found in the periphery of the nerve bundle and there is an orderly decrease in CF toward the center of the nerve bundle (this is called tonotopic organisation).

The distribution of the neural activity (as a function of CF) is called the excitation pattern, and this excitation pattern is the fundamental 'result' or 'output' of the human hearing mechanism. For instance, if you hear the word, ''bye', there is a specific excitation pattern produced in response.

Key concept: Audition takes place through excitation patterns

Excitation patterns in the **inner ear** and **auditory nerve** become automated through experience with familiar stimuli.

Not everyone hears the same thing, however, even though the excitation pattern for a particular stimulus will be similar in all of us. The difference in our perception is due to the fact that the individual neurones that make up the nerve fibres are interactive – they are affected by the action of other neurones. Sometimes, the activity of one neurone is suppressed or amplified by the presence of a second tone. In addition, since these nerves are physical structures, they are affected by our general health and level of arousal or fatigue. Another fact that interferes with accurate hearing is that these nerves sometimes seem to fire involuntarily, even when no hearing stimulus is present. This is due to the fact that the auditory nerve is intertwined with the vestibular nerve, which helps us keep our balance. Activation of the vestibular nerve will affect our hearing as well.

1.2 Consciousness

Key concept: Consciousness has specific properties that influence listening

Consciousness is the aspect of mind that has a 'self-centred' point of view and orientation to the environment.

Consciousness is the most fundamental concept when we consider listening to be an active process. We may think of ordinary consciousness as unfolding when two cognitive procedures intersect: (1) The brain encodes an outside object or event as consisting of independent properties; and (2) The brain sets up the listener as the central agent who experiences this object or event. Consciousness is the phenomenon of experiencing this integration.

Consciousness involves the **activation** of portions of the listener's model of the surrounding world: a model which is necessarily self-centred. The portions of this model that are activated which are involved in understanding the current encounter. Viewed technically, this active portion of

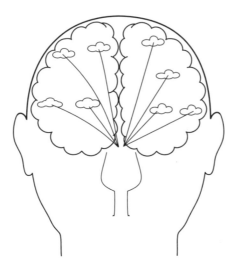

Activation of consciousness is physically represented by simultaneous neural activation of different parts of the cerebral cortex as a result of perceptual contact with an event. Activation of consciousness at any time represents only a small subset of the listener's model of the world. (This activation is apparently coordinated by the anterior cingulate cortex in the front part of the brain.)

Figure 1.2 **Activation of consciousness**

Concept 1.1   The properties of consciousness

- Consciousness is *embedded* in a surrounding area of peripheral consciousness. The active focus is surrounded by a periphery of semi-active information that provides a context for it.

- Consciousness is *dynamic*. The focus of consciousness moves constantly from one focus or item of information to the next. This movement is experienced by the listener as continuous, rather than a discrete series of 'snapshots'. (Chafe 1994 characterises this continuous movement from one focus to the next as 'flow'.)

- Consciousness has a *point of view*. One's model of the world is necessarily centred on a self. The location and needs of that self establish a point of view that is a constant ingredient of consciousness.

- Consciousness has a need for *orientation*. Peripheral consciousness must include information regarding the person's location in space, time, society and ongoing activity. This orientation allows consciousness to shift from an **immediate mode**, in which the person is attending to present references, to a **distal mode**, in which the person is attending to non-present, abstract, or imaginary references and concepts.

- Consciousness can *focus* on only one thing at a time. The limited capacity of consciousness is reflected linguistically – for both a speaker and a listener – in brief spurts of language, called 'intonation units'.

(Adapted from Chafe, 1994: 28ff.)

---

the model is constructed from perceptual contact with and subjective reactions to the external event.

Because consciousness directs the individual's attention to the external world and the individual's intentions to experience that world, we cannot discuss listening without referring to consciousness.

1.3   Attention

Attention is the focusing of consciousness on an 'object' or 'train of thought'. Attention can be directed either externally or internally. Attention is thus the beginning of **involvement**, which is the essential differentiation between simply hearing and listening. Psychologists often refer to the intuitive definition given by William James, considered the founder of modern experimental psychology.

Attention is seen as a timed process requiring three neurological elements: arousal, orientation and focus. Arousal begins with the Reticular

> **Quote 1.1**   William James on 'attention'
>
> Every one knows what attention is. It is the taking possession of the mind, in clear and vivid form, of one out of what seem several simultaneously possible objects or trains of thought. *Focalisation and concentration of consciousness* are of its essences. It implies withdrawal from some things in order to deal effectively with others.
>
> James (1890: 405)

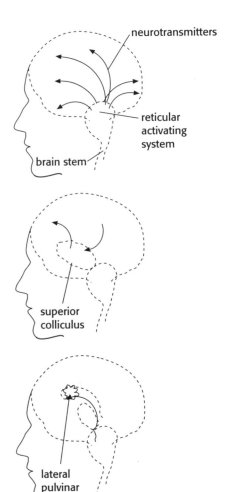

Stage 1
Arousal: Neurotransmitters fire throughout the brain, activating brain chemical, (dopamine, noradrenaline) and creating oscillations of electrical activity

Stage 2
Orientation: The superior colliculus regulates the process of disengaging neurotransmitters from the previous stimulus and sending increased neurotransmitters to the new stimulus.

Stage 3
Focus: The lateral pulvinar (part of the brain that experiences 'consciousness') locks neurotransmissions on to parts of the cerebral cortex needed to process the stimulus.

Figure 1.3   **Three elements of attention**

Activating System (RAS) in the brainstem becoming activated. When this happens, the RAS releases a flood of neurotransmitters to fire neurons throughout the brain. Orientation is a neural organising process performed near the brain stem (actually, the superior colliculus part of the brain above the brain stem). This process engages the brain pathways that are most likely to be involved in understanding and responding to the perceived object (i.e. the external event or the internal 'train of thought'). Focus is achieved in the higher cortex of the brain (the lateral pulvinar section). This process selectively locks onto the brain pathways to the frontal lobe of the brain involved in processing the incoming stimulus, thus allowing for more efficient use of energy (Carter, 1998).

Two notions are central to understanding how attention influences listening: limited capacity and selective attention (or 'choice of focus').

Quote 1.2 Attention and constraints

Attention has been used to refer to all those aspects of human cognition that the subject can control...and to all aspects of cognition having to do with limited resources or capacity, and the methods of dealing with such constraints.

Shiffrin (1988: 739)

Quote 1.3 Schmidt on attention

- Attention is a **limited capacity system**.
- Automatic activities which require little or no attention do not interfere with each other.
- **Controlled processes** require attention and interfere with other control processes.
- Attention can be viewed as three separate but interrelated networks: **alertness, orientation**, and **detection**.
  1. Alertness represents a general readiness to deal with incoming stimuli.
  2. Orientation refers to a specific aligning of attention.
  3. Detection is the cognitive registration of sensory stimuli.
- Detected information is available for other cognitive processing.

Schmidt (1995: 20–21)

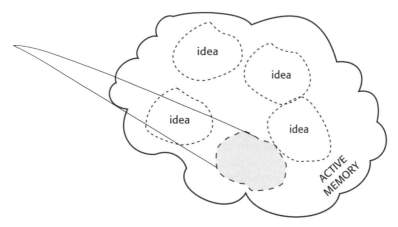

Selective attention is the process of focusing processing resources (electrical activity in the brain) onto one idea, and allowing the processing of other ideas or thoughts to terminate.

Figure 1.4   **Selective attention**

The notion of limited capacity is important in listening. Essentially, consciousness can deal with only one source of information at a time, although we can readily switch back and forth between different sources. When multiple sources, or streams, of information are present, **selective attention** must be utilised. 'Selective attention' involves a commitment of our limited capacity process to one stream of information or train of thought.

Concept 1.2   **Dichotic listening**

Among the best known experimental studies dealing with selective attention are **dichotic listening** studies in which subjects are presented with different messages through left and right earphones. When told to attend to one message only or shadow it, subjects can readily comply, switching attention to the second message. However, subjects can shift attention only at pauses in the attended message, which suggests that we can shift our attention only at suitable 'processing breaks' in the input.

Just as importantly, results from these studies also show that attention is needed not only for monitoring input, but also for effective storage and retrieval of a message. A consistent finding in these experiments is that only information in the attended channel (i.e. the ear with the attended input) can be remembered.

An everyday example of this is the 'cocktail party effect'. In a cocktail party environment, numerous streams of conversation are taking place, yet you can attend to only one at a time. It is possible to focus on a conversation taking place across the room, while ignoring a conversation that is closer and louder. Attention is directional and under the control of the listener, within certain constraints.

Although attention can usually be controlled, shifts in attention are not always voluntary. For example, while we are watching TV, our baby starting to cry takes over the attention system momentarily whether we want it to or not. Instinctively, we respond to what is perceived to be most relevant to our needs. Beyond obvious examples of overt emergency signals (such as a baby's crying signalling a need for us to take care of it) taking over our previous attentional focus (such as watching the news), our needs are complex and subtle and may be prioritised in ways that are not fully conscious to us, and will thus lead us to respond to more subtle distractions when we are listening.

Key concept: Attention

- The limitations of attention and short-term memory necessitate the use of selective attention in order to listen to speech.

Chapter 2

Linguistic processing

This chapter...

- outlines the phonological procedures for how we perceive speech;
- explains why word recognition is the central process in linguistic processing and outlines some common research techniques and explanatory models;
- outlines the kind of phonotactic rules that a listener must acquire;
- explains the process of parsing or 'applying grammatical rules' while listening;
- describes the basic unit of speech processing, the 'pause unit' and shows how it helps the listener 'manage' incoming speech;
- shows how prosodic features assist the listener in understanding speech;
- outlines the non-verbal cues available to the listener.

2.1 Perceiving speech

The fundamental goal of perception is to categorise input in ways that help the perceiver make sense of it.

In the case of speech perception, the task of assigning categories to the sound waves is achieved in three complementary ways. The first way is the experience of **articulatory causes** for the sounds that strike the ear. For language, the perceptual objects are the effects of particular vocal configurations in the speaker (the lip, tongue and vocal tract movements that cause the proximal stimulation in the ear). The second way is through

psychoacoustic effects. The perceptual objects are identified as auditory qualities (the frequency, timbre and duration of sounds that reach the ear). The third way is the listener's perceiving the speaker's **linguistic intentions**. The perceived sounds are drawn from a matrix of **contrasts** at one or more levels of a language (phonemic, morphological, lexical). The listener's knowledge of the articulatory causes of sounds, the psychoacoustic effects of sounds, and the likely linguistic intentions of a speaker all influence speech perception.

Concept 2.1   **Complementary sources in speech perception**

Four **psychoacoustic elements** are available to the listener in the speech signal. By identifying the unique combinations of these elements, the listener differentiates sounds.

Frequency, measured in hertz (Hz). Humans can hear sounds from 20 to 20,000 Hz, but human languages typically evoke sounds in the 100–3,000 Hz range. Detecting the movements in the fundamental frequency of sound is an important element in speech perception.

Tone, measured in sine wave forms. Every configuration of the vocal tract produces its own set of characteristics, which are represented as sound-pressure variations and mapped as sine waves. Further, each sound will have a simultaneous set of overtones or harmonic tones or frequencies, above the fundamental frequency. The relation of the fundamental frequency to the overtone frequencies (i.e. the 'sound formants') assists the hearer in identifying particular speakers.

Duration, measured in milliseconds (ms). Languages differ in the average sound of a syllable; for instance, in American English, syllables average about 75 ms; in French, syllables average about 50 ms. However, differences in duration between sounds and syllables in any language vary widely. Duration is an important feature in speech perception.

Intensity, measured in decibels (dB). Whispered language at one metre is about 20 dB, while normal speech at one metre is about 60 dB. However, there is a normal fluctuation of up to 30 dB in a single utterance of any speaker in a typical conversation. Intensity is particularly important for detecting prominences in an utterance (i.e. what the speaker considers focal information).

Key concept: Perception

Humans perceive speech through sampling of frequency, duration and amplitude of the speech signal. The redundant nature of the speech signal allows for selective sampling.

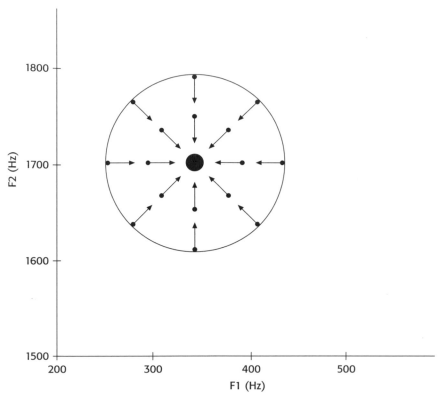

A native listener recognises sound variations according to a prototype for each phoneme. This is called 'the perceptual magnet effect'. The illustration shows the prototype for the sound /i/ (F1 = 350 Hz; F2 = 1700 Hz). Sounds within a small physical range (e.g. 100 Hz) of the target or prototype are recognised as that phoneme. Sounds too far from the prototype are not recognisable. This phenomenon allows for comprehension of individual and dialect variation.

Figure 2.1   Perception of sound

Whenever we create a speech sound, we simultaneously create that sound in several harmonic ranges. The ratio between the frequencies in these harmonic ranges vitally affects our differentiation of the sound from other similar sounds. In other words, each individual phoneme of a language has a unique identity in terms of frequency ratios between the fundamental frequency of a sound (f_0) and the frequency of the sound in other harmonic ranges (f_1, f_2, f_3). This is called the 'perceptual goodness' of the sound (Kuhl, 1991). When we learn to articulate the sounds of a language, we learn to manipulate these frequencies, without any conscious attention to them. Although there is an ideal prototype for each phoneme of a language, there is of course also an acceptable range of ratios between frequencies, that is, sound variations, within a given phoneme that allows us to recognise it.

2.2 Recognising words

Recognising words in fluent speech is the basis of spoken-language comprehension. The two main tasks of the listener in word recognition are identification of words and activating knowledge of word meanings.

Identification of words is a complex process. As Cutler (1997) notes, in listening to continuous speech, there is no direct auditory equivalent to the white spaces in reading continuous text. Because there are no reliable cues marking every word boundary, word recognition is often the most problematic process in listening. Further, if a listener 'recognises' a word but has limited or no knowledge of its basic meaning, the entire process of word recognition is subverted, and the listener must resort to compensatory strategies for understanding. Misunderstanding or non-understanding of words in speech, whether through faulty identification of word boundaries or inadequate knowledge of word meanings, is the major source of confusion in language comprehension, particularly second-language comprehension.

Assuming that a listener possesses adequate knowledge of the lexis of the language spoken, there are several simultaneous processes involved in the way words are recognised:

1. Words are recognised through the interaction of perceived sound and knowledge of the likelihood of a word being uttered in a given context.
2. Speech is processed primarily in a sequential fashion, word by word. Recognition of a word achieves two goals:
   - it locates the onset of the immediately following word
   - it provides syntactic and semantic constraints that are used to recognise the immediately following word (in other words, it allows for 'proactive processing').
3. Words are accessed by various clues
   - the sounds that begin the word
   - lexical stress
4. Speech is processed in part retrospectively, by the listener holding unrecognised words in a '**phonological loop**' of a few seconds duration (Baddeley, 1986) while subsequent cues are being processed.
5. A word is recognised when the analysis of its acoustic structure eliminates all candidates but one – in other words, when the listener identifies the most likely or most relevant candidate.

It is important to note that each individual process may produce imperfect or erroneous recognition of all of the words in an utterance. Fortunately, spoken language comprehension can usually continue successfully even if all words are not recognised because the listener can make inferences about the meaning of an utterance through other sources of information.

Concept 2.2   **Segmentation and variation**

Any model of word recognition needs to account for two characteristics of fluent speech: segmentation and variation.

Segmentation refers to the problem of locating word boundaries in a continuous signal in which physical cues are rarely present.

  Each language has preferred strategies for locating word boundaries. In English, the preferred **lexical segmentation strategy** is identifying stressed syllables and organising word identification around those stressed syllables. Since 90 per cent of all content words in English have stress on the first syllable (many are monosyllabic, of course), and since non-content words are generally not stressed, the listener can use stress as an indicator of the start of a new word (Cutler and Butterfield, 1992; Sajavaara, 1986).

Variation refers to the problem of recognising words that are characterised by 'sloppy' articulation, so that words must often be recognised from partial acoustic information.

  Proficient listeners hold **prototypes** of particular sounds in a language in memory, though they seldom expect to hear a pure prototype in actual speech. Rather the prototype serves as a basis from which **allophonic variations** can be interpreted.

Because a normal speaking rate has about eight words per every two- to three-second burst of speech, word recognition must occur very quickly in speech comprehension. To achieve this speed with efficiency, it is accepted that there are multiple sources of information supporting word recognition. The listener integrates all these sources, in a probabilistic fashion, in order to recognise words. Several models of how recognition takes place are summarised here.

'Logogen' model

Morton (1969) proposed that each word that an individual knows has a neural representation in long-term memory. To describe this representation, Morton uses the term 'logogen' (*logos* – word + *genes* – born). Each logogen has a 'resting level' of activity, a level which can be increased by contextual information in the input. When a logogen reaches a 'threshold', it 'fires', and the word is 'recognised'. The threshold is a function of word frequency: more frequent words have a lower threshold for recognition. The time to recognise a word like 'speech' is dependent on its frequency of occurrence in the individual's lexicon. One complicating factor in this theory of word recognition is the existence of 'competitors'. For example, a word like 'speech' has 'competitors', words with similar phonological forms, such as 'speed' and 'species' and 'peach'. The threshold level for word recognition must not be reached until the competitors have been overruled by either phonological evidence or contextual evidence or both.

Cohort model

Marslen-Wilson (1984) proposed that word recognition basically proceeds in sequential fashion, phoneme by phoneme. Each phoneme in a word is recognised categorically, that is, as a representative of a prototype phonological category (/b/ vs. /p/ vs. /f/ etc.). Each phoneme in a string is analysed only until it is identified as a member of a category. Recognition of the first phoneme in a word eliminates all candidate words that do not have that initial phoneme; recognition of the second phoneme eliminates further candidates in the initial 'cohort', and so on. Recognition of phonemes and the elimination of alternative candidate words in the cohort continues in this fashion until the word is recognised. Proponents of this theory claim that this recognition process happens in a very rapid – almost instantaneous – fashion in any listener who has acquired the phonological and lexical system of the language being spoken.

TRACE model

McClelland and Elman (1986) proposed that three levels of information are used in word recognition: phonetic feature, phoneme and word. Features (such as the voicing of a /b/ or /v/) activate all phonemes that contain these features, which in turn activate words in the mental lexicon. An important feature of this kind of interactive activation model is that higher-order units also activate lower-order units. According to the TRACE model, word recognition takes place in successive 'time slices'. Processing of the input goes through a number of cycles in which all of the levels update their respective activations at the same time, in an interactive fashion.

Fuzzy logic model

Massaro (1994) proposed that word recognition proceeds through three perceptual operations: feature evaluation, feature integration and decision. Incoming speech features are continuously evaluated, integrated and matched against prototype descriptions in memory. An identification decision is made on the basis of a goodness-of-fit judgment at all levels. With a fuzzy logic model, the most informative feature in the input is always the one that has the greatest impact on the decision phase. For example, if the listener clearly hears 'veer' but the context is about 'things to drink' and the syntactic phrase was 'bring me a veer', the semantic and syntactic features of the input will outweigh the phonological features of the input, and the listener will decide that the word 'beer' was uttered.

These four models share common features of activation and decision-making, and all attempt to account for the typical speed and efficiency that occurs in word recognition in speech, at least among native speakers of a language.

Concept 2.3   Research techniques for word recognition

Research on word recognition in speech has employed these basic techniques.

Detecting mispronunciations

Abstracting meaning is a function of combining perceptual and contextual information. Tasks requiring listeners to detect mispronunciations can gauge the relative importance of each factor. For example, in a study by Cole and Jakimik (1978) subjects were asked to identify mispronunciations in the following sentence:

He sat reading a *book/bill* until it was time to go home.

Mispronouncing the /b/ as /v/ was detected much faster for 'book' (a more expected word) than for 'bill' (a less expected word). The conclusion is that the quickest way to detect a mispronunciation is to first determine what the intended word is and then notice a mismatch with what has been said.

Gating tasks

Language perception involves quickly processing incremental additions of input. Gating tasks eliminate – or 'gate out' – portions of spoken messages to model how these incremental perceptual decisions are made. Successive presentations involve longer and longer portions of the words by increasing the duration of the input by fractions of a second. Subjects attempt to name the word after each successive presentation.

Probability of the correct recognition of the test word increases as additional 'word information' is presented in the gating task, although most subjects do not require more than half the word before recognising it. For example, a subject may identify the word 'spring' after the gated presentation of /sprI/. This is due in part to the fact that phonetic information of the last part of the word is contained in the way the first part of the word is articulated. In addition, studies have shown that gated words presented in sentence contexts are recognised more quickly, that is, with less actual phonetic information. For example, the word 'spring' is likely to be 'recognised' with only /s/ or /sp/ gated in a sentence context such as, 'My favourite season is /sp/ . . .'

Phoneme restoration tasks

Phoneme restoration tasks help researchers understand the relative import-ance of phonemic vs lexical information in the input during perception. In this type of task, a phoneme in a word is removed and replaced by some stimulus, such as a tone. For example, the word 'spring' may be presented as a 'spr[-buzzing sound-]'. Subjects most often have difficulty in identifying where the tone appeared as the lexical context increases. For example, in a presentation of 'Spr[-buzzing sound-] is my favourite season', a subject may report hearing the word 'spring' in full and hearing the 'buzz' following the word 'spring'. This type of experiment can indicate the extent to which 'top–down' information about the context is used during perception (Massaro, 1994).

Word-spotting

Misperceptions of speech in the real world ('slips of the ear') provide evid-ence of how listeners use segmentation strategies to interpret faint speech signals or partially attended speech. For example, if a speaker says 'analogy' and the listener hears 'and allergy', we call this a 'slip of the ear'; in this case, the hearer has inserted a sound. Word-spotting tasks aim to induce such misperceptions of speech by presenting listeners with faint speech, usually at a level (pre-set for each subject) at which only 50 per cent of the words can be correctly identified. Researchers examine the boundary placements and misplacements made by the hearers. With data from multiple subjects, the researchers can postulate the kinds of segmentation strategies that lis-teners use in an attempt to 'spot words' in the input (Cutler and Butterfield, 1992).

Key concept: Word recognition is the central process in listening

Words are recognised essentially in a linear fashion, though context influences speed of recognition and words may be recognised retroactively.

2.3   Employing phonotactic rules

Speech recognition involves knowledge of prototypical sounds and sensitisation to the sound variations of these prototypes, which are brought about through co-articulation processes of assimilation, reduction and elision.

Concept 2.4   **Connected speech patterns**

Many variations can be described in terms of assimilation, reduction and elision:

assimilation	nasalisation, labialisation, palatalisation, glottalisation, voicing, de-voicing, lengthening that results from two sounds being pronounced in sequence
reduction	centring of vowels, weakening of consonants that results from a phoneme being in an unstressed syllable
elision	omission of individual phonemes that results from simplifying a cluster of sounds for easier pronunciation

Read the expressions below aloud, as you would in normal speech. Can you notice how the sounds indicated by the letters in bold are changed from their 'ideal' form?

assimilations

has a ni**ce sh**ape	ni(s) shape
thie**ves st**ole most of them	thie(z)stole
there see**ms t**o be a mistake	see(m)z-to
was qui**te d**ifficult	quite(t)ifficult
it **c**an carry four people	i(c)can
owi**ng t**o our negligence	owin(g)-to
di**dn't y**ou see her	di(d)n(t)-chu
What'**s th**is	wat-s(th)is
who a**sked h**im	as(k)-t(h)im
your hand**b**ag	ham-bag
not that **b**oy	tha(t)poy

reductions and elisions

where **he** lived	where (h)e lived
comfor**t**able chair	comf(or)table
goi**ng to** be here	go(i)n(gt)o be here
I'll pay for it	a(l) pay
given to **the**m	given to (th)em
succeed **in im**agining	succeed in (i)magining
terro**r**ist attack	terr(or)ist attack
in the enviro**n**ment	in the envir(on)ment

2.4 Applying grammatical rules

Speech-processing requires the mapping of incoming speech on to a grammatical model of the language. As with other processes in speech comprehension, because of redundancy in communication, it is not essential that this mapping be complete in order for understanding to occur. Indeed, from a functional perspective, because the listener has limited processing resources, he will attend primarily to communicative function of the communication and only secondarily to the formal (i.e. grammatical) manifestations of that function (MacWhinney, 1994).

It is possible, but only with slow speech, for a listener to do a complete parsing of incoming speech: assign all recognised units (words) into grammatical constituents and compute a precise relationship between these constituents. However, under normal (fast) speech conditions, listeners need only draw upon a set of grammatical cues to assist them as needed in interpretation of form-function mappings. The primary grammatical cues that are used are word order, subject–verb agreement, pro-form agreement and case inflections. Selective use of these syntactic and morphological cues, along with the use of semantic cues, such as animacy (i.e. the logical viability of a given subject acting upon a given verb) and pragmatic cues, such as topic–comment relationship and contrastive stress, allow the listener to draw upon grammatical knowledge of the language while listening (Braidi, 1998).

In a full **parsing** of incoming speech, the listener would assign recognised words into grammatical categories (**content words**, such as noun, verb, adjective, adverb or **function words** attached to a content word) and assigning **structural and semantic relations** between them. This parsing would allow the listener to create a complete **propositional model** of incoming speech, although again, it is doubtful that this process is ever carried out explicitly in actual speech comprehension.

Key concept: Propositional model

A propositional model of speech represents, in the listener's mind, text referents (lexical items in the text) and their relationship to each other.

To understand this process explicitly, we can use any functional grammar, such as 'case grammar' (Fillmore, 1968), which defines 'case relations' such as Agent, Object, Instrument, Goal, Temporal, Locative to a central 'theme' (verb), or 'case theory', which describes how lexical items behave in relation to a verb (Cook, 1988). In Case Grammar, constituents in an utterance are defined by their relationship to a 'theme' or verb. The listener can construct a hierarchical map of how the words recognised in speech fit into the semantic possibilities of the verbs in the utterance, for instance if the verb (such as 'give') requires an agent, a recipient, an object, and can also entail a time, a place, etc. Based on this kind of structural-functional map, the listener can reconstruct an utterance and be said to have understood the grammar of it.

Concept 2.5   **Semantic roles**

In most languages, and particularly in English, the most commonly identifiable cases in an utterance are agent, object and patient, and are typically required in a grammatical utterance. Other semantic roles occur less explicitly, but other relevant case-roles (e.g. time, location, source) still must be inferred in order for an utterance to make sense.

agent (A) (primary do-er of an action)
patient (P) (receiver of an action)
object (O) (that which is acted upon by the agent)

instrument (I) (means of doing an action)
goal (G) (destination or desired end point)
temporal (T) (when action is carried out)
locative (L) (where action is carried out)
path (P) (way of motion)
source (S) (origination, starting point)
manner (M) (way of doing)
extent (E) (how far completed)
reason (R) (motivation for action)
beneficiary (B) (for whom action is carried out)

Stated another way, if the verb, or 'theme', is central to parsing an utterance, a listener cannot fully complete a parsing without first identifying the verb. Once the verb is identified, the listener can then relate the other constituents to it. For example, if the listener hears 'Tom and Mary took us to dinner last night', she may parse the utterance as:

(A)   VERB   (P) (G)   (T)
Tom and Mary | took | us | to dinner | last night.

A more abstract, propositional representation, would be:

THEME: took (past of 'take')
– Agent = Tom and Mary
– Patient = us (= speaker + someone)
– Goal = to dinner
– Time = last night.

Both of these views have psychological validity. The linear model represents the temporal nature of parsing, though it is clear that the listener has to hold constituents in short-term memory without completely parsing them until the utterance, or the larger grammatical unit, is judged to be complete. The hierarchical view may be a closer psychological representation of what the listener does in real time, because it addresses how short-term memory holds input only until it can be related to the theme of the utterance and fit into a developing hieararchical (situational or propositional) model of the text (Kintsch, 1998).

Concept 2.6   **Experimental methods used in studying parsing** (based on Ferreira and Anes, 1994)

Click-detection tasks

This classic methodology was pioneered by Fodor, Bever and Garrett (1975). Subjects listen to a sentence and at the same time monitor for a 'click' (or some other nonlinguistic sound). The basic assumption on which the task is based is that perceptual units of any kind resist interruption, and so if a syntactic phrase is a perceptual unit, clicks will tend to be perceived as occurring at constituent boundaries, regardless of where they actually occur. (For example, in a heard sentence such as: 'They found that the (click) house had been burglarised', subjects are likely to report hearing the 'click' before 'the' or 'that' rather than after 'the' to preserve the processing unit.

Research using these detection tasks have suggested that listeners' segmentation of speech is facilitated by correspondences between prosodic and syntactic structures.

Sentence-gating tasks

In this type of task subjects are presented with only a portion of an ambiguous sentence, and they have to indicate how they think the sentence will continue. For example, in a typical study a subject would hear 'The man believed the gossip/' and be asked to predict the continuation: (a) 'about his neighbour was true' or (b) 'about his neighbours right away'. The experimenter controls the syntax and intonation of the stem presentation to find clues as to what elements of input facilitate resolving ambiguities during speech-processing.

Research from sentence-gating tasks suggests that listeners can make interpretations on line when required, but prefer to wait for entire utterances to be completed before committing to an interpretation.

Sentence-memory tasks

These tasks are used to examine how configurations of input affect aural memory. In a typical sentence memory study, Gernsbacher and Shroyer (1989), subjects listened to texts in which a concept was introduced with the article *this* or *a*, as in 'She found this egg' vs 'She found an egg.' They are later asked to recall the text. In recalling multisentence texts, subjects add their own system of anaphoric references, and 'revise' the syntax in the text to construct a version of the text they can recall. Studies such as this demonstrate that some syntactic structures in sentence chains can promote processing and recall.

Reaction-time tasks

Reaction-time methods are used to determine facilitating or inhibiting effects of various syntactic structure. Subjects listen to a sentence and are asked to answer true or false or select a picture that matches the input. Relative reaction times and accuracy of responses help define these effects. Early studies showed, for example, that listeners take longer to make judgements or decisions when a passive sentence (e.g. 'The book was taken from the table.') is presented than when an active sentence is presented (e.g. 'Someone took the book from the table'). A generalisation that has emerged from these studies is that complex sentences are more difficult to verify as having been heard than sentences that are syntactically and propositionally simpler (Ferreira and Anes, 1994). Later studies have shown, however, that as context increases, these syntactic effects noted for isolated sentences decrease.

Key concept: Grammatical parsing contributes to comprehension by assigning semantic roles to words

Parsing is essentially a theme-based (verb-based) process, and occurs prospectively and retrospectively.

2.5 Managing spoken language

Speech is rapid, transitory medium, with most speech taking place at a rate of two to three words, or three to five syllables per second (cf. Tauroza and Allison, 1994).

In order to manage speech in real time, it is essential that the listener quickly separates the speech into a small number of constituents that can be worked with in short-term memory. The metaphor of a sausage machine is sometimes used to describe the nature of the listener's task: taking the language as it comes out and separating it into constituents. Apparently, spoken language has evolved in a way that allows the listener to parse speech 'in real time', in the most parsimonious manner given the specific resources of our short-term memory.

In examining corpora of 'authentic' spoken language, that is, language spoken in a naturally occurring context, and without explicit preparation (called 'unplanned discourse' by Ochs, 1986), researchers have found a number of following characteristics to be representative of oral English, (see Figure 2.2).

Many of these features of speech are considered to be 'sloppy' – imprecise or showing poor command of the language code – particularly when viewed from the perspective of written standards. However, linguists now assert that written and spoken language, while based on the same underlying grammatical and lexical system, simply follow different realisation rules (Carter and McCarthy, 1997). The conventions for spoken language have apparently evolved interactively, in ways they have to allow the listener the needed time to understand.

A specific cause for the realised differences in speech and writing is the difference in planning time. Brazil (1995) has observed that speakers put their speech together 'piecemeal', in real time, without detailed planning time, in part because of their need to adjust messages based on listener response, and in part because of their need to adjust their message based on their own response to what they are saying! We might expect to get closer to an understanding of what spoken language is like for the users – both the speakers and the listeners – if we take this piecemeal planning into account from the outset. Because speakers and listeners typically operate in the context of a need to meet specific communicative goals, they are more likely (than writers and readers) to utilise time-sensitive and context-sensitive strategies to compose and understand language, and to abandon them, even in the middle of utterances, when the strategies seem to be unsuccessful.

Feature	Example
Speakers speak in short bursts of speech, that is, in 'pause units'.	*The next time I saw him/* *He wasn't as friendly/* *I don't know why*
Spoken language contains more topic-comment structures, and more topic restatement.	*The people in this town – they're not as friendly as they used to be.*
Speakers frequently use additive ('paratactic') ordering with *and, then, so, but.*	*He came home/* *and then he just turned on the TV/* *but he didn't say anything/* *so I didn't think much about it/*
Speech is marked by a high ratio of function (or structure) words (particles, preposition, proforms, articles, 'be' verbs, auxiliary verbs, conjunctions) to content words (nouns, verbs, adjectives, adverbs, question words).	*written version: The court declared that the deadline must be honoured.* *(content words 4: function words 5)* *spoken version: The court said that the deadline was going to have to be kept.* *(content words 4: function words 9)*
Speech is marked by incomplete grammatical units, false starts, 'abandoned' structures.	*It's not that... I just wanted to...* *But, only...*
Speakers frequently use ellipsis – omitting known grammatical elements and unstated topics.	*(Are you) Coming (to dinner)? (I'll be there) In a minute.*
Speakers use the most frequent words of the language, leading to more 'loosely packed' language.	*the way it's put together vs its structure*
Topics may not be stated explicitly.	*I'm not sure it's a good idea for us to do that. (the topic = 'that' action referred to earlier, or never explictly mentioned in this discourse)*
Speakers use a lot of fillers and interactive markers.	*And, well, um, you know, there was, like, a bunch of people...*
Speakers employ frequent 'exophoric reference', and rely on gesture and non-verbal cues.	*that guy over there, this thing, why are you doing that?*
Speakers use variable speeds, accents, paralinguistic features and gestures.	

Figure 2.2   **Features of oral English**

2.6   Utilising prosodic features

Because planning constraints are central to speaking, it is important for the grammar of spoken language to take the effects of this planning into account. Speech is typically uttered not in a continuous stream but in short bursts. (Psychologist Eric Lenneberg [1967] has pointed out that in addition to whatever communicative function this may have, it is a biological necessity: it allows the speaker periodically to replace air in the lungs.) These units of speech have been identified by various terms, but the term '**intonation units**' may be preferable. This term emphasises that an intonational contour is constructed by the speaker to indicate a *focal centre of attention*.

Intonation units typically consist of phrases or clauses and average two or three seconds in length. Bounded by pauses, these temporal units mark the speaker's rhythm for composing and presenting ideas. (Chafe [1992] has argued that, from an evolutionary perspective, it makes sense that the duration of phonological short-term memory generally coincides with the length of the unit of articulation.) Because these units are bounded by pauses, we often refer to them as '**pause units**'.

Quote 2.1   Units in studying spoken language

The units of description for spoken language have proven to be more difficult to define than those for written language. Linguist Wallace Chafe comments on this problem:

> Researchers are always pleased when the phenomena they are studying allow them to identify units ... It would be convenient if linguistic units could be identified unambiguously from phonetic properties: if, for example, phonemes could be recognized from spectrograms, or intonation units from tracings of pitch. For good or bad, however, the physical manifestations of psychologically relevant units are always going to be messy and inconsistent.

Chafe (1994: 58)

Although it appears that the speaker has broad choices in which words to stress, the main decision in this regard comes in formulating the syntax of each intonation unit. In most intonation units, all content words (. . .) receive some stress, and the last new content word (i.e. a word that has not occurred in the previous discourse or a word that is not closely related

---

Concept 2.7   **Intonation units**

Speech is best described in intonation units. By reading a spoken text as
intonation units, we can better recreate the sense of the listener hearing it
for the first time. Syllables in CAPITAL letters indicate **prominence**, where
stress occurs (// indicates boundaries of the unit, the pauses between bursts
of speech).

//she'd been STANding in the CAR park//
and it was FREEZing COLD//
and she asked her to TAKE her round to her DAUGHTer's//
so she aGREED to take her round//
WHAT else could she DO//
she COULDn't leave her STANDing//
in this CAR park//
and they GOT back in the CAR//
and she STARTed to drive OFF//
and she was BIT sort of conCERNED/
that this woman DIDn't SAY anything//
and she kept VERy very QUIet//
but SHUFfled about in her SEAT a lot//
and sort of SEEMED a bit NERvous//
at ONE point//
she TOOK her HAND out//
from i DON'T KNOW//
where she HAD it//
in GLOVES//
or under a JACKet//
and when she SAW her hand//
she got REALly FRIGHTened//

(Brazil, 1995: 100)

---

lexically to a word in the previous discourse) usually receives the primary
stress in an intonation unit. (Note: Even though tonic prominence can
often be identified at a single syllable in a pause unit, the onset of the
stress and the decline of the stress are usually spread over several syllables,
almost always encompassing more than one word. What is identified as
'focal' in a pause unit then will usually be a 'lexical item' that consists of
one to three words.)

Another type of information available in a pause unit is given by the
intonational contour the speaker chooses. Speakers may choose either
referring tones, which rise at the end, or proclaiming tones, which fall

at the end (Brazil, 1985). (More rare are 'neutral tones', which neither rise nor fall. We use these for continuations or when we give 'impersonal information' such as the spelling of a word.) The choice of tones appears to be related to an assessment of the listener's current state of knowledge, that is, what the speaker considers 'shared with the audience' or 'new to the audience' at the time of utterance. Speakers select rising tones for pause units which remind the listeners of what they presumably already know. For example, when a lecturer says, 'You will remember that last week we talked about social norms' , she does so with a referring, rising tone, since it is clearly a reminder of a shared reference. When she continues, 'This week I want to talk about social deviations', she uses a falling, proclaiming tone since this part of the utterance is a realisation of new information in the discourse.

Most sequences in any connected turn by one speaker will consist of a rhythm of pause units with a typical 2 (referring) to 1 (proclaiming) ratio, although this varies with speaker and discourse type. It is reasonable to assume from this observation that speakers in conversation seek to maintain a balance of new versus shared information as they speak, in relation to their audience's information requirements. For example, speakers will often backtrack to shared information (referring tones), whether previously referred to in the current discourse or previously known by their interlocutors in their own experience, when they see that their audience is not responding to new information.

A third type of information available in sequences of pause units is related to connectivity. Speakers signal through intonational and 'pausal bracketing' which pause units are to be interpreted as connected. Sequences of connected pause units will end with a falling, proclaiming tone, and although a speaker may add on other units with falling tones, an experienced listener of English assumes that these are linked with the previous group. When the speaker starts back on a high rise, he indicates the start of a new group of tone units.

Typically, speakers will utilise pauses in conjunction with this tonic bracketing. Relatively short pauses before the next pause unit will typically be intended to link pause units, while relatively long pauses before the next pause unit may indicate the speaker is beginning a new topic or type of elaboration. This type of pausal and intonational coordination helps listeners identify 'paratonic units', which correspond to global planning units of the speaker text.

In addition to the purposes of indicating tonic prominence in an utterance, assumptions about the 'newness' of the information, and idea groupings, intonation can help the speaker express various nuances of meaning. Brown (1977) developed a framework of paralinguistic features that any speaker can use to shade linguistic meaning of an utterance: pitch-span, placing of voice in the voice range, tempo, loudness, voice-setting

(breathy–creaky), articulatory setting (unmarked–tense), articulatory precision (precise–slurred), lip-setting (smiling–pursed), timing and pause.
Through combinations of features, a speaker can create a range of emotional tones including warmth, thoughtfulness, anger, and sexiness (see
figure 2.3).

Concept 2.8   **Types of information available in speech**

Crystal (1995) has noted six types of tonation that are typically available in
speech. Intonation has several important functions. The central ones are:

1. Emotional: the intonation is used to express speaker's attitudinal meaning,
   such as enthusiasm, doubt, or distaste for the topic.

2. Grammatical: intonation can be used to mark grammatical structure of
   an utterance, like punctuation in written language.

3. Informational: intonation indicates the salient parts of an utterance like
   sentence stress, so a higher pitch marks the important information.

4. Textual: the intonation is used to help large chunks of discourse contrast
   or cohere, rather like paragraphs in written language

5. Psychological: the intonation is used to chunk information into unit
   which are easier to deal with. (For example: lists of words, or telephone
   or credit card numbers are grouped into units to make them easier to
   memorise.)

6. Indexical: intonation is used by certain people as a sort of identifier. For
   example, preachers and newscasters often use a recognisable intonation
   pattern.

(Adapted from Crystal, 1995)

Key concept: Paralinguistic information

The listener has access to a range of phonological information, 'paralinguistic'
information that adds to and shades the linguistic information. The listener
must simultaneously process both linguistic and paralinguistc information.

2.7   Integrating non-verbal cues

Not all input that is used by the listener is oral. Indeed, in many situations,
a great deal of information is communicated independently of the language

	replied answered said	retorted exclaimed	important pompous responsible	depressed miserably sadly	excited	anxious worried nervous	shrill shriek scream	warmly	coldly	thoughtfully	sexily	crossly angrily	queried echoed
Pitch span													
unmarked	✓				✓	✓?	✓	✓		✓	✓	✓	✓
extended		✓	✓?			??	✓		✓	✓		✓	✓
restricted				✓									
Placing in voice range													
unmarked	✓	✓?	✓		✓	✓	✓	✓	✓	✓		?	✓?
raised		??		??				?				?✓	
lowered									✓		✓		
Tempo													
unmarked	✓	✓??	✓	✓	✓	✓	✓	✓	✓	✓	✓	✓	✓
rapid										?			
slow													
Loudness													
unmarked	✓	✓	✓?	✓	✓	??	✓?	✓	✓	✓	✓	✓	✓?
loud			?						?				
soft								?					
Voice setting													
unmarked	✓	✓	✓	✓	✓?	✓?	✓?	✓	✓	✓	✓	✓	✓
'breathy'			?					?					
'creaky'													
Articulatory setting													
unmarked	✓	✓	✓	✓?	✓?	✓	✓	✓	✓	✓	✓	✓	✓
tense													
Articulatory precision													
unmarked	✓	✓	✓?	✓	✓	✓	✓	✓	✓?	✓	✓	??	✓
precise				?							?		
slurred													
Lip setting													
unmarked	✓	✓	✓	✓	✓	✓	✓	✓	✓	✓	??	✓	✓
smiling										?			
pursed													
Direction of pitch													
unmarked	✓	✓	✓	✓	✓	✓	✓	✓	✓	✓	✓	✓	✓
rise													
Timing													
unmarked	✓	✓	✓?	✓	✓	✓	??	??	✓	✓	??	✓	✓
extended													
Pause													
unmarked	✓	✓	✓?	✓	✓	✓	✓	✓	✓	??	✓	✓	✓
pause													

Speakers can regulate emotional effects in their speech through intentional manipulations of pitch, voice range, tempo, loudness, pausing and various articulatory settings of lips, tongue and glottis.

Figure 2.3   Phonological features (Brown, 1977)

that is spoken. Because of the prevalence of visual information, particularly with advancing use of visual media and multimedia, it is important to understand how visual information enhances linguistic input, distorts or replaces it, and sometimes even contradicts it.

Visual signals must be considered as 'co-text', an integral part of the text which the listener is able to utilise for interpretation. Visual signals are of two basic types: exophoric and kinesic. Exophoric signals, such as a speaker holding up a photograph or writing some words on the blackboard, typically serve as references for the spoken text and are critical for text interpretation. Exophoric signals are particularly crucial in situations of high information flow, such as scientific documentaries and academic lectures.

Kinesic signals are the body movements, including eye and head movements, the speaker makes while delivering the text. There are numerous continua for describing a speaker's body movements (e.g. Goffman, 1974; Birdwhistell, 1970; Key, 1975; Ruesch and Kees, 1969; Harrigan, 1985). From these sources, the most commonly occurring set of kinesic signals are baton signals, directional gaze and guide signs.

Baton signals are hand and head movements which are typically associated with emphasis and prosodic cadence. For instance, a speaker will often indicate with rhythmic, bounding motions of her hands the number of stressed syllables in a pause unit. Emphatic motions of the lips or chin or cheeks associated with articulation are also baton signals.

Directional gaze is eye movement and focusing used to direct the listener or audience to an exophoric reference or to identify a particular moment in the discourse as relevant in some way to the listener. Even in lectures, when there is little or no direct verbal interaction between speaker and audience, lecturers will often make and maintain eye contact with several individuals intermittently throughout the lecture to amplify and personalise meaning. In all live discourse, the main function of eye contact is to maintain the sense of contact with the listeners and to allow for them to give back channel signals to the speaker about their state of interest and understanding of the conversation or speech.

Guide signals are the systematic gestures and movements of any part of the body, such as extending one's arms or leaning forward. Many guide signals may be purely idiosyncratic, with no clear meaning, but most will have some clear role in a speaker's emphasis or shading of a particular point. For instance, speaking with one's arms outstretched may be a way for the speaker to attempt to persuade the listener to take a particular point seriously. Needless to say, guide signals will vary from culture to culture, and from speaker to speaker, and it is possible to increase comprehension by learning the guide signals of a particular speaker. However, it is difficult to discern a systematic 'grammar' of guide signal gestures that consistently contributes to discourse meaning across speakers. (The exception to this is 'lip-reading', which can be considered as interpreting guide signals.)

Some guide signals, however, do serve to specify or amplify the locutionary meaning of lexical items and relationships among lexical items. Rost (1987) found regular examples in academic lectures of lexical items and propositions being 'illustrated' through gestures such as miming (e.g. a speaker points and wags his index finger as if admonishing someone when saying, 'she *must* take the initiative and . . .'), tracing (e.g. a speaker enclosing imaginary object in his hands as he says 'is part of', widening hands to approximate length as he says, 'about 70 centimetres long'), indicating temporal relationships (a series of actions (e.g. speaker's hands moving upward in a step-like fashion), narrating (speaker tilting face upward and wide opening of eyes miming admiration while recounting, 'gee, this is a lovely house'), using emblematic signs (e.g. patting open palm on chest saying 'in our own group'). In this sense, visual variables function similarly to prosodic variables – they provide communicative and stylistic weighting to the text – and are available to the listener as part of the text.

As with paralinguistic cues, the listener assumes that non-verbal cues are intended to confirm the speaker's linguistic meaning. However, when messages in the linguistic and paralinguistic or non-linguistic channels are detected to be inconsistent, the listener may have reason to believe that the speaker is being **deceptive**, and is likely to attend to the non-verbal cues (McCornack, 1997). Similarly, in intercultural communication, when the speaker uses a gesture or body language that may connote something to the listener in her native language culture that is not intended by the speaker, it will be difficult for the listener to process the verbal message separately from the non-verbal message (cf. Scollon and Scollon, 1995; Roberts, Davies and Jupp, 1992).

Key concept: Non-verbal cues

Listening face-to-face, particularly to a familiar speaker, makes listening easier because it provides an extra layer of information: non-verbal cues. Non-verbal cues serve to amplify meaning or to confirm/disconfirm linguistic meaning.

Chapter 3

Pragmatic processing

This chapter . . .

- explains the ways that we infer speaker intention through the use of conversational conventions and inference;
- defines the notion of social frame and shows how the listener uses social frames and perceived social roles to construct meaning;
- defines the crucial concept of listener response and outlines the types of listener responses that can be used in conversation;
- details the concept of listener collaboration and the notions of goal-oriented communication and benchmarks.

3.1   Inferring speaker intention

> **Quote 3.1**
>
> Verbal communication is a complex form of communication. Linguistic coding and decoding are involved, but the linguistic meaning of an uttered sentence falls short of encoding what the speaker means: it merely helps the audience infer what she means.
>
> Sperber and Wilson (1986: 27)

As we have seen, the listener has access to several layers of language. However, at the same time, the listener understands not only 'language' but also contextual meaning. Contextual meaning includes the social status and interpersonal relationships that are signalled in the language use and also the intentions of the speaker to utilise the norms of language for particular purposes. Both of these aspects of meaning are addressed in this chapter on the pragmatics of language understanding.

Pragmatics, the study of linguistic resources in terms of their usage properties and processes in context, always addresses the context of language use first. A pragmatic view of listening likewise addresses context first, since language use is always directed by and toward actual people in real settings and meaning is generated by and for the participants within those settings.

From a pragmatic perspective, listening is an **intention** to complete a communication process. In order for this completion to occur, there must be **engagement**, in which a listener switches from becoming a mere 'presence' to an 'interpreter' (Verschueren, 1999). The implicit assumption in a pragmatic view of communication is that language resources – the listener's knowledge of phonology, morphology, syntax, lexis – cannot be activated until he takes on a pragmatic perspective.

Such a perspective includes the degree of coordination and collaboration between speaker and listener on the goals of the interaction and the rules for conducting the interaction. It is important to note that this coordination is always a less than perfect heuristic: there are never guarantees of successful coordination, successful assumptions or inferences, or mutual understanding.

There are four key pragmatic notions that contribute to an understanding of listening: (1) deixis; (2) intention; (3) strategic use; and (4) conversational meaning. These notions will be introduced in this section and integrated into the later discussion of comprehension, inference and memory.

1. Deixis

Language used in communication is 'anchored' in the real world. The listener and speaker continuously point to variables of time (then, now, today . . .), space (there, here, come back . . .), objects (that, it, those . . .), persons (he, she, we, they . . .), status (e.g. 'tu' vs 'vous' in French), as they interact. These deictic elements of an utterance can only be interpreted with respect to the context in which they are uttered. This is a crucial notion in understanding how listening occurs in context.

Hymes (1964) set forth these elements as features of 'context':

addressor (the speaker or 'author' of the utterance), addressee (the intended 'recipient' of the speaker's utterance), audience (any overhearers)
topic (what is being talked about)

setting (where the event is situated in place and time)
code (the linguistic features of the utterance)
channel (how the communication is maintained – by speech, writing, images, etc.)
event (the social norms affecting the interaction and its interpretation)
message form (the conventional categories of speech events)
key (the evaluation of the event)
purpose (the intended outcome of the event)

Hymes's features serve as an anthropological checklist that would allow an observer of a communication event to describe its various layers of potential meaning for the participants.

A more useful checklist, from a listener's perspective, was drawn up by Lewis (1972). This list provides an 'index' ('a package of relevant factors') (1972: 173) of those coordinates which a listener would need to have specified in order to interpret an utterance:

listener coordinate	example
possible world	to account for references to current and possible states of affairs: *Our situation is really serious, and it's not likely to get better anytime soon.*
time	to account for adverbials and tenses, necessary for example, to interpet the utterance: *I'll see you next week.*
place	to account for deictic utterances such as *I found it. Here it is.*
speaker	to account for personal reference: *Give it to me, please.*

audience	to account for direction of utterance: *This is your assignment. Do it yourself.*
indicated object	to account for demonstratives: *This is the right room.*
previous discourse	to account for reactivation of elements in an utterance: *The guy I told you about is . . .*
assignment	to account for ordering, inclusion, exclusion: *The second choice is better.*

2. Intention

As Berlo (1960) stated, the purpose of communication is always 'to influence people with intent'. Situated speech can thus be understood at two levels – by its 'objective' truth value and by the speaker's intention. The speaker intends to exert some influence on the listener in each instance of speaking.

Austin (1962) first made the distinction between '**constatives**' and '**performatives**' in speech. Constatives are the aspect of a speech act that can be evaluated in terms of their 'truth value'. For example, the utterance 'I sent the letter yesterday' can be evaluated as true or nearly true or false.) Performatives are the aspect of the speech act that can evaluated in terms of 'felicity', or 'what the speech act' does in the interaction. For example, the same utterance, 'I sent the letter yesterday' can be evaluated in terms of its 'felicity' as a response to the accusation, 'Why didn't you mail the letter yet?'

Austin later replaced the constative–performative distinction with a threefold contrast:

(1) **locutions**: the act of saying something as true (e.g. 'I sent the letter yesterday.');

(2) **illocutions**: what is done *in* saying something (e.g. 'I did not!', denying an accusation);

(3) **perlocutions**: what is done as a result of saying something (e.g. the speaker makes the listener believe that the accusation is false).

3. Strategic use

Speakers create meaning in part through their uses of language conventions and norms, or conversational maxims (Grice, 1969). Listeners understand speakers' meanings by evaluating speakers' utterances in the light of the cooperative principles of conversation:

1. **The maxim of quantity**: Make your contribution to the conversation as informative as is required. Do not make your contribution more informative than is required.
2. **The maxim of quality**: Do not say what you believe to be false. Do not say something for which you have inadequate evidence.
3. **The maxim of relation**: Be relevant. Say only those things that are relevant to the situation.
4. **The maxim of manner**: Avoid obscurity of expression. Avoid ambiguity. Be brief ('avoid unnecessary prolixity'). Be orderly.

However, speakers can also use language to create specific nuances of meaning by strategically failing to observe (**flouting**) these maxims. Indeed, in many conversational settings, particularly those in which the speaker feels in competition with his or her interlocutors, normal principles of 'politeness' will not be valued, speakers will deliberately violate conversational maxims (McCornack, 1997). By doing so, the speaker feels he or she may gain distinct strategic advantages:

1. By flouting the maxim of quantity, the speaker may prevent an interlocutor from getting the floor and presenting information that may contradict the speaker's assertions or intentions.
2. By flouting the maxim of quality, the speaker may gain the perception of authority without needing to provide adequate evidence for assertions.
3. By flouting the maxim of relevance, the speaker may derail the interlocutor's intentions.
4. By flouting the maxim of manner and creating ambiguity, the speaker may later exploit this ambiguity and turn it into a desired result.

Although flouting maxims may be used for deceptive or competitive purposes, more often flouting is done simply to save face, to make a situation more comfortable for the speaker or listener. These typical ways of intentionally 'failing to observe' maxims are noted by Thomas (1995):

Flouting a maxim: deliberating providing uninformative contributions, false contributions, etc., often because of a conflict between intentions to observe the maxims or to save face. The following example from Thomas (1995: 66) shows that B flouts the maxim of quantity by giving a 'less than informative' response.

A: Is he nice?
B: She seems to like him.

Violating a maxim: deliberately providing false information, often to preserve face (and avoid ridicule).

Mother: Where were you until 2 a.m. last night?
Teenage Son: I was at Jarrod's, watching a video. I lost track of the
               time.

Violation of a maxim can also be used to create **sarcasm**, as in the following example from the film *Splash* (quoted in Thomas, 1995: 63):

(B *has accidentally locked herself out of her house. It is winter, in the middle of
the night, and she is stark naked. A approaches on the street*:)

A: Do you want a coat?
B: No, I really want to stand out here in the cold with no clothes on.

Similarly, a speaker may violate this maxim for purposes of **irony**, to
convey exactly the opposite of the literal meaning:

A: Alex left me stranded in the city. I had to take a taxi home.
B: Well, he's a fine friend.

As Sperber and Wilson (1986: 200) point out, in cases like these, the
listener must use the available information ('it's freezing and you don't
have a coat' or 'you had to take a taxi') to confirm that the speaker is
violating the truth maxim and to infer that the speaker wishes to create
a particular shade of interactional meaning (here, possibly: 'Of course,
I want a coat. Why ask such a silly question!' or 'I'm sorry to hear that.
I share your frustration with Alex.')

Infringing a maxim: Naïvely and with no intention at deception or
face-saving, a speaker may fail to observe a maxim. Infringements often
occur because of a person's incomplete command of a language, such as a
young child or a non-native learner, or due to some kind of temporary
impairment, such as nervousness, drunkenness, or excitement.

Father: (*to five-year-old child*) Leon, come here. This is my boss, David
          Cameron.
Boss: Hi, Leon.
Child: My daddy says you're the strangest person he's ever worked for.

(*A carpenter, a native speaker of English, asks K., a non-native speaker of
English, about the kind of wood she wants to use for a shelf.*)

Carpenter: I'm not sure what kind of wood you want to use for the
             shelves.
K: Yes, we want to have wood shelves.

Suspending or opting out of a maxim: Deliberately being uncooperative
in delivering the most felicitous or expected response, perhaps for political, legal, cultural or moral reasons.

A: Mr President, have you considered resignation in the face of these charges?

B: No comment.

A: So when are we going to have a drink together sometime?

B: I've really got to go.

A: Tell me more about your family.

B: Oh, there's nothing to tell.

4. Conversation meaning

Although language forms embody some level of 'meaning potential', conversational or interaction meaning emerges from the context and is not determined in advance. Unexpressed information in the form of shared background knowledge (also called common knowledge, common ground, or mutual knowledge) must be recovered by the listener in order for communication to occur.

Concept 3.1   **Universals in conversation**

Even though conversational styles appear to be very different among people in different societies, a number of universals have been noted. The sociologist Erving Goffman (1974) listed the following universal elements in conversation:

1. **Openings** All societies have developed routine ways of beginning conversations.

2. **Turn-taking** All groups have subtle systems for deciding whose turn it is to speak.

3. **Closings** All societies have ritual ways of drawing conversations to a close.

4. **Backchannel signals** We all have developed verbal and non-verbal systems for the listener to give feedback to the speaker.

5. **Repair systems** All social groups have ways of 'fixing' a conversation if understanding breaks down.

Meaning expressed in conversation is mutually built incrementally and through an interactional structure created by both the speaker and listener. This incremental nature of conversation – an ongoing give and take between the speaker and listener – is essential because so much inference is involved in activating relevant assumptions and arriving at mutually acceptable meanings. This interactional structure is worked out in the actual interaction and is realised as a system of turn-taking. The variables in turn-taking are: (1) ways of getting the floor (self-selection or other-selection); (2) interruptions and overlaps; (3) back-channelling; (4) insertion sequences; and (5) repairs.

Quote 3.2

Failures in communication are to be expected: what is mysterious and requires explanation is not failure but success... Human beings somehow manage to communicate in situations where a great deal can be assumed about what is manifest to others, a lot can be assumed about what is mutually manifest to themselves and others, but nothing can be assumed to be truly *mutually* known or assumed.

Sperber and Wilson (1986: 45)

Effective listening involves the listener taking an active role in constructing meaning with the speaker. The listener must be aware of deixis, speaker intention, implicit meaning and strategy use. In addition, effective listening will involve attention to cooperative social interaction, as that is where conversational meaning is monitored and negotiated.

Concept 3.2   **What pragmatic aspects of meaning are available to the listener?**

* speaker attitudes about what he/she is saying

* speaker's intended conformity with vs infringement of language conventions

* speaker's tactics, e.g. indirectness

* speaker's dialect and register indicating personal background of the speaker.

3.2   Invoking social frames

All 'genuine' language is situated: the language is used by real speakers for a meaningful purpose and the user desires a meaningful response from one or more listeners. As a result, all understanding of genuine language requires an accounting for the '**context of situation**' (a term coined by Malinowski, 1923): the variables of speakers, purposes, setting, relevant objects, prior action. According to this view of language, the very meaning of an utterance is seen as the function of the situational and cultural context in which it occurs.

Concept 3.3   How does the listener use social frames to understand speech?

• identify prototypical elements in the text

• assume prescribed meanings.

Stanley Fish (1994) claims that all language comprehension is filtered through the norms of the '**interpretive community**' that you belong to. An 'interpretive community' is defined as any group that shares common contexts and experiences. In any complex situation requiring comprehension, such as watching a political debate, the listener will invariably draw upon expectations of the 'group' he or she identifies with in interpreting the actions and the language within that event. As Lakoff (2000) points out, people who share the same expectations as the listener will be deemed to 'get it', while those who don't share those expectations 'just don't get it'. Much of our understanding of events, particularly complex and socially significant events, is heavily influenced by our membership in various discourse communities, and much of the progress that second language listeners experience is attributable to becoming part of a native speaker discourse community (cf. Swales, 1990).

At a personal level, that of one-to-one interaction, this social phenomenon is more readily observable. Interaction takes place within social frames that influence the ways that the speaker and listener act. The social frame for an interaction involves two interwoven aspects: the **activity frame**, which is the activity that the speaker and listener are engaged in, and the **participant frame**, which is the role that each person is playing within that activity (Tyler, 1995). From a pragmatic perspective, a good deal of conversation is, in effect, using context cues to negotiate and establish the exact nature of the activity frame and the participant frame,

---

Concept 3.4   Conversation and culture

Part of what makes natural conversation of so much interest for language learning is that it is a container of culture. As Goffman (1974) says, 'Talk is like a structural midden, a refuse heap in which bits and oddments of all the ways of framing activity in culture are to be found.'

rather than simply exchanging information (e.g. Szymanski, 1999; Beach, 2000).

Once the frame is established, all conversational behaviour is interpreted within that particular context. Thus, the interpretation that a listener gives to any utterance is heavily dependent on the frames that he or she assigns to the interaction, and the expectations about how those frames are enacted in conversation. While activity frames can vary widely, participant frames are more simply divided into 'knowledge superior' (K+), 'knowledge equal' (K=), or 'knowledge inferior' (K–).

The determination of the participant frame, and the concomitant decisions about superiority or inferiority of knowledge, encompasses the notions of social class, social status, and rank. Carrier (1999) notes that the societal nature of status can be predicted from knowledge of existing social mores (e.g. doctors are seen as 'superior' in knowledge to their 'patients'), the situational nature of status is less predictable because it is co-constructed by both interlocutors in each particular encounter.

Concept 3.5   **Interpretation**

Different listeners understand different things from the same text.

The differences in interpretation are due to:

- familiarity with the language

- familiarity with the speaker

- background knowledge of the topic

- motives for listening

- what the listener finds relevant

- social frames enacted for understanding

- influence of 'interpretive communities'.

How interlocutors in a conversation define their status relative to the other – that is, how they wish to set up the participant frame – will determine a great deal about how they will communicate with each other. Not only will the participant frame influence what is and is not said, it will also influence the **affective involvement** of both participants.

One aspect of affective involvement in an interaction is the raising or lowering of anxiety and self-confidence, and thus the motivation to participate in interactions in meaningful, open and self-revelatory ways.

For listeners, greater affective involvement promotes better understanding through better connection with the speaker, while lower affective involvement typically results in less connection, less understanding and minimal efforts to evaluate and repair any misunderstandings that arise. For example, Yang (1993) found in a study of Chinese learners of English a clear negative correlation between learners' levels of anxiety and their listening performance. Aniero (1990) noted that anxiety (she called it '**receiver apprehension**') correlated with poor listening performances in pair interactions. One implication is that 'receiver apprehension' may indeed be triggered by social factors, such as perception of roles and status, and the sense that one's interlocutor does or does not have a parallel recognition of these roles.

One known effect of **perceived social distance** is a reduction in the amount of **negotiation for meaning** – that is, the work that interlocutors do to resolve communication difficulties (Pica, 1992). A vital line of research relating to listener perceptions of social role and status is based on **Uncertainty Management Theory** (Gudykunst, 1995). This theory maintains that (a) initial uncertainty and anxiety about another's attitudes and feelings in a conversation are the basic factors influencing communication, and (b) uncertainty inhibits effective communication. This theory predicts that the amount of information-seeking and 'openness' that will take place in an interaction will be determined by the degree of uncertainty. (It is interesting to note that Carrier [1999] hypothesised that social status would have an effect on listening comprehension because opportunities for negotiation of meaning are likely to be limited in socially asymmetrical interactions, such as between a university student and a professor. She further hypothesised that comprehension of the NNS by a NS interlocutor would also be influenced negatively by an asymmetrical status relationship because the NNS would have fewer opportunities to restate unclear information. Neither hypothesis was supported by her research: she found that the superior party often used politeness strategies to affect the status relationship between the NS and NNS and to allow for more negotiation of meaning and more attempts at output by the NNS.)

Uncertainty itself refers primarily to lack of clarity about how one's social or situational status affects the interaction. The **equality position** of both parties in an interaction sharing common ground is considered the starting point for effective communication. The central prediction of this theory is that when equality is in doubt, or when a **superior position** is claimed by one party without the consent of the other party, communication will be strained and ineffective. In strained encounters of this type, politeness ('**face-saving**') strategies must be used to establish **common ground** (Brown and Levinson, 1983).

Concept 3.6   **Gender roles in listening**

The role of gender and perceived effects of gender differences on communication has been the focus of numerous linguistic studies. Misunderstandings in male-female communication arise, it is often claimed, because men and women approach conversation differently. They may implicitly disagree on the appropriate activity frame and participant frame for a given conversation and thus proceed to develop the conversation according to different sets of rules.

Tannen (1990) reports the following incident, which suggests how expectations about the purpose of an interaction influence affective involvement. A woman is out walking on a pleasant summer evening and sees her neighbour, a man, in his yard. She comments on the number of fireflies that were out that evening: 'It looks like the Fourth of July.' The man agrees and then launches into a lengthy commentary on how the insects' lighting is part of a complex mating ritual. The woman becomes irritated, abruptly finishes the conversation, and walks on.

According to Tannen, this incident illustrates that people sometimes have different orientations to the purpose of a conversation. The woman made her comment about the fireflies as a way to show her feeling of appreciation for the pleasantness of the evening and to share that feeling with her neighbour. The neighbour apparently took this opening as a chance to reveal his knowledge of insects and to teach his neighbour some of the things he knows. While both neighbours had the good intention of engaging in a friendly conversation, and perhaps even of opening up to each other to establish a deeper connection, they had differing expectations about the direction such a conversation should take. The man may have believed that a 'good conversation' is one with interesting, factual content that shows the speaker's knowledge, while the woman may have believed a 'good conversation' to be one with personal content which discloses more directly our own feelings and beliefs.

3.3   Listener response

Although it is often ignored in language analysis, the listener has a subtle but powerful role in conversation, shaping the meaning of the interaction in collaboration with the speaker. By examining listener response in discourse we can see how the listener contributes to the conversation and achieves meaning, and at times clarifies or even 'creates' meaning in the speaker.

Discourse analysis, as part of pragmatics, is a useful tool for structuring observations in conversation. The setting up of a discourse analysis framework is a two-way process in which linguistic concepts and models, which provide the theoretical motivation for the framework, are tested by data, and data in turn provides the insights and bases for revision of the framework (Tsui, 1994). For understanding listening, the contribution of discourse analysis is in showing how to examine a conversation in terms of the 'real time' structuring of meaning by both the speaker and the listener.

Conversation can be seen as organised around a series of **initiating acts**, such as a request. A speaker initiates an act in conversation and the listener has the choice of '**uptaking**' the initiating move or ignoring it. Typically, the speaker **intends** the listener to uptake the act in a specific way, in a way that is 'normal' within the speaker and listener's 'discourse community'. In discourse-analysis parlance, the speaker intends to elicit a '**preferred**' **response**.

This preferred response from the listener completes the exchange.

A: Can I stay at your place for a few days?
B: Um, no, not this month.

For example, the request 'Can I stay at your place for a few days?' is designed to elicit a yes or no response. In a discourse-analysis sense, either 'Yes, sure' or 'No, not this month' would be 'preferred' responses in that they 'comply' with the structure of the request. (This is different from the normal sense of a speaker 'preferring' (hoping) that the other person says 'yes'.) 'I don't know', 'Why do you always ask me that?', and 'The sky is blue' are all '**dispreferred**' **responses** because they do not comply, they do not complete the initiating act in the expected way.

In a conversation, a listener is expected to **comply** with a speaker's initiating move. A listener response that expresses inability or reluctance to provide information, or otherwise comply with the speaker's initiating move, realises a '**challenge**', because it challenges the presupposition that the addressee has the information or resource the speaker needs and is willing to provide it, or it challenges the speaker's right to make the initiating move.

Son: I've got this term paper due tomorrow and I was wondering if you could read over my draft tonight.
Father: You're a busy guy.

In this case, the father issues a 'challenge' by not responding directly to the son's request for help, by withholding the information or resource that the son is seeking.

Challenges are **face-threatening** – they upset the participation frame by 'demoting' one interlocutor's power. Of course, some challenges are less face-threatening than others. Specifically, challenging the presupposition that one is *able* to provide the information is less face-threatening than challenging the presupposition that one is *willing* to provide it. This is why in most cultures it is more 'polite' to declare ignorance than refuse to comply with a request (Tsui, 1994).

Another type of listener response is **backchannelling**, which are short messages that the listener sends back during the partner's speaking turn or immediately following the speaking turn. These messages may include brief verbal utterances ('yeah, right'), brief semi-verbal utterances (e.g. 'uh-huh', 'hmm'), laughs or chuckles, and postural movements, such as nods. Backchannelling, with norms of meaning and use differing from culture to culture and within subcultures, is important in conversation for showing a number of listener states: reception of messages, readiness for subsequent messages, agreement on turn-taking and empathy.

Backchannelling occurs more or less constantly during conversations in all languages and settings, though in some languages and in some settings, it seems more prevalent. Maynard (1997) in her analyses of Japanese casual conversation notes clear backchannelling every 2.5 seconds. She terms the interplay between speaker and listener as the 'interactional dance'. When backchannelling is withheld or disrupted, the interaction becomes perceptibly disrupted, and the speaker will usually seek to repair the interaction.

Quote 3.3   Maynard on listener response

In observing conversation we usually notice the speaker's actions more than the listener's. It is obvious, however, that conversation cannot go without a listener. The brief comments and utterances (often accompanied by head movements or other gestures) offered by a listener are called **'back channels'**. These expressions, since they often do not have an easily identifiable meaning, have sometimes been considered marginal and insignificant semantically, but they are quite meaningful in conversational interaction...

Back channels apply to a... broad range of behaviour, including:

1. continuer: a signal sent by the listener to the speaker to continue the talk
2. displaying of understanding of content
3. giving emotional support for the speaker's judgement
4. agreeing
5. strong emotional response.

Adapted from Maynard (1997: 139–41)

A third class of listener response in discourse is the follow-up act. Follow-up acts are responses to a discourse exchange, and can be provided either by the listener or the speaker from the previous exchange. Follow-up acts can be endorsements (positive evaluations), concessions (negative evaluations), or acknowledgements (neutral evaluations). In the following extracts, we see examples of each type.

A: How long will you be staying with us?
B: 'Til next Sunday.
A: Great.

A: Are you joining us tonight?
B: Sorry, I can't. Too much work.
A: I understand.

A: How did he hurt himself?
B: Skateboarding.
A: Oh.

Listener responses, in the form of uptaking (accepting) or challenging the speaker's initiating act, providing backchannelling, or providing follow-up acts, are an integral and active aspect of conversation. Expectations about how listeners should respond is part of the cultural knowledge that is acquired when one learns a first or second language (see for example, Rost and Ross, 1991; Vandergrift, 1999; Ohta, 2000).

In professional encounters (e.g. doctor–patient, manager–employer, mediator–client), the notion of listener response has received increasing attention because of the acknowledged importance of listening in various phases of problem assessment, 'gatekeeping' and treatment. Increasingly, training in 'responsive listening' has become part of many professional curricula.

Sarangi and Roberts (2001) present a framework that is used to describe and help train medical professionals in better understanding and responding to patients.

Types of listening: empathetic and retractive

(Extract from doctor–patient interactions in the study;
act = patient; *can* = candidate, professional in training)

Empathetic

Responsive listening (focusing)
act: That doesn't do me any harm.
can: You're not worried about that at all.

Inclusiveness ('we' + affect; eliciting patient awareness/perspective and aligning with it)
can: We obviously want to sort out your problem.
can: OK seeing it is only for one day.
can: What do you understand about why we did the test in the first place?

Framing (framing intention and social relationships, often conveyed as 'talk about talk')
can: I wanted to ask you . . .
can: Do you have any idea about . . .

Hedging (acknowledging own difficulty and using softeners)
can: It's very difficult for us to say . . .
can: Would it be OK if I just tell you a little . . .

Evaluating (may also be part of responsive listening)
can: OK that's good.

Checking understanding/commitment
can: OK. Anything you don't understand so far?

Retractive

'Trained empathy'
can: I can understand.
can: How did the chest X-Ray go?

Labelling/high inferencing
can: You don't feel guilty?

Take in/ storage failure
can: How did your husband pass away?
act: I told you he died of cancer.

Inappropriately designed response
avoidance or minimal response

A key notion in this type of listening training is 'metacognition'. As the professional or service provider learns to monitor his or her 'responses' to clients, those responses become more amenable to observation, control, and adjustment depending on the kinds of outcomes desired or 'undesired'.

> **Key concept: Listener response**
>
> Listeners have three types of responses in face-to-face interaction: (1) uptaking of speaker's moves; (2) backchannelling; and (3) follow-up acts.

3.4 Listener collaboration

In communication theory, listening is viewed as part of a transactional process in which all participants are simultaneously 'sending' and 'receiving' messages. In a communicative transaction, a listener is 'speaking' continuously through non-verbal responses as well as through periodic verbal responses. The speaker simultaneously 'listens' to these non-verbal and verbal messages and adapts his or her communicative behaviour, attitudes, and affective states according to an assessment of how he or she is being 'understood'. Listening then becomes an interactive process in which the outcomes of any communication include renewed perceptions of self, other and the relationship. In this view, the goal of listening is not primarily comprehension of messages, but rather establishing interactive connections with one's interlocutors and mutually moving toward goals. These goals may be related to mutual comprehension of messages in the discourse, but they will also be related to adjustments in the 'relationship system' between the speakers.

Key concept: Connection vs comprehension

In collaborative listening, the purpose of listening is not primarily comprehension of messages but rather establishing interactive connections with one's interlocutors and mutually moving toward goals.

Listening can thus be studied as part of a theory of action in human behaviour. Systems theory is one theory of action that views interactions dynamically, in that each person in an interaction is seen as contributing to stated or unstated goals of the group. Each person's actions, in the form of verbal and non-verbal behaviour, are reflected in the **communicative states** of the system. The communicative states of the system – a dyad or a larger group – can be determined by examining the **communication patterns** formed during the interaction (Wilmot, 1979; Rhodes, 1987). Because listening is part of the behaviour in the system, listening effectiveness will affect progress toward an assigned or agreed goal.

The goals for any communicative dyad or group will of course vary, and may shift during an interaction. For instance, one dyad may have the goal of agreeing on an acceptable remedy for a problem, as in a service encounter at a complaint desk. Another dyad may have the prescribed goal of achieving empathy, as in a counselling session, in order to help the client eventually move toward solving a particular problem. In either case, what a systems theory approach seeks to invoke is a means of examining and evaluating 'frames' of interactions in terms of their contributing to or detracting from achievement of a defined goal.

In any intentional or **goal-directed communication**, the participants' success or failure depends upon a number of factors:

• the understanding each has of the situation
• the clarity of their goals
• their perception of and sensitivity to one another's needs
• the strategic choices they make

- their ability to put their choices into action
- their ability to monitor their progress toward the goals
- their ability to provide feedback about their perceived progress.

These last two factors are considered so vital in effective communication that they have become the cornerstone of definitions of listening in communication theory: 'These processes of monitoring progress toward a goal during and through communication and providing feedback about one's perception of that progress can be referred to as listening' (Rhodes, 1987: 34–5).

Other communication theorists argue further that listening includes not only **monitoring** and **feedback** but also **response**. 'The response stage of listening is especially crucial for judging the success of the listening act as a whole' (Steil, Barker and Watson, 1983: 22). In this view listening includes four stages: (1) **sensing** (taking in messages); (2) **interpreting** (arriving at a degree of understanding); (3) **evaluating** (judging, weighing evidence, deciding on degree of agreement with the speaker) and (4) **response** (non-verbal feedback to show understanding, and verbal contributions, such as asking questions or paraphrasing).

The response stage is crucial for two reasons. First, it is one concrete aspect of listening from which other participants can determine whether they have been understood. Second, the speaker must incorporate these **'listener messages'** in order to monitor goal achievement and to select further strategies in the interaction. In short, and as noted above, pursuit of goals through communication requires effective listening, including feedback and response, on the part of the listeners.

Effective listening from a systems theory perspective requires evaluation of communication patterns in the interaction. Numerous scales for such evaluation have been used for various settings and goals.

An example of one type is provided by Rinvolucri (1981), based on the Truax–Carkhuff scale used in psychotherapy:

Level 1: The listener fails to attend and thus detracts significantly from the message the speaker is trying to get across.

Level 2: The listener subtracts noticeable affect from the communication

Level 3: The listener seems to be listening at a depth similar to the depth intended by the speaker.

Level 4: The listener communicates his or her understanding of the speaker's expressions at a deeper level than they were expressed.

Because goal orientation and maintenance of communication assumes a high priority, communication research has devoted much attention to factors that promote, maintain or erode interaction. These factors are often discussed as **'benchmarks'**, that is, criteria against which interactions can

Quote 3.4 Listening as monitoring

... if we assume that the degree to which the participants in a goal-oriented communication event succeed or fail depends largely on whether or not their communicative choices produce a desired effect... then we need to include additional factors... [including] each participant's ability to monitor his or her progress toward the goal(s) and to provide the other person with feedback... These processes of monitoring progress toward a goal and providing feedback about one's perception of that progress can be referred to as listening.

Rhodes (1987: 34–5)

Concept 3.7   **Benchmarks**

Various interactive behaviours and attitudes that have been utilised as benchmarks for communicative behaviour (cf. Rubin, Palmgreen and Sypher, 1994):

- Conversational appropriateness (Canary and Spitzberg, 1990): patterns of responding appropriately to the speaker's message.

- Conversational effectiveness (Canary and Spitzberg, 1987): overall effect of listening behaviour on achievement of communication goals.

- Communicative impact measure (International Communication Association, 1978): memorability of the listener (i.e. how well the speaker recalls the listener's effect on the communication).

- 'Argumentativeness' scale (Dowling and Flint, 1990): communication patterns that indicate a tendency to approach or avoid arguments or confrontations.

- Interpersonal communication motives scale (Rubin et al., 1988): patterns of exhibiting and discovering reasons or motives for communicating with others.

- Interpersonal solidarity scale (Wheeless, 1976): patterns of communication that demonstrate solidarity with the speaker.

- Syntonic adjustment measures (Elgin, 1989): patterns of responses between participants (evaluative vs summative), and the use of positive vs negative affect in those responses.

Other studies of communicative behaviour patterns have concentrated on: affinity-seeking, audience activity, communication anxiety, compliance-gaining, interpersonal attraction, personal involvement, receiver apprehension and self-disclosure (cf. Rubin et al., 1994; Burgoon and White, 1997).

be evaluated and through which effective listening may be modelled and learned. Benchmarking is the practice of identifying specific patterns of behaviours or attitudes or affective signals that contribute to the success or failure of an interaction.

The focus on these patterns for purposes of training listeners is intended to counter the natural effects of 'accommodation' (Giles, 1979) or 'interaction adaptation' (Burgoon and White, 1996): Once an interaction is underway, the communication patterns of our interaction partner may gain potency over our own affect and cognitions as determinants of the way we communicate (both speaking and listening) in the interaction.

Chapter 4

Psycholinguistic processing

This chapter...

- outlines the processes of comprehension, in terms of 'given' and 'new' information, and updating mental models;
- discusses the concept of knowledge activation, the notions of schema and constructive memory;
- discusses the process of inference, which is central to all language understanding, and presents different systems of categorising inferences;
- presents fundamental concepts of memory that are used during listening, including phonological loop or echoic memory, short-term memory, long-term memory;
- presents a basic neurological (connectionist) view of what happens during learning in the listening process.

4.1 Comprehension

Comprehension is often considered to be the first-order goal of listening, the highest priority of the listener, and sometimes the sole purpose of listening. Although the term 'listening comprehension' is widely used to refer to all aspects of listening, the term 'comprehension' is used in a more specific sense here. Comprehension is the process of relating language to concepts in one's memory and to references in the real world. Comprehension is the sense of understanding what the language used refers to in one's experience or in the outside world. 'Complete comprehension' then refers to the listener having a clear concept in memory for every referent used by the speaker.

Because comprehension involves the mapping and updating of references that the speaker uses, the process of comprehending occurs in an ongoing cycle, as the listener is attending to speech. A concrete starting point of discussing how comprehension – the mapping and updating procedure – takes place is the notion of '**given**' and '**new**' information.

Each intonation unit uttered by a speaker unit can be seen as including both 'new' or 'focal' information and 'given' or 'background' information. 'New' refers to the assumed status, *in the speaker's mind*, that the information is *not yet 'active'* in the listener's working memory. 'New information' does not necessarily mean that the speaker believes the information itself is novel for the listener. 'Given' refers to the status, again in the speaker's mind, that information is already active in the listener's mind. (The speaker may, of course, be mistaken about either assumption.) The interplay of 'given' and 'new' information in spoken discourse is reflected in the prosody of speech, which in turn provides fundamental clues to the listener in how to attend to the speech.

Concept 4.1   **Chafe on the status of information in discourse: active vs accessible**

The concept of 'given-new' is helpful in understanding the links between speaker and listener. This concept provides a basis for negotiation of what the speaker wants to become active or salient in the conversation.

A more accurate characterization of 'new' is . . . '*newly activated* at this point in the conversation.' Conversely, 'given' can be characterized as already active at this point in the conversation. We can add a third possibility to (these) distinctions by labeling information that has been activated for a previously 'semi-active' state as 'accessible' (Chafe, 1994: 72).

Chafe views the process of bringing inactive or semi-active information into a conversation as involving mental effort or 'activation costs'. Given information is obviously least 'costly' because the information is already active. Accessible information is more costly, and new information most costly. New information is most likely to receive prominence, in order to signal that this unit of information will require greater attention and processing. This prominence can be signalled through phonology and through syntactic placement in the utterance.

The most fundamental aspect of comprehension is the **integration** of the information conveyed by the text with information and concepts already known by the listener. Comprehension occurs as an internal model of the discourse by the listener, in which the information in the text plays only one part. This process of integration is necessarily sensitive to whether the information conveyed by a sentence provides 'given' information (already known to the listener) or 'new' information (not already known to the listener). Without this interplay of 'new' and 'given', there can be no comprehension. The listener may already 'know' everything that the speaker is saying, but there is no comprehension unless the listener integrates information from the speaker's text.

The speaker conveys his or her own distinctions between 'given' and 'new' information through presentation cues. In English, these cues are primarily intonational. The main stress or prominence within an intonational unit falls on the word that is the **locus of the new information**. While all content words receive some stress according to basic phonological rules of the language, the prominent word will receive even greater stress, usually indicated by lengthening the vowel sound. For example, in the following extract (Brazil, 1995: 100) the prominent words in each intonation unit (underlined) guide the listener to the focal information.

//she'd been STANding in the CAR park//
and it was FREEZing COLD//
and she asked her to TAKE her round to her DAUGHTer's//
so she aGREED to take her round//
what ELSE could she DO//
she COULDn't leave her STANDing//
in this CAR park//

These prominent words guide the listener in comprehending the extract by indicating what should be processed as 'new' information. The listener would have difficulties comprehending the extract if it were delivered with intonational cues that did not provide such guidance, as in the following composed example:

//she'd BEEN standing in THE car park//
and IT WAS freezing cold//
and she ASKED her to take her ROUND to her daughter's//
so SHE agreed to take HER round//
WHAT else COULD she do//
she couldn't LEAVE her standing//
in THIS car park//

With the latter text, the listener may have the distinct feeling of being misled by the apparent signalling of 'new information', rather than guided toward a mutual understanding of the story.

To return to the issue of comprehension, it is important to consider what the listener actually takes away from the listening event. While attending to speech over a period of several intonation units, the listener has to store a **mental representation** of the discourse and continuously update the representation with new information. The listener's representation of a comprehended text is stored as sets of interrelated **propositions** (Goetz et al., 1981; Johnson-Laird, 1984). Propositions may be seen as units in memory, which are used both in encoding and retrieval of comprehended information.

4.2   Knowledge activation

Listening is primarily a cognitive activity, involving the activation and modification of concepts in the listener's mind. One might assume that due to evolutionary causes, the conceptual knowledge that the listener brings to text comprehension is organised in ways that allow him to activate it efficiently. As a way of referring to activated portions of conceptual knowledge, cognitive psychologists and linguists often refer to modules of knowledge as **schemas** (or **schemata**). It is estimated that any adult would have hundreds of thousands of schemas in memory, which would be interrelated in an infinite number of ways. Further, new schemas are created and existing ones are updated constantly: every time we read, listen to, or observe something new we create a new schema by relating one fact to another through logical or semiotic links (cf. Kramsch, 1997)

For example, if you are listening to a news broadcast on an international conflict, you bring to mind numerous existing schemas about the countries involved, their leaders and past history. Indeed, you will need to bring them into your short-term memory in order to comprehend the news story. These schemas built from your understanding of the world, including your experience with comprehending language, will be organised in your mind in ways that make them accessible to you. Schema organisation is influenced by a number of factors, such as their relative importance to your personal value system, as well as their frequency (how often you activate particular schemas) and their recency (how recently you have activated similar schemas).

Under normal circumstances, when you are in the act of listening, you activate only a small number of schemas that you might consider relevant to understanding the text (e.g. the news story) adequately. In comprehending a news story, you update these schemas rather than simply comprehending the text as a unique and distinct source of information. Indeed, several minutes after listening to the news story, you may no longer remember where or how your knowledge became updated, and may not even realise that it has been updated.

Because schemas contain a shorthand code for our experiences, a main function of activating appropriate schemas in comprehension is to allow the listener to induce the presence of people, events and things that *are not explicitly referred to in the text.* For example, if the speaker is describing an incident at a train station, the listener can presume the presence of people, noise, trains, ticket vendors, and so on. The speaker need not make explicit whatever he or she can assume the listener already knows through activated schemas. The listener's schema contains prototypical (or default) referents for items that are not explicitly signalled as 'new' information.

The speaker and the listener do not need to have identical schemas relating to the conversational topic in order for language understanding to take place. Simply activating an appropriately related schema allows the listener to make the inductions that are essential to comprehending the text. When there are significant mismatches between the speaker's and the listener's schemas, we say that **misunderstanding** has occurred. When there are critical lapses and the listener is unable to activate any appropriate schema, we say that **non-understanding** has occurred (Rost, 1990).

Understanding what a speaker says depends to a large degree upon shared concepts and shared ways of reacting to the world. Although it is impossible that two persons would share identical schemas for train stations or historical events, or whatever the conversational topic may be, it is indeed possible that they will share common **activation spaces** in memory. If schemas, or conceptual frameworks, consist of activation patterns across the brain's neurons (estimated to be about 10^{11}) the 'activation space' (or 'activation vector space') has a distinct 'weight', or activity level, for each neural synapse that is involved in the concept. A specific configuration of synaptic weights will partition the activation space of a given neuronal pathway into distinct 'prototypes' or 'universals' (Churchland, 1999). A connectionist concept such as this is essential to explain how mutual understanding, or mutually acceptable understanding, of any concept can occur between a speaker and a listener.

As we listen, prototype patterns get activated as we respond intellectually to certain language inputs (Rosch, 1975). While there will be differences in the synaptic weights of concepts we respond to (some will be more important to us than others), the actual neural space in which these differences occur is similarly partitioned in speakers and listeners of similar backgrounds. People react to the world in similar ways not because their underlying synaptic configurations in memory are closely similar, but because their activation spaces are similarly partitioned (Churchland and Senjowki, 1992).

In virtually every listening situation, calling on knowledge from stored prototypes and universals is absolutely crucial to comprehension. When this knowledge is activated during comprehension, additional information, stored as related schemas, becomes available to the listener. At the same time, whenever a knowledge structure is activated, the listener also experiences an affective response which further influences connections with the speaker and her ideas, and empathic responses to what she has said.

Quote 4.1 Constructive memory

The influence of background knowledge on comprehension has long been of interest to psychologists. Charles Bartlett, often considered the founder of cognitive psychology, notes in his book, *Remembering*:

> Every social group is organized and held together by some specific psycholog-
> ical tendency or group of tendencies, which give the group a bias in its dealings
> with external circumstances. The bias constructs the special persistent features
> of group culture ... [and this] immediate settles what the individual will observe
> in his environment and what he will connect from his past life with this direct
> response. It does this markedly in two ways. First, by providing that setting of
> interest, excitements, and emotion, which favors the development of specific
> images, and secondly, by providing a persistent framework of institutions and
> customs which acts as a schematic basis for constructive memory.

Bartlett (1932: 55)

4.3   Inference

Quote 4.2 George Miller on listening

In order to understand what another person is saying, you must assume it is true and try to imagine what it could be true of.

George Miller (quoted in Hall, 1980: 46)

Since the listener does not have direct access to a speaker's intended meaning in producing an utterance or series of utterances, she has to rely on a process of inference to arrive at an acceptable interpretation of the utterance and the connection between a series of utterances. One part of the process of inference by the listener is achieved through conventional procedures involving language use and another part is achieved through problem-solving procedures involving logic and real-world knowledge.

When a speaker makes an utterance, she is presenting successive bits of information about a topic or set of topics. The references for information within any one utterance and the connections between the bits of information across utterances will be signalled by the speaker through conventional use of cohesion devices, such as anaphora, lexical substitution,

conjunction and ellipsis (cf. Halliday and Hasan, 1983; Cook, 1989; Carter and McCarthy, 1997). A primary inferencing process in listening is determining what cohesion devices are being used by the speaker.

Concept 4.2   **Cohesion devices**

Language comprehension involves finding coherence across utterances. The listener must be able to construct coherence by following the speaker's use of cohesion devices.

Anaphora: reference back to an item previously mentioned in the text: ('My brother stayed at my apartment last week. He left his dog here.')

Exophora: reference to an item outside the text (*pointing*: 'That's his dog.')

Lexical substitution: using a similar lexical item to substitute for a previous one ('His dog . . . that stupid animal . . .')

Lexical chaining: using a related lexical item as a link to one already mentioned ('The dog makes a mess . . . it sheds everywhere, it tears up newspapers . . .')

Conjunction: using links between propositions, such as *and, but, so* ('The dog is too much for me, but I promised I'd take care of it.')

Ellipsis: omission of lexical items that can be recovered by the listener through conventional grammatical knowledge ('I promised to take care of it, so I will' [take care of it]).

Understanding an extended text (or extended speaking turn) involves making use of this conventional 'discourse grammar'.

Although an understanding of cohesion through conventional means is essential to language comprehension, a great deal of language understanding cannot be explained in terms of conventional knowledge. As we have seen, language comprehension requires representation of knowledge that is not contained or signalled explicitly in the text. The speaker leaves much of that supplementing work to the listener. The process of providing these supplements in order to understand texts is often called 'making inferences' or 'inferencing'.

As Kintsch (1998) points out, this use of the term **inferencing** is confusing, for much of what psychologists call inferencing has very little to do with real inferences. According to Kintsch, real (or 'generated') inferences are **problem-solving processes** employed when there is evidence from which some conclusion can be drawn. The broader use of 'making inferences' in language education also includes general knowledge-retrieval processes in which any piece of prior knowledge is retrieved.

Inferences involve operations on a mental model that a listener has produced while listening. Several types of inferencing have been identified.

1. estimating the sense of ambiguous references
2. supplying missing links in ellipted propositions
3. filling in schematic slots
4. supplying plausible supporting grounds for logical arguments
5. using text genres to generate expectations for the macrostructure
6. supplying plausible intentions for the speaker.

(Rost, 1990)

Through the use of inference, the listener updates a cognitive representation from one utterance to the next. This internal updating of one's cognitive representation has been called the 'flow' of consciousness (Chafe, 1979). Because of limited working-memory capacity, the exact verbal material that has been processed will be forgotten. All that may be available to the listener are a few lexical items, related to concepts in long-term memory.

Bisanz et al. (1981) have proposed that during cognitive processing of a text, new information 'chunks' are integrated into higher-order chunks ('flowing chunks'). This integration process increases the functional capacity of working memory tremendously. Working within the limitations of short-term memory, the listener will construct only the number of inferences necessary to maintain a coherent representation of the text. (In this view of text processing, the order of presentation of propositions in a text influences the fluency and ease of processing.)

Concept 4.3   **Inference types**

The main types of inferences that have been identified are set out below. Note that more than one inference type can be used to represent the link between two propositions.

Types of logical inference during text comprehension

Initiating links
A is the reason for B:
'He was afraid to fly. He wasn't getting on that plane.'
(afraid → causes → not getting on)

Enabling links
A makes Y possible:
'I sat down in the driver's seat. I felt something wet and spongy through my trousers'
(sitting down → enables → feeling wet)

Schematic links
A contains an information framework that is needed to interpret B:
'He's a real nuisance in restaurants. He always questions the waiter about the bill.'
(Restaurant → entails → waiters, bills, etc.)

Classification links
B expresses something that can be classified in terms of A:
'He eats a ton of fruit every day. I'm always finding banana peels, orange rinds and grape stems all over the kitchen.'
(fruit → includes → bananas, oranges, grapes)

Paratactic (sequential) links
B expresses something that follows A:
'She put on her raincoat. She turned to leave.'
(put on → precedes in sequence → leave)

Logical links
A and B together express a syllogism in logic:
'A lot of people say living in California is great. But they're ignoring the high cost of living. That's why I hate it when I hear people say that.'
(Condition X + Y → lead to → Z)

Reference links
Anaphoric links between items across utterances:
'I got the beer out of the car. It was very warm.'
(it → refers to → the beer, not the car.)

Elaborative inferences
Any inference that is made by the listener not necessary for text coherence. Such inferences are always culturally relative, and informed by both individual experiences and values:
'I got the beer out of the car. It was very warm'
(→ The speaker is probably over 21 years old because he drinks beer. It's probably summer time – that's why the beer got warm, etc.)

Bridging inferences
Any inference that fills in assumed facts or presupposes details in order to make a coherent representation. Like elaborative inferences, bridging inferences are culturally relative, based on cumulative experiences and personal attitudes:
'The surgeon was perspiring profusely at the completion of the heart operation. One of the attendants spoke to . . .'
(→ him/her)
While listening, the listener will form a representation of the surgeon, including unstated details such as whether the surgeon is male or female, by way of bridging inferences.

(Based on Nix, 1983)

Concept 4.4   **Inference and reasoning**

According to educator Stephen Toulmin (1987) , much of the **reasoning** we do during language comprehension (listening and reading) can be explained in terms of **claims** and **grounds** of support. In everyday reasoning, we must infer the grounds once we understand a claim. Claims are the assertions that the speaker wishes us to accept. Grounds are the supporting facts or ideas which supposedly lead us to accept the claim. It is an unspoken principle of communication that whenever a person makes a claim, let us say of the sort, 'The people who just moved in to the house next to me are good neighbours', the person is accountable, if asked, to produce the data on which the claim is based.

The following are some claims recently heard in conversations:

- The Akimbes are good neighbours.
- It's OK to cheat in exams sometimes.
- If they put a higher tax on gasoline, I'm sure it'll cut down on consumption.
- I think one of the causes of juvenile delinquency is poor nutrition.
- Mary has got to stop drinking.
- You'd better get one of those Beacon alarm systems.

If you are engaged in a conversation in which one of these claims is made, you might be willing to accept it since you understand – and accept as true – the implicit grounds of support. However, you may wish to challenge the claim by asking for specific underlying grounds for it:

- Why do you think they're good neighbours?
- When would it be OK to cheat in an exam?
- Don't you think that people who have to use gasoline will continue to buy it anyway?
- Do you mean that poor nutrition leads to behaviour problems or that good nutrition alone can prevent them?
- What do you mean? She's only a social drinker.
- Why do you think I need an alarm system?

This challenge will usually force the speaker to make the grounds of the claim explicit:

- They're good neighbours because they maintain their property well.
- Cheating in exams can sometimes be justified when a course isn't part of a student's major.
- People would use gasoline only when absolutely essential.
- I read a study in which delinquent kids got a better diet and it brought about a change in their behaviour.
- She tends to get depressed about her weight, and then she starts drinking heavily.
- Crime in this neighborhood is increasing.

Even after hearing the grounds explicitly, the listener may still disagree with the claim. She may find the grounds irrelevant, that is, not related to the claim, or she may find the grounds contradictory, leading her to reject the claim rather than accept it. Similarly, she may find the claim too strong in that there are other grounds, or counter-evidence, that would lead to an alternate claim. Or she may find the grounds too weak in that the claim is not very informative or interesting.

A central part of comprehension of conversation consists of understanding – and then accepting, rejecting, or partially accepting or rejecting – the claims that the speaker is making.

4.4 Memory

In neurological terms, memories are groups of neurons that fire together in the same pattern each time they are activated. The links between individual neurons that bind them into a single 'memory' are formed through a process called long-term potentiation (LTP) (Carter, 1998). When we refer to memory in listening, we mean both the process of activating relevant memories to assist in comprehension and the process of forming or updating memories during comprehension.

Memory is generally discussed as involving two dimensions: long-term memory, associated with the sum of all of a person's knowledge and experience, and short-term memory, associated with knowledge that is activated at a particular moment. Cowan (1993) notes that the popular term **'short-term memory' (STM)** is ambiguous because it is used to refer to either (1) the set of representations from **long-term memory** stores that are currently and temporarily in a state of heightened activation, or (2) the focus of attention or content of awareness that can be held for a limited period of time. Cowan argues for a more coherent conception of STM that is hierarchical, with the focus of attention a subset of the activated set of neural connections in long-term memory.

Over the past century, research on **working memory** has been dominated by the construct of memory as a structural entity. Characterisations of short-term memory have emphasised storage, with the role of STM described as specialised for information maintenance for retrieval after a brief interval, such as when we try to retain a new phone number before we dial it. There has been little emphasis on STM as a means of activating or transforming information or as a means of integrating selected portions of long-term memory with new material.

More recent models have challenged this traditional model of a single short-term 'store'. For example, newer models posit *multiple* working

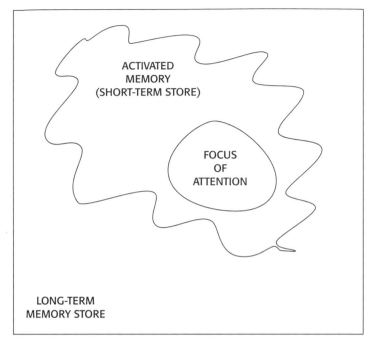

Our focus of attention is the active part of our short-term memory, which is part of our long-term memory store.

Figure 4.1   Focus of attention (based on Cowan, 1997: 31)

memories, modules that are associated with different modalities (e.g. speech vs writing) and with different kinds of **representations** (e.g. spatial, serial, verbal) (Cowan, 1993).

Another new proposal is a computational model of working memory. Working memory is seen as a 'computation space' in which various operations, such as rehearsal, phonological looping of input, and information reductions, generalisations, and inferences occur. A computational version of working memory still has strict temporal-span limitations. Cowan (1998) has discussed two phases of short-term memory with very different properties: (1) a brief sensory unresolved **afterimage** lasting up to two seconds (sometimes called **echoic memory**) and (2) a more perceptually resolved short-term memory lasting up to 20 seconds. Under this conception, the second phase of short-term memory, lasting 10–20 seconds, is just one of a series of activated features in memory.

Short-term and long-term memory can be associated with **active information** and **inactive information** respectively. For purposes of understanding verbal communication, psychologists now consider it preferable to speak in terms of memory activation rather than in terms of memory size.

Concept 4.5   **Schank's 'dynamic memory'**

Schank (1986) uses script theory as the basis for a dynamic model of memory. His model suggests that events are understood in terms of scripts, plans and other knowledge structures as well as relevant previous personal experiences. Important aspects of dynamic memory are the explanatory processes (XPs) that represent stereotyped answers to events when there is a perceived anomaly in the event. Schank proposes that XPs are a critical mechanism of human creativity.

Script theory is primarily intended to explain language-processing and the application of higher-level thinking skills to discourse comprehension. A variety of computer programs have been developed to demonstrate the theory. Schank (1991) applies his theoretical framework to story-telling and the development of intelligent tutors. Shank and Fano (1995) describe the application of these ideas to educational software.

Example:

The classic example of Schank's theory is the restaurant script. The script has the following characteristics (scenes, events and 'cognitive moves'):

Scene 1: Entering

S PTRANS S into restaurant, S ATTEND eyes to tables, S MBUILD where to sit, S PTRANS S to table, S MOVE S to sitting position

Scene 2: Ordering

S PTRANS menu to S (menu already on table), S MBUILD choice of food, S MTRANS signal to waiter, waiter PTRANS to table, S MTRANS 'I want food' to waiter, waiter PTRANS to cook

Scene 3: Eating

Cook ATRANS food to waiter, waiter PTRANS food to S, S INGEST food

Scene 4: Exiting

Waiter MOVE write cheque, waiter PTRANS to S, waiter ATRANS check to S, S ATRANS money to waiter, S PTRANS out of restaurant

There are many variations possible on this general script having to do with different types of restaurants or procedures. For example, the script above assumes that the waiter takes the money; in some restaurants, the cheque is paid to a cashier. Such variations are opportunities for misunderstandings or incorrect inferences.

Note: TRANS, ATTEND, BUILD refer to cognitive movements of information

4.5 Learning

Once a listener has participated in a 'listening event', and the event has concluded, what has the listener 'learned'? In psychological terms, learning can be defined most simply as the modification of a concept due to an experience. This modification may of course affect subsequent behaviour as well. In this sense, all listening 'experiences' involve some degree of learning. The degree of learning is reflected initially in the way the listener represents what he or she now knows. Degree of learning is then reflected in the impact of that new knowledge on the listener's subsequent attitudes, beliefs and actions.

Learning from listening requires activating prior knowledge, or knowledge schemas and updating them in some way: through addition, negation, generalisation, reduction, or abstraction. The most basic type of learning is what Kintsch (1998) calls a '**textbase**' **model** of memory use. This type of learning tends to be temporary, fading after even a few hours, because the new learning is not sufficiently integrated with prior knowledge and can only be retrieved in specific ways related to the 'learned' text. Learning for a long-term purpose involves a **situational model** of memory that integrates prior knowledge with knowledge gained from the text. This type of learning tends to last beyond a few hours because it is better integrated, and has multiple means of being accessed.

In a cognitivist framework the relation of listening and learning requires four elements:

1. **Units** of learning – words or concepts or configurations of concepts that are represented in long-term memory. These units (words or concepts or configurations) must have 'psychological reality' for the learner; they must signify to the learner what is being learned.

2. **Activation values** for these units – the cognitive importance attached to a unit by the learner, and the recency of its prior activation in working memory. Importance (or salience) and recency will influence the likelihood of these new units being retained.

3. **Connection weighting** – the links of a unit to other units in memory, and the strength of connection. The strength of the links of the new unit (concept or configuration, etc.) to prior experience, and to the listener's own interests, views and needs, will predict strongly a likelihood of the new learning becoming permanent. The ways in which the listener 'experiences' the text (unidimensionally or multidimensionally) will also influence the weighting of new connections.

4. **Learning rules** – the ways (both innate and acquired) that the connections can be augmented or changed, or unlearned. The ways that the listener 'processes' the text – fills in the gaps in the text to achieve her

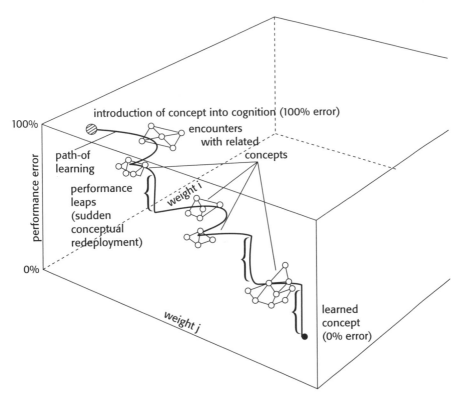

Connectionism is a model of how the brain organises neuron networks to achieve learning. In order for learning to take place, a new 'concept' must be formed and replicated with decreasing levels of error. In order to learn a new concept, the person must form 'connections' with previously learned concepts and continuously 'reapprehend' the new concept. Each set concept of concepts that the learner encounters has a particular 'weight' that alters the path of learning. The learning 'path' involves multiple encounters with the concept in new cognitive contexts and with different weightings. Progress in learning (toward 0 per cent errors) occurs in 'performance leaps' through encounters with related concepts. What drives this model of learning is the learner's desire for 'unifying' concepts in cognition.

Figure 4.2   **Connectionist view of learning (based on Clark and Millican, 1996: 32)**

own sense of continuity and completion – and the beliefs that the learner has about this processing – how his own learning can be altered – are the basic learning rules that the listener employs.

(Based on Clark, 1993)

Although these principles for learning are simple, it is impossible to depict the exact nature of learning from any particular text or listening experience. First, the sheer number of the connections of brain circuitry involving units of representations and weights cannot be determined. Secondly, this model of learning does not address the 'drive' systems of the human brain (situated in the hypothalamus and its immediate connections) which are involved in the way a person perceives a stimulus and responds to it at basic visceromotor levels, or the ways in which the brain's layered systems reinforce interactions between perception and learning (Austin, 1998: 191). In spite of these shortcomings, this type of connectionist model allows us to understand how listening and learning are related.

Chapter 5

Natural language processing

This chapter . . .

- provides an overview of some issues in natural language processing (NLP) and how they parallel human speech processing, and outlines the process of speech recognition;
- provides an outline of the kind of semantic processing that takes place in NLP.

Computer science has long had an interest in **natural language processing** – the understanding of naturally spoken language by a computer – as a means of extending the power and efficiency that computers can exert on human transactions and interactions. A review of the basic research in natural language processing is included in this section because computer science has modelled natural language processing (NLP) on the ways that humans understand and respond to speech. In turn, the insights gained from NLP are often helpful in understanding human listening.

Although the procedures required in computational listening are also required in human listening, the results are of course achieved in fundamentally different ways. Current computer programs for recognising, analysing, and responding to human speech have become remarkably effective and even human-like, though always within a restricted environment of possible meanings.

Designing a restricted natural language processor requires a great deal of research and performance checking. The computer programmer faces three main challenges in speech processing: **speech recognition, semantic analysis** and **appropriate response**.

5.1   Speech recognition

Automatic speech recognition by computers bears no resemblance to the way that the human ear and brain work, although it seeks to emulate the kinds of processing outcomes that the human ear and brain produce. The computer performs an electronic spectrum analysis of incoming acoustic signals. Nearly all automatic speech recognisers, as the first step on the way to recognition, convert the incoming sound pressure variations into a set of coefficients from which spectral information (pitch, loudness, duration) can be obtained. The key operation involved is cutting the incoming signal into a series of **acoustic snapshots**, perhaps each a tenth of a second in length, with each snapshot approximating and simplifying the true spectrum of the sound. The coefficients for the spectral information in a sequence of snapshots are analysed to determine which sequence of phonemes in the language is most likely to have generated them (e.g. /s /+ /a/ + /p/ vs /z/ + /ae/ + /b/) (Denes and Pinson, 1993) .

A sequence of frames does not actually correspond to specific words in an utterance. An additional probability calculation must be performed in order to derive the best possible match of frames to words. This calculation is fraught with problems because the frame sequence for any word can vary so widely. In addition to extraneous variables such as background noise and microphone differences, phonemic factors that contribute to this variability are

- different rates of speaking;
- different sounds preceding or following a particular word of interest (co-articulatory effects);
- different pronunciations, due to regional NS accents or NNS accents;
- different speakers – different vocal tract configurations lead to spectrum differences;
- incomplete utterances, in which sounds or whole words are omitted.

The goal of an automatic speech recogniser is to determine the words that were spoken. In order to determine, or 'recognise' words, a program must have a database. The contents of the database and how it is constructed or programmed (called the 'training' of the database) as well as the techniques used to find the best match are what distinguish one type of processor from another. All of the words in the speech recogniser's vocabulary are represented as phonemic patterns in the computer's database, against which input comparisons are made.

Three basic methods employed for pattern matching: **template-matching recognisers**, **statistical recognisers** and **neural nets**. Template-matching systems match patterns directly on sequences of spectrum frame.

Systems that use words as units for recognition will have stored templates of each word in the recogniser's vocabulary. The template contains a sequence of frames corresponding to a typical utterance of each word. When a sequence of speech is uttered, frame patterns are matched to measure the least difference or 'distance' between the input and plausible words and sequences of words. As with human speech recognition, a 'best match' can always be found, although this match may not necessarily be what the speaker uttered.

Statistical recognisers utilise a technique known as **'hidden Markov models' (HMMs)**, named after the Russian mathematician A.A. Markov. HMMs utilise statistical probabilities that characterise many aspects of speech. The basic assumption underlying the HMM technique is that a sequence of frames can always be described by probabilities. In particular, the probability of a single sound 'snapshot' (called a 'state') transitioning

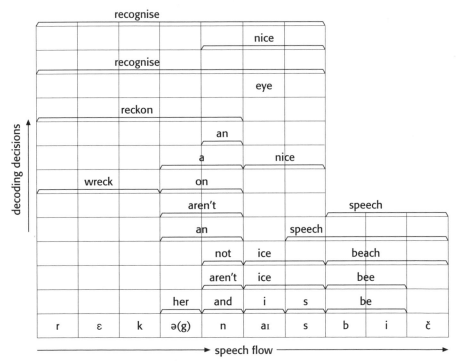

Speech is recognised sequentially as words are identified through progressive elimination of alternate word candidates. Most decoding decisions are required on unstressed parts of the utterance and the listener must often wait until subsequent syllables and words are uttered to complete the decoding of a phrase.

Figure 5.1   **Sorting out candidates in speech recognition**

to any other snapshot can be estimated, given a large database of words and phrases in the language (and a large calculating capacity). The terminology 'hidden Markov model' arises from the fact that the frame sequence for a specific word is not directly observable in the input data, and is therefore 'hidden'. HMMs are generally more efficient than template processors because they can decode full phrases rather than 'listen' word by word.

Neural net models (NNs) rely on simultaneous processing at multiple layers: phonetic, lexical and syntactic. Using information in one layer to help clarify partial information at any other layer, they can quickly rule out implausible candidates for the speech recogniser .

All three models improve their accuracy and efficiency by limiting the number of words to be considered at a given time. Automatic recognisers in general gain efficiency by imposing constraints using an underlying language model. If a language model can specify vocabulary collocation rules (or probabilities) and grammar rules, the speech recogniser can more accurately determine what words are acceptable in specific strings of speech (James, 1985).

5.2   Semantic analysis

Speech recognition is only one phase of speech understanding; in a sense, speech recognition is analogous to stenography, the goal of which is to record linguistic strings correctly (Rodman, 1988). Speech recognition then is the 'front end' of speech understanding systems. Speech understanding requires speech recognition, but also requires semantic and pragmatic analysis of the speech string once it is recognised accurately. This clear separation of phonetic and semantic processes is one obvious difference between human and machine 'listening'.

Semantic analysis by computer can be achieved by defining the 'propositions' and 'scripts' (sequences of propositions) that are possible and probable in the input. **Spoken Language Systems (SLSs)** can manage to 'understand' input on a semantic level only to the extent that propositions and scripts can be matched with an internal set of representations pre-programmed into the system. Similarly, an appropriate response can be provided only if the SLS system is pre-programmed with likely prompts for its set of responses.

For instance, if an SLS is set up to help museum visitors, it may be pre-programmed to anticipate questions such as: 'Where is the dinosaur exhibit?' 'What is the most popular exhibit in the museum?' It would provide pre-set responses once the input had been recognised as a 'request for location of (specific item)'. Effective semantic analysis assigns an input string to an appropriate content schema, in which vacant slots in the schema – those not provided in the input – can be filled by the SLS. An appropriate response effectively predicts what information the user requires and provides it in a usable form.

Concept 5.1   **Early developments in computer 'listening'**

By defining the domain in which interaction and understanding will take place, the computer programmer can predict all (or most) plausible 'meanings' and prepare a 'response'. Advances are being made continuously in the area of natural language processing. Here are some of the milestones in its development.

ELIZA: Weizenbaum (1966) – a 'simulator', which attempted to simulate basic human interaction (question and answer) through simple transformations of grammar.

DARPA (1970s): US Department of Defense – a 'transcriber', with the task of transcribing normally produced speech within limited (1,000 word vocabulary) domain, with allowable error limits (10 per cent of words spoken).

GUS (Genial Understanding System): (Bobrow and Winograd, 1977): 'Gus' was a travel agent who could arrange trips. This was a frame-driven system that prompted the user with questions to receive needed information to complete the frame.

PAM (Plan Applier Module): (Wilenski, 1981) – understood propositions in stories in terms of 'plans', as a series of propositions relating to the outcome of a story. It mapped received input onto a story structure.

HARPY: (Lowerre and Reddy, 1980) and **HEARSAY** (Ermann et al., 1980): speech recognition and understanding occur as part of the same process, attempting to arrive at 'meaning' as a primary goal.

MARGIE (Meaning, Analysis, Response Generation, Inference in English), MOPs (Memory Organising Packets): (Schank, 1982) – MOPs were scene or frame-based knowledge structures to help organise 'world knowledge', designed to understand descriptions of real-life scenes (e.g. restaurants).

BORIS (Lehnert, Robertson, Black, 1983): a text-comprehension system that understood new sentences in terms of context provided by previous sentences. It incorporated questions asked as part of the text and could be 'misled' by questions that presupposed false information.

Concept 5.2   **Ongoing issues in natural language understanding**

- **User logic problem**: How to design dialogue between computer interface and user to approximate the user's logic.

- **Recovery problem**: How to manage dialogues with the user and recover from breakdowns, how to diagnose ambiguities and potential understanding problems before they 'snowball'.

- **Sufficiency problem**: How to extract the needed information from the user's utterances.

- **Variability problem**: Because the same target speech sounds are encoded differently by speakers of the same language (speaker and dialect variations), how can the 'same' sound be recognised.

- **White-space problem**: How to handle the uncertainty about what the units of processing are, as there is no 'white space' between words in speech.

- **Time problem**: How to solve ambiguity problems, integrate relevant information quickly and still keep up with the input.

Chapter 6

Listening development and language acquisition

This chapter...

- explains how listening skill develops in first languages (L1) and second languages (L2);
- outlines key concepts in development of speech perception in our first language (L1);
- explains the role of contextualised input in L1 development;
- discusses the idea of cognitive restructuring and its relation to L1 listening;
- outlines how L2 acquisition takes places through listening;
- discusses the role of listening intake in L2 acquisition;
- outlines the notions of speed of processing and transfer in L2 listening;
- introduces the concept of learning context in L2 to explain differences in levels of L2 listening success.

6.1 First language (L1) development of perception

Under normal circumstances, we all manage to acquire our first language, and we do it primarily through listening. There is a seamless connection between learning to listen and acquiring our first language (L1). We acquire listening ability in our first language (L1), in a gradual and seemingly effortless way, and regardless of what that first language is, we tend to do it in the about same amount of time.

Developmental studies of speech perception across languages demonstrate that infants begin with a language-general capacity that provides a

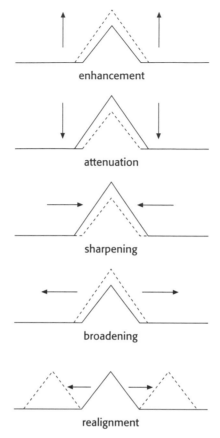

The child selectively modifies input in five different ways during language acquisition. These figures show how perceptual changes occur as a result of experience with the native language input (exposure and feedback).

Figure 6.1 Learning processes in L1 language perception (Based on Jusczyk, 1997)

means for discriminating *thousands* of potential phonetic contrasts in any of the world's languages. Over time, based on the input received from the speakers nearby, each child sifts the set of contrasts to the ones most relevant to what is to become his or her native language. This notion is consistent with other accounts about general neurological development, in which the child employs '**learning-by-selection**'. It is claimed that the nervous system of an infant starts with an 'overexuberance of connections' that are pared down in the course of development (Changeues, Heidmann and Patte 1984).

One of the first attempts to discuss the possible roles of experience in speech perception capacities hypothesised exactly these types of **directional**

Vowels				Consonants				
(1)	(2)			(1)	(2)			
i	ee	as in	beat	p	p	as in		pea
ɪ	ɪ	as in	bit	t	t	as in		tea
e	e	as in	bait	k	k	as in		key
ɛ	ɛ	as in	bet	b	b	as in		bee
æ	ae	as in	bat	d	d	as in		do
ɑ	a	as in	bought	g	g	as in		go
o	o	as in	boat	f	f	as in		fin
ʊ	u	as in	book	θ	th	as in		thin
u	oo	as in	boot	s	s	as in		sin
ə	uh	as in	cut	ʃ	sh	as in		shin
ɚ	er	as in	bird	č	ch	as in		chin
ɑɪ	ai	as in	bite	h	h	as in		honk
ɑʊ	au	as in	bout	v	v	as in		verb
ɔɪ	oi	as in	boil	ð	th	as in		then
				z	z	as in		zoo
				ʒ	zh	as in		pleasure
				ǰ	dzh	as in		jail
				m	m	as in		mail
				n	n	as in		nail
				ŋ	ng	as in		sing
				l	l	as in		line
				r	r	as in		rib
				w	w	as in		will
				j	y	as in		yes

As part of the language acquisition process, the child comes to discriminate the vowels and consonants of her native language. In General American English, there are 14 vowel and 24 consonant sounds that the child must come to distinguish from each other. Most languages have a similar number of sounds. (1) = International Phonetic Alphabet, (2) = Common Phonetic Guide.

Figure 6.2 **The sounds of English (Denes and Pinson, 1993: 13)**

changes in perception (Aslin, 1981; Aslin, Jusczyk and Pisoni, 1998). Aslin, Jusczyk and Pisoni base their arguments on the ways experience (exposure and selective attention) is known to affect the 'tuning' of neural transmissions in the cortex: through enhancement, attenuation, sharpening, broadening and realignment of sound prototypes.

During their first year of life, infants develop the perceptual ability to discriminate various kinds of differences in the utterances they hear around them. This ability provides them with a way of distinguishing one utterance from another and one speaker from another, and serves as a precursor to developing the ability to listen to connected language in context.

Words are very seldom isolated from one another in fluent speech, and even 'child-directed speech' (CDS) is generally in phrasal forms. Consequently, part of what the child must acquire has to do with learning how

Table 6.1 **Development of listening abilities in the first year** (based on Owens, 1992)

Months	Listening ability
1	responds to the sound of human voices
2	distinguishes between different sounds
3	turns head in response to direct voices
4	imitates heard tones
5	discriminates between 'negative' and 'positive' attitudes in human voices
6	imitates volume, pitch and speech-rate of heard voices
7	attends to vocalisations of adults around her
8	recognises some frequently repeated words
9	begins to imitate complex sounds
10	imitates syllables (combined phonemes) of adult speech
11	imitates inflections and rhythms
12	recognises familiar words, such as own name

word boundaries are marked in the language. Learning what features mark word boundaries in utterances from a particular language seems to involve discovering how the sounds can be ordered, phonetically and prosodically, within words in the language. This exposure and gradual discrimination of allowable features is what is known as gaining **phonotactic knowledge** of the language.

Words from other languages will frequently differ with respect to the properties of the child's first language, and the infant must acquire a sense of what is and is not allowable in the native language. Hence, one of the things that is essential for infants to learn is what sound properties are characteristic of utterances they hear in their native language. Over the course of hundreds of hours of exposure, this ability seems to emerge naturally.

By the end of the first year, sensitivity will decline for many distinctions that are not frequently found in the native language input. At the same time, infants seem to be absorbing information about regularly occurring features of the native language sound patterns. In a cumulative fashion, sensitivity is thus developing to precisely those features that are helpful in segmenting words from the input. This is an important transition in listening development. This means that infants' skills at word segmentation are developing along with their knowledge of the way sound patterns are structured in their native language. Speech segmentation and word recognition are the essential properties of perception.

In summary, there are two primary features of the early development of learning to listen:

1. Infants develop **'categorical perception'**, the capacity to discriminate speech sound contrasts in their native language in a number of different phonetic dimensions, in addition to **'continuous perception'**, the ability to hear continuous speech as combinations of sound sequences.

2. Infants develop **'perceptual constancy'**, the ability to tolerate the kind of **acoustic variability** that accompanies changes in rates of speech or differences in speakers' voices. This ability to generalise across variable input is exactly what is required to relate sound differences to changes in meaning.

Concept 6.1   **Methodology used in studies of infant speech perception**

When working with infants and very young children, researchers have to devise ways for the children to participate in experiments. Because young children cannot yet verbalise their responses, non-verbal responses have to be utilised. Here are the two main procedures that have been used.

HAS (High Amplitude Sucking Procedure)

Although this procedure seems absurd at first glance, the HAS procedure has been a highly productive tool in speech research with infants. Because infants often show increased interest in novel stimuli, it has been found that they will increase their rate of sucking on a pacifier in response to different stimuli. In order to test whether an infant can discriminate between two sounds, the researcher might present a tape of a sound sequence /a/ /a/ /a/ /ae/ /a/. If there is an increase in the HAS response (over a number of trials), the researcher may conclude that the child perceives a difference in the sounds.

OHT (Operant Headturn Procedure)

The OHT technique is based on principles of operant conditioning and can be used reliably only with infants who have successfully completed a 'conditioning phase'. In the basic experimental situation, an infant is seated on a caregiver's lap facing the experimenter across a table in the testing room. To the left of the infant is a loudspeaker, in front of the loudspeaker is a dark Plexiglas box, and concealed inside the box is a mechanical toy (such as a monkey banging cymbals) that is used as a 'visual reinforcer'. During the experiment, whenever the infant detects a change in the auditory stimulus, he is supposed to turn his heads toward the box, which of course is also the direction of the loudspeaker. An observer, outside the room looking through a one-way mirror, presses a button linked to a computer timing the presentation of the auditory stimuli whenever the infant makes a headturn toward the box. The correlations between headturns and presentation of auditory stimuli is later calculated. Because this procedure can be used successfully with infants between 6 and 12 months old, it has been used to study the development of speech-perception capacities in young children (e.g. Werker, 1991).

6.2 L1 contextualised input

While the child spends its first year of linguistic development learning to recognise the sound contrasts of a language, he or she is also being assimilated into a social unit, usually with familiar adult caretakers. The child's innate language ability, coupled with her natural curiosity about the world and her desire to integrate into the family unit provide the means and the motivation for acquisition of language. While the child motivates this acquisition process, the role of carers is critical in providing challenges, support and feedback for the child as she develops. Further, these interactions provide a useful record of the kind of linguistic and social development that the child is undertaking.

In most cultures adults and other caretakers commonly use special speech styles when talking with young children. In terms of language development, it has been assumed that 'baby talk' or 'caretaker speech' facilitates children's noticing and subsequently learning the phonology, syntax, lexis and discourse patterns of the native language. Empirical study of caretaker speech to young children, or CDS ('child-directed speech') dates back to the 1960s and flourished through the 1990s.

Gallaway and Richards (1994: 264) provide a concise overview of the interactionist traditions within L1 acquisition studies. They point out that CDS might be expected to facilitate language acquisition in a wide variety of ways, including:

- managing attention
- promoting positive affect toward interacting with others
- improving intelligibility of language directed to children
- facilitating segmentation of input
- providing feedback on comprehension
- providing correct models for imitation
- reducing processing load
- encouraging conversational participation
- teaching social routines.

There is no consensus among child language specialists, however, about all of these potential facilitating factors in language acquisition (cf. Snow, 1994; Mitchell and Myles, 1998). A couple of points seem to be agreed. One is that CDS is typically **semantically contingent**, that is, carer talk with the child tends to be about objects and events to which the child is already paying attention. Thus, it may be that semantic contingency, rather than the linguistic features of CDS itself, is what facilitates language acquisition. Studies from other cultures (e.g. Ochs, 1987) have shown that CDS

Turn	Jacqueline	Mother
1	Wash Linda's	
2	There's socks	
3		**** (looks at J)
4	Linda bought you socks Mum	
5		Yes-there's your socks
6	Lin-	
7		Mummy's washing them
8		I've got to do all that now
9	Linda brought you socks Mum	Yes
10		Linda bought you socks (softly)
11		—
12		They're dirty
13		They've got to be washed
14	Linda bought you	
15	Me got washed	
16		Pardon?
17	Linda wa-	
18	Wash them	
19		No
20		Mummy's going to wash them
21	Linda wash them	
22		No Linda's not going to wash them
23	Linda not going to wash them	
24		No
25		Mummy wash them

Analysis of caretaker–child speech across cultures consistently demonstrates how caretakers provide cognitive 'scaffolding' – making concepts explicit, repeating, reconstructing and clarifying – to help children come to understand things around them and come to participate in increasingly sophisticated discourse.

Figure 6.3   Parent–child interaction (Wells, 1981: 146–7)

is clearly not a universal practice; however, children are nearly always in the presence of **contextualised language routines**, such as eating, getting dressed, playing with toys, taking a bath, going to bed. In these situations, salient features of the context as well as habituated routines help the child understand the meaning of the language used.

Another agreed-upon point is that in CDS explicit formal correction of the child's productions is unusual, though **recasts** are quite common. These recasts (restating a correct or acceptable formulation) provide opportunities for the child to notice 'negative evidence' in the child's own speech and comprehension processes.

Child-directed speech is typically constructed to help the child understand linguistic or social concepts more easily, and to provide positive and negative evidence to help the child develop productive and receptive language skills. In Figure 6.3, Jacqueline (J), aged two, interacts with her mother (M). M attempts to understands J's meaning, to help J clarify her understanding of the situation, to help J formulate the language needed to express that understanding, and to offer opportunities to be understood. In this setting, Jacquelyn has just noticed a pair of her socks in a pile of laundry that Mother is doing and recalls that she received the socks from her Aunt Linda. She is now trying to share this interesting discovery with her mother.

Although the intensity and the style of child-directed speech varies from culture to culture, it appears that children in all language backgrounds are constantly present in group settings and are surrounded by contextualised talk routines to which they can and do pay attention. Both exposure to and attention to a wide range of live contextualised talk routines appear to be necessary conditions for language acquisition to occur. At early stages of development, language acquisition is primarily learning to understand, which means having the opportunities to work out the meaning of language in context, to 'make sense' of their social environment.

Quote 6.1 Listen on language acquisition

... the study of child language development cross-culturally supports the idea that children will only learn to talk in an environment of which they can make some sense and which has a structure of which the child is a part ... there are systematic ways in which the structure in which the child is growing up gives her/him access to ways of working out the language ...

Lieven (1994: 59)

6.3 L1 cognitive restructuring

As a child learns a first language, a number of cognitive developments are taking place simultaneously. These cognitive changes serve as an experimental playground for the child to try out new language and also as a motivator to help the child seek new language that fits new concepts that the child is experiencing for the first time. Because of this harmonious fit between growth and motivation, first language development and cognitive development cannot be separated.

The concept of **cognitive structure** is central to understanding how these two forms of development coincide in the child. Cognitive structures are patterns of physical or mental action that underlie specific acts of intelligence.

According to Piaget, who spent his entire career exploring the development of language and intelligence, these patterns correspond to definable stages of child development. According to Piaget, there are four primary cognitive structures – and thus four development stages: (1) sensorimotor; (2) preoperations; (3) concrete operations; and (4) formal operations.

In the sensorimotor stage (0–2 years), intelligence takes the form of motor actions. Intelligence in the preoperation period (3–7 years) is intuitive in nature. The cognitive structure during the concrete operational stage (8–11 years) is logical but depends upon concrete referents. In the final stage of formal operations (12–15 years), thinking involves abstractions.

Cognitive structures invariably change as the child grows older, but this change can be optimised through experience and education. Piaget calls these experiences the processes of adaptation: assimilation and accommodation. **Assimilation** involves the interpretation of events in terms of existing cognitive structure, whereas **accommodation** refers to changing the cognitive structure to make sense of the environment. Cognitive and linguistic development consists of a continual effort to adapt to the environment in terms of assimilation and accommodation. The child's use of language – both receptively and productively – is a reflection of his or her efforts to adapt to the environment. In this sense, Piaget's theory is similar in nature to other constructivist perspectives of learning (such as Vygotsky's) that posit a 'proximal zone' in which the learner is actively experimenting with structures not yet mastered. Guidance by a caretaker can facilitate the child's cognitive and linguistic development, but cannot alter the innate nature of this learning.

While the stages of cognitive development identified by Piaget are associated with characteristic age spans, they vary for every child. Furthermore, each stage has many detailed structural forms that individual children will come to master in different ways. For example, according to Piaget, the concrete operational period has more than 40 distinct structures covering classification and relations, spatial relationships, time, movement, chance, number, conservation and measurement.

Based on the child's current stage of development, caretakers and teachers can provide environments, stimulation and listening opportunities that will appropriately engage the child in concepts that the child is beginning to explore. For example, with children in the sensorimotor stage, teachers should try to provide a rich and stimulating environment with ample objects to play with, and ample discourse – and active listening experiences – about the objects and actions that are employed. On the other hand, with children in the concrete operational stage, learning activities can involve problems of classification, ordering, location, conservation using concrete objects (cf. Mercer, 2000).

Another critical aspect of the child's cognitive and linguistic development is social. It is now well established that social interaction plays a fundamental role in the development of cognition and language (cf. Vygotsky, 1978; Lantolf, 2000). Vygotsky (1978: 57) states:

> Every function in the child's cultural development appears twice: first, on the social level, and later, on the individual level; first, between people (inter-psychological) and then inside the child (intra-psychological). This applies equally to voluntary attention, to logical memory, and to the formation of concepts. All the higher functions originate as actual relationships between individuals.

A critical aspect of Vygotsky's theory is the idea that the potential for cognitive development is limited to a certain time span which he calls the 'zone of proximal development' (ZPD). Furthermore, full development during the ZPD depends upon full social and oral interaction. The range of skill that can be developed with adult guidance or peer collaboration exceeds what can be attained alone. (Vygotsky's theory was an attempt to explain consciousness as the end product of socialisation. For example, in the learning of language, our first utterances with peers or adults are for the purpose of communication but once mastered they become internalised and allow 'inner speech'.)

While the child is continuously 'restructuring' cognitive connections, she is also working on restructuring her internal 'grammar' of the L1. This is done through active processes of using intake (understood input) to formulate the underlying grammar rules of the language. This is done primarily through 'extraction' (finding recurring units in speech that are bound by silence, and hence are likely to be 'units' of communication) and 'segmentation' (breaking off pieces of extracted units to make internal comparisons). Throughout the first few years of listening to 'positive examples' of speech being used appropriately and contextually, the child gradually restructures his rules of the language until they conform to the adult standard (cf. Peters and Boggs, 1986; Bates and MacWhinney, 1989).

6.4 L2 acquisition: the role of listening

While virtually all children learn to listen in their first language as part of their language acquisition process, even when their environment is only minimally supportive of their efforts, the case for second-language learning is not nearly as optimistic. It has been noted that for a person to learn a second language three major conditions are required: (1) a learner who realises the need to learn the second language and is motivated to do so;

(2) speakers of the target language who know it well enough to provide the learner with access to the spoken language and the support (such as simplification, repetition and feedback) they need for learning it; and (3) a social setting which brings the learner in frequent enough and sustained enough contact with target-language speakers to make language learning possible. Most cases of difficulty or failure of a learner, either a child or an adult, to acquire a second language are generally due to a lack in one or more of these factors (Wong-Fillmore, 1991).

Listening is required in two of these conditions, and is therefore an essential means of language development, a point that is often overlooked in language pedagogy and research. In Second Language Acquisition (SLA) research, listening opportunities are often characterised as the **'linguistic environment'** – the stage for second-language acquisition. This environment, that is, the speakers of the target language and their speech to the L2 learners, provides linguistic input in the form of listening and interaction opportunities embedded in social and pedagogic situations. The learner, in order to acquire the language, must come to understand the input *and* pay attention to the forms in the input. As in L1 acquisition, motivation and access to developmental opportunities are required. Access is made possible in part through accommodations made by (native or otherwise fluent) L2 speakers to render their language more comprehensible and in part through strategies the learner employs to create meaning from limited linguistic resources.

In L2 acquisition there is wide acceptance that the processes of 'comprehending input' are not identical with the processes of acquiring the L2 through oral input. The former, comprehending input, refers to getting the meaning from input. The latter, acquiring the L2 through oral input, refers to processing input in order to learn the language. In this chapter, and in Section 2, it is assumed that there are two overlapping processes in L2 listening development: learning to listen in the L2 and learning the L2 through listening. The optimal goal of L2 listening development is to allow for the L2 to be acquired through listening, not only to allow the learner to understand spoken messages in the L2.

In order to listen in the L2, for purposes of message comprehension and for language acquisition, the listener must gain access to the spoken-language code. The work on speech to children learning their L1 prompted SLA researchers in the mid-1970s to enquire how much 'code modification' was typically being offered to L2 learners in order to increase their access to the L2. It is often assumed that **modified input** or **accentuated input** in SLA is of even greater potential importance, given that many learners are adults (without carers) and their opportunities for access to input in the L2 may be limited.

Because the language presented to second-language learners is often in the form of a modified input similar to child-directed speech, SLA

researchers in the 1980s began to document the kind of linguistic adjustments that were evident in this newly named 'foreigner talk'. Linguistic
adjustments were noted in several areas (cf. Parker and Chaudron, 1987;
Long and Larsen-Freeman, 1991).

- **phonology**: slower rate of delivery, more use of stress and pauses, more
  careful articulation, wider pitch range, more use of full forms/avoidance
  of contractions;
- **morphology**: deliberately well-formed utterances, shorter utterances,
  less complex constructions, more retention of optional constituents/less
  ellipsis, more questions;
- **semantics**: more redundancy of information, higher frequency of
  content words, fewer idiomatic expressions, more concrete references.

An important research and pedagogic issue arising from SLA studies of
this nature is the degree to which modified input and '**compensatory
strategies**' for dealing with difficult input actually facilitate L2 learners'
acquisition of the language. Chaudron (1988), for example, has recommended that, for purposes of pedagogy, one should favour modifying the
input in the direction of elaboration (providing rephrasing, examples,
confirmation checks) rather than syntactic simplification (slower rate of
delivery, etc.), as this is more congruent with native speaker to native
speaker (NS-NS) norms.

In response to the question that modified input may in some way be
deviant or insufficient for second-language development, SLA researchers
have also focused on interactional adjustments that NSs make in conversation with NNSs. SLA research has pointed out that in addition to
linguistic adjustments, native speakers and non-native speakers often employ
conversational adjustments to make language comprehension and participation in language exchanges more productive. **Conversational adjustments** dealing with content (narrower range of topics, more predictable
topics nominated, more here-and-now orientation, shorter treatment of
topics) and interaction (more acceptance of unintentional **topic shifts**, more
confirmation checks, more clarification requests, more question-and-
answer strings) are most often noted. These conversational adjustments,
when initiated by the NNS participant, in effect constitute tokens of
listening strategies which the learner uses to make NS messages more
comprehensible (cf. Pica, 1994; Kasper and Kellerman, 1997).

6.5   L2 listening acquisition: comprehensible input

While it is clear that input plays an essential part in second-language
acquisition, the amount and type of input that is required for a learner to

acquire an L2 has not yet been clearly described. Some of the factors involved in this matter, however, are now established.

Building on research that showed a relationship between input adjustments and message comprehension, Krashen (1982) maintained that **'comprehensible input'** was a necessary condition for language learning. In his 'Input Hypothesis', Krashen says that development from the learner's current stage of interlanguage development can be achieved only by the learner's 'comprehending' language that contains linguistic items (lexis, syntax, morphology) at a level slightly above the learner's current knowledge ($i + 1$). Krashen insisted that comprehension is necessary in order for input to become 'intake' – language data that is assimilated and used to promote further development. And the ability to understand new language, he said, is made possible by speech adjustments made to learners, in addition to the learner's use of shared knowledge of the context.

Quote 6.2   Krashen's **Input Hypothesis**

Humans acquire language in only one way – by understanding messages, or by receiving 'comprehensible input'... We move from i, our current level, to $i + 1$, the next level along the natural order, by understanding input containing $i + 1$.

Krashen (1985: 2)

Krashen's Input Hypothesis has had a strong impact on language teaching, in large part because it presented a simplified interpretation of the important educational principle of 'proximal development' forwarded by Vygotsky (Vygotsky, 1978). However, the simplifications of the '$i + 1$' theory have been widely challenged (e.g. Gregg, 1984) and its parallels to Vygotsky's theories have been called into question (e.g. Dunn and Lantolf (1998)).

Krashen's 'Input Hypothesis', particularly as it was originally formulated, has been widely criticised (e.g. McLaughlin, 1987; Mitchell and Myles, 1998) because of its lack of support through empirical evidence and its lack of testability. Further, Krashen's concepts of 'understanding' and 'noticing the gap' are not clearly operationalised, and it is not clear how the learner's present state of knowledge ('i') is to be described. Specifically, it is unknown whether '$i + 1$' is intended to refer to lexis, phonology, syntax, or discourse.

As Mitchell and Myles (1998) point out, the idea that input at the right level of difficulty being necessary and sufficient for L2 acquisition is the most serious concern. There are many cases of L2 learners who have failed to progress beyond a beginning level of the L2 despite massive amounts of meaning-oriented input. Swain (1985) and Swain and Lapkin (1999) have extensively researched English L1 students in French immersion programmes in Canada, in which students receive instruction in the target language. They have discovered that many students achieve French listening comprehension scores at near-native speaker levels, but 'fossilise' in productive control of French grammar and lexis.

On the basis of this research, Swain proposed a competing '**Comprehensible Output Hypothesis**', which recognises that listening proficiency may be gained by 'semantic-pragmatic means', making it unnecessary for the listener to struggle to process unfamiliar structures (syntax and lexis) in full. She suggests that it is the effort of composing new utterances, rather than comprehending new utterances, that is more likely to require learners to formulate new hypotheses about the L2 syntax and lexis, and to try them out on real listeners (Swain, 2000).

The common ground for most claims about the role of input in L2 acquisition appears to be that the L2 acquirer must have ongoing access to meaningful input. What is meaningful to a learner will of course change over time, and needs to be 'tuned' to the learner's interests and needs, and be at a level that is both comprehensible and also progressively closer to the native-user norms of the target language.

6.6   L2 listening development: phonological and lexical processing

It has been noted that while nearly everyone achieves first-language proficiency, there is a marked range of success in people learning second languages. Among the reasons for the varying success in L2 acquisition are external factors such as opportunities to hear and use the L2 and internal factors such as motivation and attitude toward speakers of the L2 (Dornyei, 2001).

A key difference between more successful and less successful acquirers relates in large part to their ability to use listening as a means of acquisition (Vandergrift, 1996; 1998). Successful acquirers may find listening to naturally spoken language manageable, and eventually learn to listen 'at natural speed', even if they do not have full comprehension.

A distinction between **compound bilingualism** and **coordinate bilingualism** was introduced decades ago (Ervin and Osgood, 1954) to account for the apparent slower speed of processing among some bilinguals. Response time experiments by Ervin and Osgood revealed differences in how quickly bilinguals could recognise words in their L2. Their conclusion was that the 'better' listeners were 'coordinate bilinguals', who organised their L1 and L2 mental lexicon in an integrated fashion. As a result, they tend not to be slowed down significantly by oral input in either their first or second language. Compound bilinguals, on the other hand, apparently have separate stores of L1 and L2 lexis, and recognise words more slowly in their L2.

It was found that most coordinate bilinguals are those who acquired their second language at an early age, in the same context in which they acquired their first language. Lambert, Havelka and Crosby (1958) demonstrated that separate acquisition contexts for each language will lead to a more functional separation between the two language codes and will slow down aural processing in the L2. Apparently, early bilingual experience has an effect upon neuropsychological organisation of the L2 in the user's mind and on the user's cognitive functioning in the L2. Early bilingual experience also seems to determine a cognitive and semantic organisation in which the two languages will be more or less interdependent. Apparently, when a user's L1 and L2 are interdependent, shifting from one language to the other is less difficult, less stressful and faster.

Compound bilingualism, as in the case of an adult acquiring an L2, is an example of **conceptual redeployment**. This is a process in which a conceptual framework that is already fully developed (e.g. a mental lexicon in the L1) and which is in regular use in some other domain of experience or comprehension, comes to be used for the first time in a new domain (Churchland, 1999). In the case of L2 vocabulary learning, the adult must redeploy vast amounts of semantic knowledge of words and concepts to a new domain of language use. This requires a separate 'tagging' of semantic knowledge with the new L2 codes.

Lexical processing in the L2 is the means by which the L2 user comes to use conceptual knowledge needed for understanding. The area of bilingual speech processing is particularly important as it relates to **cognitive transfer** from the L1 to the L2. Several factors are attended to in speech perception: phonetic quality, prosodic patterns, pausing, pacing and speed of the input. All of these factors influence the comprehensibility of the input. While it is generally accepted that there is a common store (or **single coding**) of semantic or 'real-world' information in memory that is used in both L1 and L2 speech comprehension, there seems to be a separate store information (or **dual coding**) of phonological for speech (Soares and Grosjean, 1984). The semantic knowledge that is required for language understanding (the background knowledge related to real-world people, places and actions) is accessed through **phonological tagging** of the language that is heard, and facility with the phonological code of the L2 will be the basis for keeping up with the speed of the spoken language (Magiste, 1985).

Use of the phonological code of an L2 has been widely studied in the context of word recognition experiments (often called 'word-spotting'

i	TOLD him to	GO and	FIND a	PLACE
	w1	w2	w3	w4

Lexical segmentation strategies allow the listener to identify some words more quickly, or with more certainty, than others. In English, stressed syllables typically (more than 85 per cent of the time) mark the start of a new content word.

Figure 6.4   Lexical segmentation

in psycholinguistic literature). The essence of phonological competence in an L2 is the appropriate use of **lexical segmentation strategies**. Each language has its own 'preferred strategies' for listening, which are readily acquired by the L1 child but often only partially acquired by the L2 learner. In English, for example, L2 listeners must come to use a **metrical segmentation strategy** that allows them to assume that 'every strong syllable is the onset of a new content word'. Because English is a **trochaically timed language**, stress peaks are important indicators of processing segments (Cutler and Butterfield, 1992; Sajavaara, 1986). Presumably, the similarity of metrical segmentation strategies between one's L1 and L2 (e.g. Dutch and English) will result in positive transfer, making aural perception in the L2 easier.

Lexical segmentation is the processes of recognising words in the stream of speech. Because there are few reliable markers in the speech code for word boundaries, even a fluent listener may require one or two seconds to recognise words in the speech stream.

Studies of error analysis focus directly on phonological coding and reveal the kind of word-recognition difficulties that L2 listeners face (e.g. Kim, 1995; Ross, 1997). In order to decode incoming speech, the L2 listener has to deal with a perceived degraded phonetic quality due to assimilation, prosodic patterns disguising unstressed words and varying speed of the input. All of these factors influence comprehensibility of speech in real time, even though the listener may 'know' all of the words being used.

Speech perception and word recognition are the **'bottom–up' processes** in listening: they provide the 'data' for comprehension. If the listener does not recognise enough of these bottom–up cues in order to process the speech in real time, he or she will rely more exclusively on **'top–down' processes**: semantic expectations and generalisations.

6.7   L2 listening development: syntactic processing

One of the important differences between L1 and L2 listening is that during the development of L2 listening, particularly for adult learners, the processes of learning to listen (that is, learning to understand spoken messages) and listening to learn (that is, learning the syntax and lexis of the language through listening) do not coincide. As a language learner or teacher or researcher knows, not everything that is understood on the message level necessarily contributes to the learner's understanding of the language. In other words, not all input becomes intake, as noted by Corder (1967).

The key distinctions that have arisen based on Corder's call to study developing L2 grammatical systems, or 'interlanguages', concern input and intake to the developing system. If listening is the primary route to language acquisition, this distinction is critical. According to van Patten (1996), it would appear that only a very small subset of input ever becomes intake that has a permanent effect on the learner's acquisition of the L2. When input does become intake, the learner 'restructures' her internal knowledge of the language, and this change becomes a permanent development in language growth.

In order for input in the L2 to become intake, the learner must address the issue of cognitive capacity for processing information. Until a learner's cognitive capacity increases, acquisition remains stagnant, and though the learner may come to understand more of the L2 through strategic compensations (e.g. inferring meanings from situational cues), her ability to process information from linguistic cues in real time remains the same.

A common point of agreement among L2 processing models (the Information Processing Models of Bialystok, Hulstijn and McLaughlin, the Input Processing Model of van Patten and his colleagues, the Competition Model of Bates and MacWhinney, the Multidimensionl Model of Meisel, Clahsen and Pienemann) is that in order to increase cognitive capacity for processing, the learner must 'detect' a new form in the spoken input. Detection (i.e. 'finding it' without being told) is the key cognitive process that makes the piece of information in the input available for further processing. In order to detect _a_ particular form (e.g. subject–verb agreement), the learner must attend to form generally. A key problem in L2 listening occurs because the learner is typically unable to attend to both content (lexical items) and grammatical form of a message (van Patten, 1990; 1996). When a learner attends to the form of the message, this attention to form competes for the processing capacity in short-term memory that is available to attend to content. As is well known, L2 listeners can attend to only so much linguistic information at a time, and under normal processing constraints, detecting any new linguistic information is unlikely.

In order for the learner to develop a capacity for increased syntactic processing in speech, the learner needs both motivation to detect new forms and a means of access to a grammar-building model. The relationship between input processing and grammar building is that input processing determines the body of data to which the grammar-building mechanisms have access. Certain types of instruction, advocated as 'processing instruction' (see Section 2) help learners use cues in the oral input that will help them detect new forms. The belief is that this type of instruction advances the strategy of 'cue noticing', which in turn helps learners engage their innate capacity for language learning (Universal Grammar).

Concept 6.2 **Van Patten's Input Processing Model**

Input processing principles:

P1   Learners process input for meaning before they process it for form.

P1(a) Learners process content words in the input before anything else.

P1(b) Learners prefer processing lexical items to grammatical items (e.g. morphological markings) for semantic information.

P1(c) Learners prefer processing 'more meaningful' morphology before 'less or non-meaningful morphology'.

P2   For learners to process form that is not meaningful, they must be able to process informational or communicative content at no (or little) cost to attention.

(van Patten, 1996: 14–15)

The link between noticing in real-time listening and eventual speech production is an important one. When applied linguists refer to grammatical processing and language acquisition, in fact, they are often referring not to speech interpretation, but to speech production. For example, Pienemann's Processability Theory (Pienemann, 1999) is based on the principle of readiness: that 'the learner cannot access [grammatical/ structural] hypotheses which he cannot process.' Though these grammatical hypotheses are accumulated and tested through speech *comprehension* ('the origin of linguistic knowledge'), it is important to note that in Pienemann's theory, acquisition is actually measured through the learner's ability to process that information during speech *production*.

6.8   L2 listening success or failure: context for learning

One of the inescapable realities of second-language education is that there is a high degree of 'failure': most adult learners who undertake to learn a second language never reach a highly proficient stage of language use in any of the four major skill areas. Many explanations have been put forward for this phenomenon: cognitive factors (intelligence, language aptitude, language-learning strategies) (cf. Gardner and MacIntyre, 1992; Dorneyi, 2001), affective factors (language attitudes, motivation, language anxiety) (cf. Ellis, 1994), environmental factors (availability of opportunities and resources, time and timing of instruction, teaching methods), genetic factors (a critical period for language acquisition) (cf. Singleton, 1995), linguistic factors (differences between the learner's L1 and L2) (cf. Gass, 1996). While all of these factors undeniably contribute to the ultimate success or failure of a given language learner, there are also societal factors underlying the 'expected success' of language learners in a given community or culture. Individual language learners are strongly influenced by these prevailing social norms.

Many people undertake to study or to learn a second language, for purposes ranging from wanting to broaden one's understanding of the world, or wanting a new learning challenge to needing to communicate for compelling social or professional purposes. Success in achieving these purposes, then, is a relative matter. Only a very few of those who do undertake second-language study actually aim to reach a high level of proficiency and persevere to the eventual attainment of that stage. Studies of those 'success stories' have become the basis for describing 'good learner' profiles, optimal learning conditions and effective teaching methods.

There are, of course, some learning contexts which clearly favour and predict a high rate of success, and others which predict a low rate of success. The type and degree of success that a *group* of second language learner reaches – whether a passing knowledge of a language, or a detailed academic knowledge of a language without communication ability, or a functional proficiency, depends to a great extent on the societal perspective toward the language being learned and the profile of the successful learner in that group (McLauglin, 1992).

11 Teaching listening

Chapter 7

Approaches to teaching listening

Because listening is so prevalent in language use and because listening is the primary means of L2 acquisition for most people, the development of listening as a skill and as a channel for language input should assume critical importance in instruction. Ironically, instruction in listening has not received much attention until recently. 'Teaching listening' is used in this section to refer to approaches to curriculum design and methods of instruction that aim to assist learners in improving their listening.

Over the past 50 years, methods for the development of listening instruction have evolved slowly, as the result of various techniques being combined and recombined. Most methodologies now in use around the world in classrooms, in materials design circles and self-access centres cannot be said to subscribe to any one philosophy or theory of learning or teaching. Most methodologies can thus be described as eclectic, drawing upon principles of education, linguistics, psycholinguistics, language acquisition and instructional design in aiming to come up with the 'best teaching practices' for particular situations and programmes.

Section II explores the teaching of listening, describing the principles that are relevant to instructional design and teaching methodology. Consistent with the goals set out in the Introduction, this section aims to promote more inclusive and better-informed approaches to teaching of listening. By 'better-informed approaches' we mean approaches that incorporate receptive, constructive, collaborative and transformative aspects of listening and work toward deepening the experience of listening for learners.

Chapter 7 outlines principles of general instructional design and second-language acquisition that can help learners activate and develop the key processes of listening that were provided in Section I. Chapter 8 provides a brief overview of teaching methods and ways of conceptualising methodology. Chapter 9 explores aspects of 'input' that are central to the teaching of listening: authenticity, relevance, genres, difficulty, grading and simplification. Chapter 10 then explores ten key areas that are part of a comprehensive methodology for teaching listening. Finally, Chapter 11 provides an overview of principles for testing listening.

This chapter...

- presents ten principles of instructional design;
- outlines second-language hypotheses and theories that exert an influence on the teaching of listening.

7.1   Principles of instructional design

The president of a famous religiously affiliated university was once asked, 'What does it take to be a top-notch Catholic university?' His answer was 'First, you have to be concerned with being a top-notch university.'

There is a parallel to language education. If we want to have top-notch language-teaching methodology, we first have to be concerned with having a top-notch *teaching* methodology. This is true whether we are considering language teaching generally, or instruction focusing on any of the particular skill areas, such as listening. We must first be concerned with educational principles.

Some methodologists will challenge this view, claiming that language learning is unique and requires unique teaching methodologies. Indeed, over the past century, a number of very specific language-teaching methodologies have emerged, including Total Physical Response, Suggestopedia, the Berlitz Method, Community Language Learning, the Silent Way, English through Drama, Peak Learning, the Natural Approach. Each of these approaches emphasises a particular **route** to language learning, although the goals of native-like comprehension and fluency are the same.

And although proponents of each of these methods have documented dramatic successes and promoted their methods on the basis of these successes, there have not been consistent, replicable findings with any of them. The reasons for their successes, when indeed they are successful, may be due to factors not integral to the methods themselves: selection of students, motivation of students prior to the course, amount of instruction time, time on task, qualifications of instructors, consistency of the methodology, outside activities of the learners, etc. Because these factors have not been controlled in studies of these methods, it is not valid to claim superiority for particular methods.

Although any instructor of listening, or any other skill, would be delighted to find a 'magic bullet' that would work in all teaching situations, this pollyannaish search is probably futile. There are simply too many variations in learner needs, goals, constraints and learning styles to prevent a single methodology from applying to multiple contexts. Nevertheless, the search for universal **teaching principles** both within language education and within other fields, has been very fruitful. Recent research on instructional design has suggested a number of principles that seem to underlie effective education. If we are to have high-quality language education, it is important to examine the principles in high-quality education generally, and adopt them where appropriate.

Out of a number of educational theories, several have been selected for their relevance to language education. Many of these views suggest concepts that may seem to be in conflict with concepts of 'traditional' teacher-led and text-led instruction. The principles that can be derived from these theories provide ways to achieve greater balance of the four approaches to teaching listening we outlined: receptive, constructive, responsive and transformative.

These theories are concerned with **intentions** of instruction:

1. **Aptitude specific instruction**: Instruction that is based on specific aptitudes, interests, abilities, and preferred learning styles of learners, rather than on a priori sequences or fixed methodologies is likely to be more amenable to learners. Instruction and feedback that is geared to individual differences in learning styles is more effective for complex skills and abilities (Snow, 1989; Gardner, 1993).

2. **Cognitive flexibility**: Presentation of input that is multimodal (e.g. video, audio, text, graphics) and features multiple perspectives (e.g. a story told from different points of view) is likely to be processed more thoroughly and be retained in a more meaningful way, and become more useful for language-learning purposes. Learning activities that provide multiple representations of content allow for more stable meaning construction on the part of the learner (Spiro, et al., 1988, Spiro et al., 1992; Clark and Paivio, 1991).

3. **Coordination of teaching and learning**: Long-term retention of material requires different kinds of 'learning events'. Teaching that is coordinated with 'learning events' that lead to long-term retention of material (reception, expectancy, retrieval, selective perception, semantic encoding, responding, reinforcement, retrieval, generalisation) is most efficient and most satisfying for learners (Gagne and Driscoll, 1988; Gagne et al., 1992).

4. **Modes of learning**: Learning takes place primarily by 'accretion', adding to existing schema in memory. Continual 'cognitive restructuring' of content requires some form of prediction and reflection. Metacognition needs to be built into the instructional process in order to allow for restructuring (Rumelhart and Norman, 1981; Norman, 1982; Ausubel, 1978).

5. **Positive climate for learning**: The role of the teacher is to facilitate learning by: setting a positive climate for learning, clarifying purposes for the learner, organising learning resources, balancing intellectual and emotional components of learning and sharing thoughts and feelings with the learners. Instruction is an interactive process and requires open two-way communication (Rogers and Freiberg, 1994; Combs, 1982; Valett, 1977).

The following theories are concerned with the **design** of a course:

6. **Anchored instruction**: A 'problem' text serves as a 'macrocontext' for teaching (Bransford, 1990; Bransford and Stein, 1993); this allows for greater interpretation and construction work by learners, greater response, development of strategies and focused feedback.

7. **Course structures**: Instruction proceeds in 'transactions' (what the student needs to find out or accomplish) rather than 'presentation units' (what the teacher has chosen to present), as outlined in Component Display Theory (Merrill, 1994). This theory suggests that for a given objective and learner, there is a unique combination of presentation forms (e.g. readings, interviews, discussions) that results in the most effective learning experience, and that unique course structures need to be designed for specific purposes, rather than reliance on traditional methods.

8. **Spiral learning**: Instruction should be designed and sequenced to facilitate noticing and extrapolation ('filling in the gaps') (Bruner, 1983; 1986; 1990). This entails a focus on inference work by the learners rather than expository work by the instructor.

9. **Elaborative sequencing**: Instruction should contain learning episodes that increase in levels of complexity and demands on reasoning; this sequence of instruction creates 'stable cognitive structures' (Reiguth, 1987; Reiguth and Stein, 1983). A principled type of grading of learning experiences is required to lead to stable learning.

10. **Criterion referencing**: Instructional goals need to be derived from 'end stage' performances that learners are targeting. They should reflect the competencies that need to be learned for these performances. Learners should be given specific opportunities to master the target objectives and obtain clear and expert feedback about the quality of their performance (Mager and Pipe, 1984; Mager, 1988).

Although these ten theories present ideals that often need to be modified by practical constraints, they none the less serve as useful reminders of the goals of instruction.

Concept 7.1   **Instructional principles**

principle	instructional design element
Aptitude specific instruction	input based on interests and needs of learners; focus on individualising learning and increasing motivation
Cognitive flexibility	input is multimodal, with multiple representations of content; focus on use of resources, keeping learning flexible and enjoyable
Coordination of teaching and learning	instruction organised into holistic 'learning events', focus on cross-cultural communication between instructor, learners, other sources
Modes of learning	inclusion of metacognitive strategies; focus on developing learning strategies
Positive climate for learning	instructor organises, facilitates, interacts; focus on positive climate for cross-cultural communication
Anchored instruction	use of 'macro-context' and 'problem texts'; focus on integrating listening with other areas of learning
Course structures	instruction organised around transactions; focus on developing learner autonomy
Spiral learning	focus on inference as primary learning strategy; focus on developing language-use strategies
Elaborative sequencing	increasing complexity and demands on learners, focus on deepening critical thinking
Criterion referencing	agreed instructional goals and clear feedback provide link between teachers and learners; focus on favourable outcomes of learning

7.2   Influences from second language learning research

This section outlines some key influences on the teaching of listening that are derived directly from second language acquisition research.

7.2.1   Affective filter hypothesis

The affective filter was first proposed by Dulay and Burt (1975) to account for how affective variables influence the process of L2 learning. In a subsequent work by Dulay, Burt and Krashen (1982) the concept was given more extensive treatment.

The filter is that part of the internal processing system that subconsciously screens incoming language based on what psychologists call 'affect': the learner's motives, needs, attitudes and emotional states.

Principles

1. Listening experiences that help students lessen their anxiety about listening will generally be beneficial.
2. By taking into account learners' motives and attitudes about listening, the instructor can better select input or point learners to the best resources and opportunities for appropriate input.

7.2.2   Input hypothesis

Krashen's (1982) Input Hypothesis, outlined in Chapter 6, has had a sustained effect on teaching approaches to listening. Krashen's promotion of the hypothesis shows that even though a proposed theory may be unsuccessful as a theory, it can still offer viable and valuable approaches for language teaching.

Krashen's Input Hypothesis claims that humans acquire language – first and second languages – in one and only one way: by understanding messages. By receiving input that is progressively more complex, the learner 'naturally' acquires listening ability.

This hypothesis has two main corollaries:

1. Speaking is the result of acquisition and not its cause. Speech cannot be taught directly, but rather 'emerges' on its own as a result of building competence via comprehensible input.
2. If input is understood, and there is enough of it, the necessary grammar the learner needs to learn is automatically provided. The language teacher does not need to teach the 'next structure' along a continuum of learnability or difficulty – it will be provided in just the right quantities and automatically reviewed if the student receives a sufficient amount of comprehensible input.

(Based on Krashen, 1985: 2)

Principles

1. Instruction should aim only to provide comprehensible input, that is, input at a 'i + 1' level, slightly above the learner's current level of

competence in terms of vocabulary, syntax, discourse features, length and complexity.

2. Comprehensible input may be aural or written, or both. Contextualised input, input with visual and environmental support, will tend to be more comprehensible.

3. Teachers do not need to force students to speak, as speaking will emerge naturally as a result of work with listening.

7.2.3   Interaction hypothesis

Participation in verbal interactions following a listening experience offers a learner the opportunity to follow up on new words and structures. By itself, participation in interaction has long been believed to be of great value for language learning, though the reasons for this vary. According to the Interaction Hypothesis (Long, 1985; Pica et al.,1996; Swain and Lapkin, 1999), interaction contributes directly to language acquisition in three ways: (1) through allowing the learner to provide herself with comprehensible input through interaction adjustments (e.g. requests for clarification); (2) by providing negative feedback that allows the learner to see where she may be producing errors (e.g. through recasts or reformulations by the conversation partner); and (3) by presenting opportunities for 'pushed output', in effect forcing the learner to try out new words and structures to get her ideas across.

In particular, the kind of 'negotiation' of meaning that routinely takes place during interactions (both NNS-NNS and NNS-NS interactions) is a primary means of listening development as well as language acquisition. Indeed, the most effective source of comprehensible input is usually conversational exchanges because the learner must use active clarification strategies to 'negotiate' meaning. Negotiation between learners and interlocutors takes place during the course of their interaction when either one signals with questions or comments that the other's preceding message has not been successfully understood. The other then responds by repeating or modifying the original message.

Principles

1. Listening instruction should allow learners to figure out meanings for themselves and not depend on presentation by the instructor.

2. Listening instruction should build in the need and opportunity for 'negotiation of meaning' (e.g. information and opinion gap tasks). A substantial portion of instructional time should focus on such negotiation.

Table 7.1   **Hierarchical task structure of listening** (Rost, 1994, based on Levelt, 1989)

In order to achieve first-order goals, one must achieve, with some degree of completeness and efficiency, the lower-order goals.

First-order goal:	respond to relevant aspects of what is heard
Second-order goals:	establish appropriate connection with speaker or content activate relevant knowledge to understand speaker and topic understand social meaning of input (including speaker's intentions)
Third-order goals:	understand gist of input understand cohesion between utterances understand words and structures understand pragmatic conventions
Lower-order goals:	understand sounds speaker uses

7.2.4   Procedural knowledge

One important distinction in learning theory is the distinction between declarative and procedural knowledge. Internalised rules and chunks of language (vocabulary, syntactic structures, discourse structures) constitute the 'what' of language learning, the **declarative knowledge** of the language. In contrast, procedural knowledge consists of knowing 'how' to employ language knowledge in specific cases of use, for comprehension or for production. Procedural knowledge then accounts for how learners accumulate and automatise rules and how they restructure their internal representations of the language to become progressively closer to target-language standards.

The acquisition of skills involved in any communicative task requires the coordination of information from multiple domains. Because all listeners, and especially L2 listeners, have finite mental capacities, many required skills must be automatised for the listener to function in communication.

Rather than being the goal of listening, however, comprehension is a lower-order goal, one that aids the listener in achieving an appropriate connection or response. This means that comprehension is one of the goals of listening, not the end goal.

Principles

1. Listening tasks and instruction should aim to help learners automise 'lower-level' processing of language so that they can devote more attention to 'higher-level' goals.

2. Regular targeted practice with 'fine-tuning' of lower-level processing skills (sound discrimination, etc.) will help learners automise these skills for use in extended discourse settings.

7.2.5   Learning strategies and communication strategies

Learning strategies refer to any mental or behavioural devices that students use to learn. These range from techniques for improved memory to better studying or test-taking. Learning strategies have been studied extensively, both in general education and in language education (cf. Cohen, 1998; Oxford and Leaver, 1996; Oxford, 2001).

The intent to promote learning strategies often involves changes to the design of instruction. Methods that attempt to increase the degree of learning that occurs have been called 'mathemagenic' (Ropthkopf, 1970). For example, the use of questions before instruction has been shown to increase the degree of learning (Ausubel, 1978), through encouraging students to engage in metacognition strategies such as planning.

Second-language learning strategies are generally divided into two basic classes: those adopted for *long-term* learning (e.g. joining a conversation club, making and reviewing vocabulary cards every day) and those adopted for using the language in a *current* contact situation. (Listening strategies fall into the 'strategies for use' class, although long-term learning strategies may of course also involve increasing one's listening experiences.)

Strategies for use include four subsets: retrieval strategies, rehearsal strategies, cover strategies (to create an impression of control), and communication strategies (to convey or receive a message) (Cohen, 1998). Language-learning and language-use strategies can be further differentiated according to whether they are primarily cognitive, metacognitive, affective, or social (O'Malley and Chamot, 1990; Oxford, 1990).

This cross-section alone creates 16 subcategories of language-use strategies, and it is easy to see ways to multiply the subcategories further (for instance, by language modality, listening, speaking, etc.). The process of creating strategy lists has obviously become unwieldy, although many teachers report benefits from perusing these kinds of lists.

The point of incorporating strategy instruction into language teaching is not to 'accomplish' as many strategies as possible, but rather to focus the learner's attention on particular cognitive plans they can employ to help them overcome obstacles in language use or language learning.

One caveat often raised about 'strategies' is that an effective 'strategy of language use' may not be an effective 'learning strategy'. For instance, a learner may substitute an L1 word in an effort to communicate (a use strategy), but this may not be with the intention or effect of learning the L2.

Strategies used in listening

grouping	translating
associating	transferring
elaborating	taking notes
creating mental linkages	summarising
using imagery	highlighting
semantic mapping	using linguistic clues
using keywords	using other clues
representing sounds in memory	overviewing and linking with
structured reviewing	already known material
using physical response or sensation	paying attention
using mechanical techniques	organising
repeating	setting goals and objectives
recognising and using formulas and	identifying the purpose of a
patterns	language task
getting the idea quickly	self-monitoring
using resources for receiving	self-evaluating
messages	using progressive relaxation, deep
reasoning deductively	breathing, and meditation
analysing expressions	using music
analysing contrastively across	using laughter
languages	making positive statements
	taking risks (wisely)
	rewarding yourself
	listening to your body
	using a checklist

(Oxford, 1990)

Principles

1. Consistent use of learning strategies helps students learn more efficiently.

2. Language use strategies can enable students to handle tasks that may be more difficult than their current processing might allow. This 'stretch' of capacity can be instructive to learners, and may motivate them to learn more.

3. Learning strategies that are associated with successful learners can be demonstrated and modelled for less successful learners.

7.2.6   Processability hypothesis

Because acquisition of the grammatical system of a second language takes a long time and seems to follow a stage-like pattern, certain linguistic forms in oral input are accessible, salient, or *noticeable* to learners *only* at specific times. Before certain forms are noticeable, they are heard by the L2 listener simply as a 'blur of sound' surrounded by other more comprehensible parts of discourse.

In order to bring parts of this blur progressively into focus, it appears that successful listeners consciously use 'operating principles' like those outlined by Slobin (1985), Anderson (1996) and Anderson and Shirai (1994). Operating principles are simply cognitive operations that link incoming sound with linguistic rules, and actually allow the listener to discover the way the grammatical system of the spoken language works.

Slobin's operating principles were as follows:

1. Pay attention to the ends of words.
2. There are linguistic elements which encode relations between words.
3. Avoid thinking about exceptions; try to find a consistent rule.
4. Underlying semantic relations should be marked overtly and clearly.
5. The use of grammatical markers should make semantic sense.

Anderson's proposed operating principles expanded on these, and they were also aimed at explaining how the learner figures out the semantic 'congruence' of grammatical rules, the 'relevance' and 'distribution' of rules, and how rules differ from those in the learner's L1. Research in the area of L2 processing strategies (e.g. Liu et al., 1992; Hernandez et al., 1994) show differences in patterns of processing based on early vs late experience with the L2.

Principles

1. Different features of the grammatical system of the language are available to learners at different times, depending on their readiness to learn the 'next' stage of the grammatical system.
2. Learners must use operating principles to notice formal features of the spoken language in order to make progress in listening.
3. Attending to grammatical forms while listening requires a gradual increase in processing capacity.

7.2.8   Social distance hypothesis

Second-language acquisition is just one aspect of **acculturation** and the degree to which a learner acculturates to the target-language group will control the degree to which he acquires the second language (Schumann, 1978).

In this view, acculturation, and hence second-language acquisition, is determined by the degree of **social and psychological 'distance'** between the learner and the target-language culture. Social distance pertains to the individual as a member of a social group that is in contact with another social group whose members speak a different language. Psychological distance is the result of various affective factors that concern the learner as an individual, such as culture shock, stress, motivation to be part of the culture and personal 'ego'.

Social and psychological distance influence second-language acquisition by determining the amount of contact the learners have with the target language and the degree to which they are open to the input that is available to them.

Principles

1. Learners who have 'positive' (little) distance, socially and psychologically, from the target language will learn more efficiently and more enjoyably. Instruction must seek to gauge the appropriate input and design based on the 'social distance' of the learners.

2. Instruction that fosters increasing the 'positive' distance will be more successful.

3. Learners who experience 'positive' social and psychological distance will more readily 'denativise' their language and use target-language standards in their language-learning endeavours.

Chapter 8

Methods

This chapter outlines...

- • the history of methods involving listening;
- • an argument for not subscribing to particular methods;
- • an approach to creating and using skills taxonomies.

8.1 The historical search for the best method

The explicit treatment of listening in language learning is a relatively recent phenomenon. From the time foreign languages were formally taught until the late 1800s, language learning was presented primarily in a written mode, with the role of descriptive grammars, bilingual dictionaries and 'problem sentences' for correct translation occupying the central role. Listening began to assume an important role in language teaching during the '**reform movement**' of the early 1900s, when linguists sought to elaborate a psychological theory of child language acquisition and apply it to the teaching of foreign languages. As a result of this movement, the spoken language became the definitive source for and means of foreign language learning. Accuracy of perception and clarity of auditory memory became focal language-learning skills.

This focus on speech was given a boost in the 1930s and 1940s when anthropologists began to study and describe the spoken languages of the world. Influenced by this anthropological movement, Leonard Bloomfield declared that 'one learns to understand and speak a language primarily by hearing and imitating native speakers' (Bloomfield, 1942). Following the Second World War, American applied linguists formalized this '**oral**

approach' into the audio-lingual method with its emphasis on intensive oral-aural drills and extensive use of the language laboratory. The underlying assumption of the method was that learners could be 'trained' through intensive, structured and graded input to change their hearing 'habits'.

In contrast to this behaviourist approach, there was a growing interest in Britain in situational approaches. Firth and his contemporaries believed that 'the context of situation', rather than linguistic units themselves, determined the meaning of utterances. This implied that meaning is a function of the situational and cultural context in which it occurs, and that language understanding involved an integration of linguistic comprehension and non-linguistic interpretation.

Other key background influences are associated with the work of Chomsky and Hymes. A gradual acceptance of Chomsky's innatist views led to the notion of the meaning-seeking mind and the concept of a '**natural approach**' to language learning. In a natural approach, the learner works from an internal syllabus and requires input data (not necessarily in a graded order) to construct the target-language system. In response to Chomsky's notion of language competence, Hymes proposed the notion of 'communicative competence' (Hymes, 1972). Hymes stated that what is crucial is not so much a better understanding of how language is structured internally, but a better understanding of how language is used.

The influence of language philosophy, particularly the work of Austin (1962) and Searle (1969; 1975), began to exert an influence on language-teaching syllabus design. The Council of Europe proposed defining a 'common core' of communicative language which all learners would be expected to acquire at the early stages of language learning. The **communicative language teaching** movement (CLT) which had its roots in the 'threshold syllabus' of van Ek (1973) began to view listening as an integral part of communicative competence. Listening for meaning became the primary focus and finding relevant input for the learner assumed greater importance.

In the late 1960s and early 1970s, applied linguists began to recognise that listening was the primary channel by which the learner gains access to L2 'data', that listening therefore serves as the trigger for acquisition. Initial methodology research suggested that '**listening first**' **methodologies**, such as those proposed by Asher ('total physical response'), Postovsky, Nord and Winitz ('the comprehension approach') would be much more successful than methodologies that did not have an explicit or consistent role for listening. However, while there are reported successes with these methods, research has not consistently borne out their claims.

8.2   Anti-methods and post-methods

Teaching methodology involves any aspect of instruction that entails a choice of learning environment, teacher–student and student–student relationships, classroom language, input, procedures, outcome, feedback and assessment.

These choices are obviously important because they affect each learner's attitude about learning, their motivation and effort in the classroom – and also the learner's rate of progress and eventual level of success in learning the language. Moreover, methodology choices affect how well teachers can do their job of helping learners learn. Teachers are constantly searching, rightly so, for ways to teach more creatively, in ways that engage them as well as their learners, in a rich and enjoyable learning experience.

In Quotes 8.1 and 8.2 we see different views of methodology: one based on the concept of teaching methods 'triggering' language acquisition and one based on the concept of teaching methods 'guiding' language-learning choices and strategies.

Candlin and Mercer (2000) have observed that because of the inconsistent applications of 'pure' methods and because of the unclear results of attempting to apply single methods there has been a shift in how methods and methodologies are viewed. Many language educators and writers have

---

Quote 8.1   Michael Long on teaching methods

I would claim that, beneath superficial differences among teaching methods, materials, and syllabuses, alternatives in second language instruction consist essentially of varied selections among options of two kinds. First, there are options in the way linguistic input to the learners is manipulated. Choices here exist in such matters as (1) the sequence in which the learner will encounter linguistic units of various kinds, along with (2) the frequency/intensity and (3) the salience of those encounters. Second, there are options in the types of productions tasks classroom learners are set. It is reasonable to expect that formal instruction may trigger such processes as transfer, transfer of training, and (over)generalization, depending on the choices that teachers and materials writers make in this area. . . . Further, if various characteristics of (1) the linguistic/and or conversational environment and (2) the performance tasks are what trigger some of the processes, it would seem reasonable to expect instructed and naturalistic acquirers (i.e. those without formal instruction) to exhibit either partially different acquisition processes or, at least, different degrees of preference for those processes.

Long (1988: 120)

Quote 8.2 Candlin and Mercer on teaching methods

In a methods-dominated classroom, the teacher is placed in the subservient position of following pathways defined by others. Teachers' expertise and local knowledge is devalued. Typically, these methods are determined without reference to, or knowledge of, particular local social and cultural conditions. They are deemed to be universally applicable. The power over what happens in the classroom is exerted from *outside* the classroom, rather than being determined by the teacher, and by the teacher and the learners together.

In a post-method condition, Kumaravadivelu (1994) argues, teachers need to develop into **strategic thinkers** and **strategic actors**. By this he means that teachers require the skills of reflection, and to be able to describe and analyse interactions among learners. They need to learn how to select different tasks and activities with their learners in a *principled* way, so as to enhance their natural language learning abilities and strategies.

Although Kumaravadivelu focuses on the teacher, it is important to recognize that it is not only the teacher who has to learn to be strategic. His or her goal is to enable learners to be as strategic as possible in achieving *their* language learning goals. With the author, we can say that these common goals of teachers and learners consist of maximizing the learning opportunities of the learner, facilitating the negotiation of interaction, and minimizing the gaps that regularly occur between what teachers plan and intend and how learners interpret what teachers do and have in mind. To these we can add, with Kumaravadivelu, the need for teachers and learners to develop a conscious awareness of the form and functions of language and always to set language in its contexts of use.

Candlin and Mercer (2000: 10)

now taken an 'anti-method position', arguing that there is little point in classifying and labelling teaching procedures that are regularly not followed in practice.

Nunan (1999) has proposed that we are now in a 'post-method condition' in which teaching is explained not in terms of classification by prescribed methodologies, but rather by actual practice of interactive teaching. By systematically observing, analysing and evaluating what actually takes place in classrooms, a teacher can establish well-grounded principles for effective language teaching and learning. Candlin and Mercer (2000) claim that such systematic study is necessary if we are to evaluate the effectiveness of instruction, the contributions to successful learning being made by learners and by teachers, and the role played the texts, tasks and activities in that process.

In this vein, it has been the specific focus on listening texts, listening tasks and listening strategies in actual learning contexts that has furthered the 'methodology' for teaching listening.

8.3 Skills taxonomies

Another approach to teaching methodology ignores defining methods altogether and relies on an analysis of component skills involved in 'expert performance' and specification of criteria for mastery of those subskills. Virtually any complex skill from riding a bicycle to listening to a lecture can be 'taxonomised' by decomposing the skills that are involved. This is done through observation, interviews with 'experts' (i.e. those who have

Table 8.1 **A taxonomy of general listening skills (based on Richards, 1990; Rost, 1994)**

- Hearing prominent words
- Hearing pause unit boundaries
- Hearing assimilations, elisions and reductions
- Hearing differences in intonation patterns
- Guessing the meaning of 'weakened words' in an utterance
- Guessing the meaning of unknown words
- Discriminating between similar words

- Parsing an utterance into relationships (agent, object, location, etc.)
- Deciding the meaning of an ambiguous utterance
- Finding correct references for ellipted forms and pro-forms
- Understanding the function of an utterance when the speaker is indirect

- Using gestures to guide our understanding
- Activating images or memories when we listen to a story or description
- Making predictions as we listen
- Filling in missing information (or information that was not heard clearly)
- Using reasoning as we listen, such as filling in the 'supporting grounds' of an argument and making 'bridging inferences'

- Understanding the speaker's intended function for an utterance
- Understanding differences in conversational styles and discourse patterns
- Understanding organisational patterns of the speaker
- Holding information in short-term memory, building up long-term memory of relevant information
- Responding to what the speaker says

gone through the stages of mastering the skill) and introspection. Although it is relatively easy to come up with a taxonomy for a skill, a valid and useful taxonomy needs categories that are perceptible to learners and have demonstrable criteria for improvement.

The primary intention of most taxonomy writers is to aid in instruction or test-writing by identifying subskills that can be practiced or tested in isolation. A taxonomy is created with two assumptions in mind: (1) that subskills can indeed be practised and tested in isolation in a sensible way; and (2) that when the learner improves measurably on a subskill, his or her performance on the holistic skill will improve also.

A number of taxonomies of listening skills have been proposed, from the detailed 'enabling skills' (e.g. phonemic discrimination) (Munby, 1978) to more focused taxonomies dealing with particular listening situations (e.g. getting information in service situations such as hotels) (Richards, 1990; Rost, 1994).

Taxonomies are often used to analyse deficiencies in performances, but this use has very questionable value for teaching or testing. Indeed, use of taxonomies to identify deficiencies (e.g. 'the learner does not recognise low frequency vocabulary' or 'the learner does not have the ability to process complex structures') may be very *un*helpful in identifying the kind of work that will actually lead the learner toward improving global listening ability.

For teaching and testing, the most useful taxonomies are those that posit progressive, rather than fixed, criteria. Buck et al. (1997), based on an analysis of test performances, identified a taxonomy of listening skills that utilise this kind of **progressive framework**:

Concept 8.1   **Ten important listening abilities**

The ability to:

- process faster input
- process lower-frequency vocabulary
- process texts with higher vocabulary density
- process more complex structures
- process longer segments
- process texts with a higher information density
- scan short segments to determine listening purpose
- synthesise scattered information
- use redundant information.

The advantage of this kind of taxonomy for teaching is that it suggests progressive grading of materials and tasks, provides a framework for feedback to learners and points out areas in which they need additional exposure and practice.

The following chapter (Chapter 9) outlines considerations for the teaching of listening in terms of decisions about texts, tasks and strategies, whilst Chapter 10 presents specific plans and activities for teaching listening.

Input

The selection and use of input is the central aspect of teaching listening. How we identify sources, select among them and construct tasks around them are the most salient decisions in the teaching of listening. Chapter 9 deals with six important notions in the teaching of listening.

It will . . .

- define the concept of relevance and argue that relevance should assume a central role in the teaching of listening;
- outline the concept of authenticity and argue for a modified student-oriented view of authenticity;
- examine the notion of genre, how it relates to teaching listening, and exemplify teaching approaches with two different genres;
- define the notion of 'difficulty' in terms of cognitive load and suggest using this measure for grading listening material;
- examines the practice of simplification, and argues for a user-oriented notion of simplification;
- looks at the role of 'teacher talk' in teaching listening and examines the variables that make teacher talk more or less effective.

9.1 Relevance

The term 'relevance' has been widely discussed in educational and communication contexts.

According to Sperber and Wilson (1986), human cognition has a single goal: we pay attention *only* to information which seems to us relevant. If our entire cognition – our powers of attention, perception and interpretation

– is organised most naturally and most readily around 'relevance', it certainly makes sense to place relevance of input as the top priority in teaching. Relevant material, 'the right stuff' according to Beebe (1985) is central to all progress in language learning.

Relevant material for listening can be obtained through selection or adaptation. An example of a pedagogic study for selecting material to maximise relevance was conducted by Day and Yamanaka (1998). They surveyed a target population of students to identify the types of topics that students found most interesting and most useful for their English study. Given a list of topics and subtopics, students ranked the topics in terms of interest or relevance to them as discussion topics. Materials for listening were then found or developed for each of the topics selected as relevant by a majority of students. While no approach can guarantee relevance for all students, the approach used in this materials design study used the aim of relevance as its guiding principle.

Teaching principle: Relevance

Learning materials (topics, inputs, tasks) are relevant if they relate to learner goals and interests, and involve self-selection and evaluation.

Adaptation can be realised through adapting or adding to existing input material in order to make it more relevant to the needs of a learner group. A materials design study Rost (1999) added recorded topical interviews conducted by students to assigned course listening material in order to increase student motivation and course relevance. Students rated the value of the course more highly than a control group that did not use the additional material.

9.2 Authenticity

Situated language is the basis of natural, real-time language use, and comprehension of this situated, **'authentic' language** is the target of virtually all language learners.

This issue of **'authenticity'** is one of the most controversial issues in the teaching of listening, one that engenders heated discussion among teachers in both SL (second language) and FL (foreign language) settings. At one end of the spectrum are those who define 'authenticity' as any and all language that has been actually used by native speakers for any 'real purpose', that is, a purpose that was real for the users at the time the language was

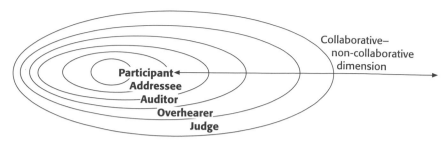

Participant – a person who is being spoken to directly and who has speaking rights equal to others involved in the discourse (e.g. a conversation between two friends on a topic of mutual interest and shared background).

Addressee – a person in a discourse who is being spoken to directly and who has limited rights to respond (e.g. a student in a traditional classroom in which the teacher is lecturing).

Auditor – a person in a discourse who is a member of an audience that is being addressed directly and who has very limited rights to respond and is not expected to respond (e.g. a bus driver announcing the name of the next bus stop to the passengers (audience) on the bus).

Overhearer – a person who is not being addressed, but who is within earshot of the speaker, and who has no rights or expectations to respond (e.g. hearing the conversation of a bank teller and the customer who is in front of you as you stand in line waiting).

Figure 9.1   A schematic representation of listener roles in discourse (Rost, 1990: 5)

used by them. While this approach is laudable in its valuation of 'real context' and 'real language' as central to language instruction, it devalues the role of the 'addressee' in *making* the language authentic.

As is now well-established in pragmatics (cf. McGregor, 1986; Rost, 1990; Goodwin and Duranti, 1992), the closer a participant is to the 'control centre' of an interaction, the more immediate is the purpose for the interaction, and the more 'authentic' and meaningful the discourse becomes.

If we accept the notion of discourse control as leading to authenticity, then for purposes of language education, only those inputs and encounters that involve the students' own purposes for listening can be considered 'authentic'. In this sense, any source of input and interaction that satisfies the learner's search for knowledge and allows the learner the ability to control that search is authentic.

What many teachers are referring to when they seek 'authentic input' is the characteristic of 'genuineness'. Genuineness refers to features of colloquial style of 'real-time' planning (many people say 'lack of planning') that characterise everyday spoken discourse:

• natural speed
• natural phonological phenomenon, natural pauses and intonation, use of reduction, assimilation, elision

> ### Quote 9.1 Authenticity in the virtual world
>
> One of the correlates of connectivity, community, and shared knowledge is that online education is highly authentic in nature. Ironically, the virtual world is more real than the usual classroom. Because students can access actual databases and experts, their learning activities are realistic. The lack of realism in traditional instruction has often been identified as a major weakness of education at all levels. Indeed, one of the reasons that students often give for disillusionment with school or college is that it lacks 'real-world' relevance.
>
> Greg Kearsely (2001)

- high-frequency vocabulary
- colloquialism, such as short formulaic utterances, current slang, etc.
- hesitations, false starts, self-corrections
- orientation of the speech toward a 'live' listener, including natural pauses for the listener to provide backchannelling (e.g. nodding, 'um-hmm') or responses (e.g. 'Yes, I think so').

The reasons for preferring 'genuine' input are obvious. If the target of the learners is to be able to understand 'genuine' spoken language, as it is actually used by native speakers, then the targets need to be introduced into instruction.

If at one end of the spectrum are those who argue for 'authenticity' (or at least genuineness) at all times for use as input, then at the other end of the spectrum are those who believe that 'authentic' input is too difficult for the students to handle or impossible for the instructor to provide. A mediating factor in the use of authentic listening material has been task design (Nunan, 1999). By designing tasks which preview key vocabulary and discourse structures in the input, by 'chunking' the input into manageable segments and providing selective focus on its particular elements, teachers can utilise authentic material in ways that are motivating and useful to learners at all levels.

Teaching principles: Authenticity and genuineness

1. Language input should aim for 'user authenticity', first, by aiming to be appropriate to the current needs of the learners, and second, by reflecting real use of language in the 'real world'.

2. Language input should aim to be 'genuine', i.e. involving features of naturally occurring language with and between native speakers: speed, rhythm, intonation, pausing, idea density, etc.

9.3   Genres

One aspect of the 'authenticity' and 'genuineness' arguments that often goes unexplored is the treatment of genres. In principle, learners should be exposed to a wide range of oral genres in order to 'develop a feel' for the range of spoken language. 'Developing a feel' goes beyond becoming familiar or comfortable with different genres and discourse types. By becoming familiar with the understanding of different genres, learners can begin to adopt 'point-driven' strategies for understanding rather than 'information-driven' strategies for understanding (Olsen and Huckin, 1990; Tauroza and Allison, 1994).

Genres differ, not primarily in the situations in which they are most often found, but more in their underlying organisation and purposes for use. The five main types of 'rhetoric' that have been used since ancient times often serve as a basis for an initial classification of genres. These types apparently correspond to universal thinking processes, although there are countless variations and cultural styles associated with each of them.

From a purely cognitive perspective, part of the listener's initial task is to determine the 'genre' – what kind of text it is – and then to activate the kind of listening orientation that is most useful to interpreting the text. Knowledge of a genre allows the listener to focus on essential information, as outlined in Table 9.1.

Of course, texts seldom exist outside of a social context in which they are composed and intended to be understood; rather, they are always embedded in a social context and often intertwined with various other speech acts (e.g. persuasion, apology, congratulations). For this reason, understanding a text is always more complex than simply decoding its information and argument structure.

The following subsections provide illustrative overviews of the general understanding processes for two main categories of texts, narratives and descriptions.

Teaching principle: genres

Learning materials should include a range of genres and discourse types that learners are likely to encounter in their contact with the target language.

9.3.1   Narrative

The narrative is the most universal rhetorical form. Narratives follow a time, event, change sequence that is understood and enjoyed by people in every culture. Narratives are an unparalleled teaching device for cultural

Table 9.1   **Genre and listening purpose** (based on Rost, 1987)

Type	Information organisation	Purpose for listening	Speaker focus
1. Narrative	temporal sequence	to find out what happened	events, actions, causes, reasons, enablements, purposes, time, proximity
2. Descriptive	spatial/sensory sequence and coherence	to experience what something looked or sounded or felt like	objects, situations, states, attributes (definitions)
3. Comparison/ contrast	point-by-point organisation, leading to single conclusion	to discover how two things are alike and unalike	instances, specifications, equivalences
4. Causal/evaluation	syllogistic/logical explication	to understand the causes and effects of certain actions	value, significance, reason
5. Problem/solution	problem/proposal/ effect of proposed action	to hypothesise on the effects of proposed solutions	cognition, volition

values and facts as well as for morals. Narratives also have great value as second-language teaching devices.

Narratives vary in complexity, but always involve some element of time orientation, place orientation, character identification, events, complications, goals and meaning.

Time orientation: When are the actions happening? What is the historical setting? In what order, what events are left out? (Listeners typically assume paratactic organisation [that is, the first event is told first, followed by the next event, etc.], unless time-markers indicate backtracking or jumping forward in time.)

Place orientation: Where is the action happening? What aspects of the setting are significant for the narrative. (Listeners typically assume prototypical settings – that is, prototypes, or 'typical cases', based on their personal experience – unless specific descriptions contradict them).

Character identification: Who is in the story? who is/are the main character(s)? Who are minor ('supporting') characters? Who are peripheral ('throw-away') characters? How are they all related?

Events/problem/complication/goal: What about the setting is 'problematic'? What complicates it? How can it be solved?

Meaning of the story: Most stories are told with some 'point', often with a moral lesson or a principle that confirms some aspect of the relationship between the speaker and listener.

Although the underlying 'semantic structure' of narratives have a great deal in common, the surface features of narratives vary widely. In order to teach listening to narratives, the teacher also needs to familiarise learners with transitional elements that help them decode the story as well as content themes in the story (cf. Hatch, 1992).

9.3.2 Descriptive

Like narratives, descriptions – of people, places, and events – are universal. However, unlike narratives, there are many more variations, and cultural differences in how descriptions are likely to unfold.

Oral descriptions of people, places, and things tend *not* to follow a fixed pattern, but often exhibit – *somewhere* in the text – characteristics of pro-totypical descriptions: features that are specific or peculiar or otherwise memorable, features that evoke a feeling or strong impression in the speaker, features that lead to a story or anecdote about the object or place or person being described, features that provide a link to other topics shared by the speaker and listener.

objects – appearance, parts, functions

places – spatial/geographical organisation (left to right, front to back, etc.)

Linde and Labov (1975) analysed apartment descriptions and found that many speakers gave their listeners a spatially oriented 'walking tour', pointing out their own likes and dislikes in terms of layout and furnishings as they proceeded. They also found that much of the description of an apartment – or other place assumed to be familiar to the listener – is considered 'given' and not described. Only those aspects of the description that differ from the norm, and are therefore 'new' are included in the description.

Hatch (1992) notes that when we listen to certain genres, we expect characteristic syntactic and lexical patterns. For example, in descriptions, we tend to find copula sentences (it's very warm, it's basically blue), relative clauses (it's a narrow room that leads to the outside porch), presentatives (there's a big oak door, there are two small windows in the back wall), as well as descriptive adjectives of size, shape, colour and number.

9.4 Difficulty

The organisation of a text (often called a 'formal schema') contributes to the ease or difficulty of understanding it. For example, understanding a three-minute segment of an academic lecture is considered to be more challenging than understanding a three-minute story. Similarly, the language that is used in the text contributes to its difficulty. For example, a text with a lot of complex and embedded sentences may be more difficult to understand than one with shorter, simple sentences. However, Brown (1995) has argued that the central feature in difficulty of a text is not the language itself, but the content.

> **Quote 9.2** Brown on cognitive difficulty
>
> It is usually supposed that listening comprehension is difficult for foreign or second language learners simply because aspects of the language are difficult for learners.... There remain, however, other aspects of the input which may contribute to making listening comprehension difficult. One aspect, which still appears to be strangely neglected is the question of the intrinsic cognitive difficulty of the text.
>
> Brown (1995: 59–60)

Brown defines cognitive difficulty in terms of factors that make four central listening processes (*identify* information, *search* memory for information you already have, *file* or store information for later cross-referencing, and *use* the information in some way) easier or more difficult to perform. Having conducted a long series of interactive listening experiments (Brown et al., 1984), he and his colleagues proposed six principles of cognitive load that affect listeners:

Cognitive load, principle 1: It is easier to understand any text (narrative, description, instruction, or argument) which involves FEWER rather than MORE individuals and objects.

Cognitive load, principle 2: It is easier to understand any text (particularly narrative texts) involving individuals or objects which are clearly DISTINCT from one another.

Cognitive load, principle 3: It is easier to understand texts (particularly description or instruction texts) involving simple spatial relationships.

Cognitive load, principle 4: It is easier to understand texts where the order of telling matches the order of events.

Cognitive load, principle 5: It is easier to understand a text if relatively few familiar inferences are necessary to relate each sentence to the preceding text.

Cognitive load, principle 6: It is easier to understand a text if the information in the text is clear (not ambiguous), self-consistent and fits in readily with information you already have.

The implications for teaching and testing are that if we wish to grade the texts and tasks that listeners will encounter, we need to take into account the cognitive load of these texts and tasks we are presenting. If we wish to simplify a text (e.g. by shortening it) or a task (e.g. by providing initial vocabulary or other information), we need to consider first the factors of cognition – the listening processes – that make a listening activity difficult.

9.5   Simplification

Simplification of input is a form of '**social accommodation**', a term first used in social psychology (Giles, 1979) to refer to mutual movements of interlocutors toward the discourse and behaviour standards of the other. Simplification of input is one common method of making discourse accessible to L2 users and rendering 'difficult' texts usable for language-learning purposes.

Simplification of input can be achieved in two basic ways:

1. **Restrictive simplification**: operates on the principle of using and highlighting familiar linguistic items and frames:

- **Lexical**: using a simpler term (or higher-frequency term) for a more complicated one (or lower-frequency one), less slang, fewer idioms.
- **Syntactic**: using simpler syntax, shorter utterances, topic-fronted utterances (e.g. 'The man at the reception desk, I gave the package to him'), less pre-verb modification ('I only want coffee' vs 'I want only coffee') to make utterance easier to process and analyse.
- **Phonological**: emphasising word boundaries by slowing down or exaggerating speech patterns.
- **Discoursal** (for conversation): using prototypical question–answer patterns (yes/no questions), non-inverted questions ('You can sing?'), either-or questions ('Where do you live?' 'Do you live in the city?') or other familiar, recognisable patterns (e.g. tag questions: 'You're from Osaka, aren't you?').
- **Discoursal** (for monologues): using prototypical rhetorical patterns such as direct temporal organisation, avoidance of tangential information.

It is important to note that not all intended simplifications by the speaker have the effect of simplifying the input for the listener. In research (e.g. Pica et al., 1987) and in teaching, it is known simplifications do not have consistent effects at making listening texts more accessible or comprehensible.

2. **Elaborative simplification**: operates on the principle of enriching the input:

- **Phonological**: use of higher pitch and more pitch variation to promote attention.
- **Lexical**: providing rephrasing of key words and ideas, use of definitions, use of synonyms.
- **Syntactic**: providing rephrasing of difficult syntactic constructions, to provide more time for processing of meaning.
- **Syntactic**: use more subordinate clauses and embeddings to make utterance relationships more transparent (e.g. 'That's the place where I grew up').
- **Syntactic**: supply optional syntax ('I think that he's here' vs 'I think he's here').
- **Discoursal**: providing explicit frame shifts ('well', 'now', 'so', 'okay', 'the next thing I want to mention is', 'One of the main issues is . . .') to assist in identifying of idea boundaries and relationships. (Temporal relationships: and, after that/ causality: so, then, because/ contrast: but, on the other hand/ emphasis: actually, in fact).
- **Discoursal**: providing direct repetition of words, phrases, whole utterances.
- **Discoursal**: providing narrative examples of key ideas.

Teaching principle: Simplification

Simplification of input is effective for language learning only if it helps the listener become more active, that is, more able to activate background knowledge, make inferences, and more willing to respond to what she hears.

Simplification often has the immediate beneficial effect of helping learners understand the ideas in what otherwise might be an inaccessible text, and thus reducing frustration. But because simplification of the input itself necessarily alters the original text and mitigates against the satisfaction of having a 'genuine' listening experience, it is important for teachers to use simplification judiciously.

Other means of achieving greater comprehension without altering a text are often preferable and typically much easier to administer. They include:

1. **Direct repetition**: Repeating the text by replaying the audio or video extract or repeating the text orally.
2. **Simplification of the context**: Preparing for key concepts in advance is the chief means of simplifying the context for the listener. Presenting or eliciting vocabulary and ideas that will be part of the text generally help adjust the listener's 'cognitive context'. As Lynch (1996: 26) says,

'the more we know, the less we need to rely on language to understand the message'.

3. **Chunking the input**: Presenting the input in short chunks (e.g. one- to three-minute segments), followed by opportunities for clarification before continuing.

Table 9.2   **Range and types of discourse structuring** (Bremer et al., 1996: 180)

Encouraging participation	Raising expectability	Raising transparency	
		Raising accessibility	Raising explicitness
open-topic management	DISCOURSE: metadiscursive comments on: activity type, topics, shared knowledge	(a) perceptual: short utterances salience of elements (articulation, volume) segmentation (pauses, rate of delivery, chunking, avoid false starts)	Full forms instead of: ellipsis pro-forms reduced forms lexicalisaton of important information
slow down rhythm for turns	TOPICS: announce by paralinguistic markers, announce content explicitly	(b) of lexical meaning: high-frequency vocabulary, recourse to L1 code-switching	metadiscursive comments on: discourse function of utterance discourse structuring discourse context
(if relevant) acknowledge language problems	LOCALLY: left topic dislocation	(c) of conceptual meaning: linking complex topics to 'here and now' absolute instead of relational reference to time	possibility of reruns by (modified) repetition
giving room: offer turns open questions allow for pauses help other with formulations			

Focusing particularly on interactive discourse between a native and non-native speaker, Bremer et al. (1996) offer a helpful summary of the range (encouraging participation, raising transparency and raising expectations) and types of discourse structuring (offering turns, segmenting and slowing down, 'meta' comments, etc.) that will help prevent understanding problems and promote repair of problems when they occur (see Table 9.2).

Teaching concept: Simplification and shared knowledge

Speakers often do not consciously script features of 'simplified language' into their speech. Rather, they tend to 'pitch' their discourse at their intended audience, taking into account their own perceived importance of the topics and subtopics as well as the interests and expectations of their audience and the amount of background information available to them.

Lynch (1996: 25) provides an interesting example of two pieces of spoken discourse on the same specific topic to illustrate how texts on the same topic differ, in terms of simplification as well as features of assumed shared knowledge and interests.

> The two examples below are transcripts of reports on the same event, covered by different BBC1 television news programmes on the same day. Most people find one of the reports simpler than the other. Do you? If so, why?

Example 2.5
The film *Amadeus*, about Mozart, picked up eight Oscars at last night's award ceremony. The award for Best Supporting Actress went to Dame Peggy Ashcroft in *A Passage to India*. She has got flu and did not collect it herself but is said to be delighted. She was also to have been present at the funeral today of Sir Michael Redgrave. He was buried this morning. His three children were there, and many other acting friends.

Example 2.6
The film world's most famous awards, the Oscars, were announced in Hollywood last night, with the usual mix of surprise and disappointment. British films did not do as well as was hoped, although there was one top award for a British star. Most of the Oscars went to the American film *Amadeus*. This is a story about the composer Mozart and won eight Oscars, including Best Film of the Year. Some people had been waiting three days for a glimpse of the celebrities arriving for the ceremony. The American pop star Prince was among them, dressed in purple. But one of the top awards did go to a British star. Dame Peggy Ashcroft won her first Oscar at the age of 77, for Best Supporting Actress in the film *A Passage to India*.

> ### Teaching principle: Use of simplified vs genuine texts
>
> Although simplified texts have an important role in the development of listening ability, if the simplified texts no longer reflect features of 'genuine texts' – those used for authentic purposes among users (not learners) of the language, they have less long-term learning value. Whenever possible, simplified texts should preserve features of naturalness and include some language that has not been modified for learning purposes.

9.6 Teacher talk

'Teacher talk' – how the teacher talks to students – is one of the vital sources of listening input for learners, and the art of appropriately engaging teacher talk is something that all teachers strive to develop. This aspect of listening instruction varies from highly interactive casual talk with learners to less interactive extended academic lectures.

In any kind of 'teacher talk', we will find that teachers typically accommodate their speech to the comprehension abilities of their students. Although it is desirable to expose learners to genuine language (rather than overly simplified versions of the target language), it is likewise desirable for learners to become engaged in the processes of understanding in order to trigger both listening development and language acquisition. For this reason, the continual adjustment of discourse in speech to learners needs to be monitored.

Penny Ur (1984) in her book *Teaching Listening Comprehension* advocates the use of the 'live' instructor as a main source of oral input for listening instruction:

> . . . the speaker is actually visible to the listener in most real-life situations, and his facial expression and movements provide some material aids to comprehension, so that it does not seem right to consistently deprive the learner of his presence in classroom exercises. Also if the speaker is (as is generally the case) the teacher herself, then she can adapt the material as she goes through it, varying, pausing and repeating parts to suit the needs of her students (p. 25).

Ur goes on to talk about the benefits of informal 'teacher talk' for the purposes of enhancing students' listening opportunities:

> [It is important for students to] have plenty of opportunity of listening to good speakers of English – of whom the most conveniently available one is their teacher. Informal teacher-chat is excellent listening material, arguably the best there is. It can be interpolated at any stage of the lesson, serving as

a relaxing break from more intensive work. It is easy to listen to, since it is 'live' and personal – intended specifically for the ears of these particular students by this particular teacher here and now (p. 62).

She gives suggestions for such informal 'teacher talk' topics:

- a member of your family
- a friend or someone you have met
- something you like doing
- a place you know or have known
- your childhood
- a happy/unhappy/frightening/amusing/surprising experience
- something you did that are proud or ashamed of
- a film or play your have seen/ an article or book you have read
- your favourite hobby/food/clothes
- stories or anecdotes you have heard or read.

Teaching principle: Teacher talk

To develop students' listening ability, teachers should aim to give all teacher talk (classroom instructions, social chat, praise, as well as content instruction and explanations) in the target language. When necessary to maintain student attention, interest and comprehension, the teacher should simplify language, but attempt to keep 'genuine' features of real spoken language.

Quote 9.3 Teresa Pica on 'wait time'

Research findings suggest that teaching a second or foreign language should be an interactive process between teachers and students and among the students themselves. Students need to comprehend new language, but can best do this when allowed to ask about what it is that they do not understand rather than rely on their teacher or textbook to anticipate areas of comprehension difficulty ... what (the research) also suggests is that simply giving students enough **wait time** to ask questions about or to internalize input that they do not initially understand may have very positive results on their comprehension, without the need for much talk on the teacher's part at all.

Pica (1994)

On the other end of the spectrum is the less interactive but equally essential aspect of listening that is characterised in lectures. In lecture situations, or other 'distance' situations in which the listener exerts less direct influence on the speaker's ongoing speech adjustments, 'teacher talk' is realised more as a priori decisions by the speaker on how best to 'deliver' content.

In this realm, as outlined by Flowerdew (1994), the speaker must use rhetorical signalling devices in order to guide the listener, both 'micro-markers' such as 'well', 'now let's', 'so' and 'macro-markers' such as 'Next I will be talking about . . .' and 'Finally, I'd like to look at . . .'. More importantly, the teacher must use global structuring devices such as graphic organisers and explicit tie-ins to prior knowledge (e.g. reading material) to accommodate the input to the listener.

Chapter 10

Instructional design

The presentation in this chapter starts with the simplest types of tasks and moves toward more complex activities and curriculum design. Three types of listening are discussed:

- intensive listening
- selective listening
- interactive listening.

Three aspects of learner involvement are outlined:

- learner response
- paused tasks
- pre-listening.

Specific principles for listening instructional design are considered:

- grammar processing
- multi-media
- strategy training
- listening awareness training.

Finally, four more elaborate procedures for listening instruction are profiled:

- listening projects
- lectures
- sheltered content
- self-access listening.

Many educators and materials designers have contributed to the clarification, refinement and illustrations of the concepts and principles in this chapter. In most cases, only one specific illustration and author may be mentioned for each concept or principle. In the resources section (Section 4), additional sources are provided.

10.1   Intensive listening

Intensive listening refers to listening for precise sounds, words, phrases, grammatical units and pragmatic units. Although listening intensively is not often called for in everyday situations, the *ability to* listen intensively *whenever* required is an essential component of listening proficiency. As such, intensive listening needs to be included in listening instruction, although to be an effective practice it need not be more than a small part of each class session.

The prototypical intensive listening activity is dictation, the transcription of the exact words that a speaker utters. Dictation is often claimed to be an excellent integrative test (e.g. Cohen, 1994; Buck, 1992) because it involves listening, vocabulary, grammar and the ability to make inferences from context. However, the administration and scoring of dictations can be very time-consuming, and may be best used for self-study outside of classroom time.

Variations of 'pure' dictation have been developed in order to provide greater ease of use, more interaction, 'forced' output, and better focus on specific language items.

Dictogloss

Dictogloss started as an experimental method of Merrill Swain (1995) in her research on 'comprehensible output', and has since been developed by both researchers and language teachers, such as Wanryb (1990) and Kuiken and Vedder (2001). With a dictogloss technique, learners hear an extended passage, perhaps two minutes long, on a relatively complex exposition or story (e.g. 'The Ivory Soap Story', in Section 3, Chapter 13). The passage deliberately contains complicated facts, difficult vocabulary and structures, and more information than can be recalled. The learners do not take notes. Following the hearing of the passage, the learners are asked to reconstruct the passage as completely and as accurately as they can.

The students can work in pairs or small groups to construct a 'group account'. This collaborative goal-oriented interaction 'forces comprehensible output' beyond what normally happens in a topical group conversation where the politeness strategy of deference (not pressing someone for precise meaning) normally outweighs the need for clarity.

For teaching purposes, the passage can be read again after each group has constructed their passage. Indeed, the entire cycle can be repeated. This version of dictation focuses initially on inclusion of ideas and gradually focuses on details.

> **Teaching principle: The need to supplement 'comprehensible input' with 'comprehensible output'**
>
> Though working with comprehensible accessible listening input is vital in language acquisition, it is not sufficient for lasting progress toward proficiency. Learners must not only come to understand increasingly complex input but they must also be compelled to *produce* (in speaking and in writing) increasingly complex output that is comprehensible to others.

Other variations of dictation are:

Fast-speed dictation: The teacher reads a passage at natural speed, with assimilations, etc. The students can ask for multiple repetitions of any part of the passage, but the teacher will not slow down her articulation of the phrase being repeated. This activity focuses students attention on features of 'fast speech'.

Pause and paraphrase: The teacher reads a passage and pauses periodically for the students to write paraphrases, not the exact words used. (Indeed, students may be instructed not to use the exact words they heard.) This activity focuses students on 'vocabulary flexibility', saying things in different ways, and in focusing on meaning as they listen.

Listening cloze: The teacher provides a partially completed passage that the listeners fill in as they listen or after they listen. This activity allows focus on particular language features, e.g. verbs or noun phrases.

Error identification: The teacher provides a fully transcribed passage, but with several errors. The students listen and identify (and correct) the errors. This activity focuses attention on detail: the errors may be grammatical or semantic.

Jigsaw dictation: Students work in pairs. Each person in the pair has part of the full dictation. The students read their parts to the other in order to complete the passage. This activity encourages negotiation of meaning.

10.2 Selective listening

Joan Morley offered perhaps the first cohesive approach and comprehensive set of materials for selective listening in her work *Improving aural comprehension* (1972). She states in the introduction: 'The only way to improve aural comprehension is to spend many hours practicing listening. However, a directed program of purposeful listening can shorten the time' (p. vii). Morley considers the two tenets of improving aural comprehension ('listening with understanding') to be (1) concentrated, disciplined listening and (2) immediate writing to provide an urgency for remembering. Morley sees selective listening as a prerequisite for more complex and more extended listening: 'It is the purpose of this workbook to provide carefully planned and graded listening lessons to help students learn to listen and get facts – so they are ready to listen and get ideas' (p. viii).

Unit contents (about 15 tasks per topic area; each input about two minutes long) are as follows:

1. numbers and numerical relationships
2. letters, sounds, abbreviations, spelling and alphabetising
3. directions and spatial relations
4. time and temporal sequences
5. dates and chronological order
6. measurements and amounts
7. proportion, comparison, and contrast
8. getting the facts (factual 'readings').

For extended texts, a popular and useful form of selective listening is note-taking. As reviewed by Flowerdew (1994), note-taking is widely viewed as an important macroskill in the lecture-listening comprehension process, a skill that often interacts with reading (when integrated with reading material accompanying the lecture), writing (the actual writing of the notes or writing based on the notes) and speaking (oral reconstruction of the notes or discussion based on the notes).

Note-taking may be guided by the instructor through previewing macrosections of the lecture which will help students with headings and main points and through overt signalling of subordinate parts of the lecture (e.g. 'one example of this is . . .'). For purposes of developing students' selective listening ability, instructors may give specific requirements in note-taking, such as writing down certain words or phrases, copying material on board in appropriate places in their notes, listing topics, or labelling

---

Teaching principle: Selective listening

Selective listening tasks encourage learners to approach genuine spoken texts by adopting a strategy of focusing of specific information rather than trying to 'understand and recall everything'. Reconstruction of the spoken material based on selective listening tasks can help students link selective listening to global listening.

SUPER-X GROCERY

'Where is the meat? Where are the frozen foods?'

In large grocery stores the clerks can tell you where to find certain foods. Let us locate some items.

Listen carefully. Practice the vocabulary. Then write the names on the diagram as you hear them.

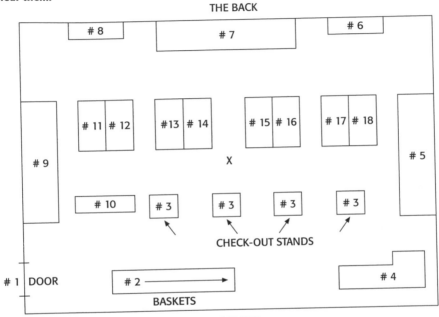

THE BACK

8   # 7   # 6

11 # 12   #13 # 14   # 15 # 16   # 17 # 18

9   X   # 5

10   # 3   # 3   # 3   # 3

CHECK-OUT STANDS

1 | DOOR   # 2   # 4

BASKETS

THE FRONT

Door – Number _____1_____	Canned Fruit – Number _____
Baskets – Number _____2_____	Canned Vegetables – Number _____
Check-out Stands – Number ___3___	Drugs – Number _____
Dairy Products – Number _____	Frozen Food – Number _____
Meat – Number _____	Soaps and Cleaners (cleaning _____ products) – Number
Produce (fresh fruits and vegetables) – Number _____	Paper Products – Number _____
Ice Cream – Number _____	Coffee, Tea, etc. – Number _____
Cookies – Number _____	Soft Drinks – Number _____
Bread – Number _____	Dishes (and utensils) – Number _____

This early example of a selective listening exercise demonstrated the trend toward using quasi-authentic situations and information as part of classroom listening training.

Figure 10.1   Selective listening task (Morley, 1972: 131)

examples. As noted by several researchers, it is not the note-taking itself that fosters increased listening ability, but the preparation for note-taking, and the follow-up reconstruction and review activities based on the learner's own notes (Rost, 1990; Chaudron, Loschky and Cook, 1994).

An important aspect of selective listening is the **pre-listening** portion of the task.

Quote 10.1 Underwood on pre-listening

It is unfair to plunge students straight into the listening text, even when testing rather than teaching listening, comprehension, as this makes it extremely difficult for them to use the natural listening skills (which we all use in our native language) of matching what they hear with what they expect to hear and using their previous knowledge to make sense of it. So before listening, students should be 'tuned in' so that they know what to expect, both in general and for specific tasks.

Underwood (1989: 30)

'Pre-listening work' can be done in a variety of ways and occurs naturally when listening is part of an integrated skills course, and a listening task is linked to a previous content-based activity.

Underwood summarises a variety of ways that pre-listening work can be done in the classroom, including:

- the teaching gives background information before students listen to the text
- the students read something relevant to the topic
- the students look at pictures that prepare them for the topic
- there is a class discussion of the topic or situation in the upcoming text
- there is a question–answer session with the class as a whole
- the teacher gives written exercises to preview the content
- the students go over the procedures for the upcoming listening task.

Any of these activities, alone or in combination, will serve to activate the knowledge and vocabulary students will need to listen 'fluently'. The key to effective pre-listening activities is to heighten the degree of relevance for listening, so that students feel motivated to listen and will activate what they know as they listen (Schmidt-Rinehart, 1992).

10.3   Interactive listening

Interactive listening refers to listening in collaborative conversation. Collaborative conversation, in which learners interact with each other or with native speakers, is established as a vital means of language development. Its potential benefits seem to be both in 'forcing comprehensible output' (Swain, 2000), that is, compelling the learner to formulate ideas in the target language and in 'forcing negotiation', that is, compelling the learner to come to understand language that is initially not understood. Learners acquire new linguistic forms (syntactic structures, words, phrases) as a product of attending to them in the communicative contexts that true collaborative discourse provides, where they are concerned primarily with meaning. Because learners frequently experience difficulty in attending to and producing accurate forms, collaborative discourse provides the ideal opportunity to give focal attention to target forms that are necessary to arrive at meaning (Long and Robinson, 1998; Ellis, Loewen and Basturkmen, 1999).

In order for learners to benefit from collaborative discourse, it is important for there to be a communicative task, that is, a tangible outcome of the interaction, and for there to be a 'problem' that requires negotiation of linguistic form to achieve that outcome. (Factors that make the task motivating and relevant, etc., are important but not the key features that make it useful for listening development and language acquisition purposes.) Most purposes for collaborative speaking in the real world involve a problem or a query (however small, such as asking if someone has gone home for the day) requiring negotiation and clarification of meaning, although most real-world communicative outcomes are incremental, intangible, or unstated. Therefore, for pedagogic purposes, tasks are often contrived to make problems and outcomes explicit. Commonly used texts are information gaps (e.g. Lynch, 1996) or ambiguous stories (e.g. Rost and Ross, 1991).

For purposes of tracking learner interactions, Lynch (1997) has developed a framework based on the work of Brown (1980; 1986; 1990) and Yule and Powers (1994). The framework focuses on ways that learners come to achieve communicative outcomes, (see Figure 10.2).

Another aspect of interactive listening is developed in whole-class activities, with the teacher providing the oral input, in the form of story-telling

---

Teaching principle: Interactive listening

Interactive listening is a key component of listening ability. It can be developed through collaborative speaking tasks that focus primarily on meaning but also entail negotiation of linguistic form.

1. **No Problem**: A problem exists but is not identified by either the sender or the receiver.

2. **Non-negotiated Solutions**

   a. **Unacknowledged Problem**: A problem is identified by the receiver but not acknowledged by the sender.

   b. **Abandon Responsibility**: A problem is identified by the receiver and acknowledged by the sender, but the sender does not take responsibility for solving the problem, either by saying they will skip it, leave it, never mind it or forget it, or by telling the receiver to choose any location or path.

   c. **Arbitrary Solution**: A problem is identified by the receiver and acknowledged by the sender who then makes an arbitrary decision about some defining feature of the location or path. The key element here is not accuracy, but the arbitrariness of the decision which does not attempt to take the receiver's world into account or to make the receiver's world match the sender's.

3. **Negotiated Solutions**

   a. **Receiver's World Solution**: A problem is identified and acknowledged by the sender who then tries to find out what is in the receiver's world and uses that information to instruct the receiver, based on the receiver's perspective.

   b. **Sender's World Solution**: A problem is identified and acknowledged by the sender who then instructs the receiver to make the receiver's world match the sender's, ignoring whatever information the receiver provides which does not fit the sender's perspective.

Figure 10.2 Communicative outcomes: an assessment category system (Lynch, 1997)

Quote 10.2 Ur on 'real-life' listening

We may say that most . . . of our real life listening activity is characterised by the following features:

1. We listen for a purpose and with certain expectations.
2. We make an immediate response to what we hear.
3. We see the person we are listening to.
4. There are some visual or environmental clues as to the meaning of what is heard.
5. Stretches of discourse are heard in short chunks.
6. Most heard discourse is spontaneous and therefore differs from formal spoken prose in the amount of redundancy, 'noise', and colloquialisms, and in its auditory character.

Ur (1984: 9)

or explanations (often accompanied by visuals). As Ur (1984) has pointed out, in order to approximate 'real-life' listening, we need to provide opportunities for immediate and ongoing responses by the listener (see Quote 10.2). For purposes of classroom management these responses can be oral, non-verbal, or written (Lund, 1991).

One structured method of using ongoing listener response is a **paused task**. Listening task design using short inputs (typically one or two minutes long) and overt listener response have great benefits for listening training. There are known limitations to short-term memory that occur after about 60 to 90 seconds of listening (cf. Bostrom and Waldhart, 1988; Cowan, 1993; Carpenter, Miyake and Just, 1994). Because of these limitations, one minute may be an optimal 'training window' for new listening skills and strategies. When learners are listening beyond this time limit, it is often not clear what mental activities they are performing. Guided instruction and feedback becomes more difficult in extended listening activities.

One way to work within the limitations of short-term memory and still employ longer texts is to utilise paused tasks. Paused tasks require the instructor to pause at specific points during the input phase of the activity – either by pausing the audio tape/CD or video or by stopping the narration if the teacher is providing the input directly.

Teaching principle: Paused texts

By pausing the spoken input (the tape or the teacher) and allowing for some quick intervention and response, we in effect 'slow down the listening process' to allow the listeners to monitor their listening more closely.

Example of a paused prediction task (for beginners, younger learners)

Purpose: The purpose of this kind of task is to encourage students to make explicit predictions about what they will hear next.

Focus of the activity: Students have to comprehend enough of the story plot and characters to be able to predict.

Input: A text with frequent pause points, one pause after each 15–30 seconds of input at which points the students will be asked to make a prediction.

Procedure:

- say/play the text
- stop at pre-set points to have students write or say their predictions for the missing parts

- check predictions at each pause point, then proceed with remaining part of the text.

Strategy focus: Students make explicit predictions, without worrying if their prediction is exactly correct.

Outcome: statements of predictions for each pause point.

Example (beginning level)

A folk tale

Once there was a very proud fox. One day, he was walking in the woods and [(pause point) he stepped into a trap.] His tail was caught in the trap. He pulled and pulled and [(pause point) he escaped], but his tail was left in the trap. He was very sad that he lost his tail, but he was also very [(pause point) proud.] When he went back to the pack, he said [(pause point), 'Look, everybody, I cut off my tail. Life is great without a tail.]' All of the other foxes . . .

Possible follow up

Students write their own short story or folk-tale (or translate one) and select three 'prediction points' in the story. Working with a partner (or the whole class), the student reads the story and pauses at the prediction points. Their partner tries to guess the next idea.

Notes on adjusting this task

Students often do not want to state a prediction or make only a vague prediction. The 'prediction points' the teacher selects may be too constrained, or the text itself is too difficult. It is best, initially at least, to select prediction points that have many possible completions, and can be answered by someone with only a fair understanding of the details of the text.

(Rost, 1999)

10.4 Grammar processing

Teaching principle: Amplifying input

Amplified or flooded input features multiple exemplars of a target grammatical feature or set of features in a genuine listening input. By using amplified input with noticing tasks, we can assist learners in acquiring grammar.

Most language teachers have noticed that when communicative listening or speaking tasks require learners to focus on meaning, they often 'forget' the grammar they have presumably acquired. They tend to revert to the 'lexis first' principle of communication: if you have limited capacity for processing, attend to content words first.

In communication tasks, learners focus – often very effectively – on 'getting the meaning' in listening or 'getting across their meaning' in speaking, often through the use of words in ungrammatical strings. On the other hand, structured language tasks (e.g. language drills or memorised exchanges) seemingly allow learners to focus on correct form, but it is clear that they are not practicing 'communication'. Teachers have often wondered about the best procedures to have students focus on both form and meaning at the same time.

Carr and Curran (1994) note that

> The syntax of natural language presents a very complicated hierarchical organisation with many interrelated conditional rules on what elements can combine with one another. Therefore, it seems plausible that natural language learning taxes the system's (i.e. the brain's) ability to keep track of context more severely than learning the model grammars used in structural learning tasks . . . syntactic learning may well require, or at least benefit from, focal attention (p. 224).

In order to focus learner's attention on form, Ellis (1999) proposes working with 'grammar through listening', an extension of 'input enhancement' and van Patten's (1990) 'processing instruction'.

1. Teach only one thing (i.e. grammatical structure or contrast) at a time.

2. Keep meaning in focus.

3. Learners must do something with the input.

4. Use both oral and written input.

5. Move from sentences to connected discourse.

6. Keep the psycholinguistic processing strategies (e.g. use of word order, word endings, inflections) in mind.

(van Patten, 1990: 67–70)

Ellis's approach involves:

> providing learners with data (in the form of a listening or reading text) to illustrate a particular grammatical feature and getting them to analyze it so as to arrive at an understanding of how the feature works. In effect, this requires learners to become active-thinkers in order to discover for themselves how the grammar of the language they are studying works.
>
> [A teaching unit in this approach is] based on a grammatical problem that we know learners of English as a second language commonly experience (e.g. the use of the present progressive tense with stative verbs as in * *I am weighing 60 kilos*). The learners begin by listening to a text that contains examples of correct usage. They first process this for meaning. Then they

Fantastic Toys

ERROR BOX

✗ A tamagochi is a computerized toy. Tamagochi has
become very popular

Have you ever had a pet?
What did you have to do to take care of it?

LISTENING TO COMPREHEND

Listen to the newspaper report about the tamagochi.
Answer these questions:

1. What is a tamagochi?

2. What does the owner of a tamagochi have to do?

3. What kind of tamagochi did the Chinese street seller make?

4. Why did Mariko Tada lose her job?

WORD BOX

* hatch	* insect
* cage	* discipline
* chick	* fired
* bamboo	* gadget
* chirping	* invent

LISTENING TO NOTICE

Listen again. Choose *a* or *the* to complete the newspaper report.

   A   tamagochi is a computerized toy invented in Japan. The name means a cute little egg.
     tamagochi has become very popular all around the world. The gadget hatches ____
chick. ____ chick makes a chirping noise every few minutes. ____owner has to push buttons
to feed, play with, clean up and discipline the chick. If ____ owner stops caring for the chick,
it dies.

    However, the electronic toy is expensive and many people cannot afford to buy one.
____ street seller in China had a good idea. He decided to make a live tamagochi. He
made ____ small cage out of bamboo. Then he caught ____ insect. He put ____ insect inside
____ cage. ____ street seller was able to sell the tamagochi for three yuan (about 40 cents).
Now he has become rich selling live tamagochis.

    Some people think that the tamagochi is a bad thing. 'I bought a tamagochi and
spent a lot of time looking after it,' explained Mariko Tada, a sales assistant in ____
downtown Tokyo store. She spent so much time caring for her tamagochi that ____ store
fired her!

Figure 10.3   Grammar through listening (Ellis and Gaies, 1999)

UNDERSTANDING THE GRAMMAR POINT

1. Read the story again. Fill in the table.

a(n) + noun	the + noun
a tamagochi	the tamagochi

2. When is *a* used? When is *the* used?

3. Look through the story again. Study the other noun phrases with *a* and *the* (a computerized toy; the gadget). Can you see why *a* is used in some noun phrases and *the* in others?

CHECKING

Read the following descriptions of other toys. Fill in the blanks with *a(n)* or *the*.

1. TUGGLES is _a_ cuddly pet with a leash. When you pull on ____ leash the pet walks by
   itself. Kids love taking Tuggles for ____ walk.

2. JOSEPHINA MONTOYA is ____ realistic doll that looks Hispanic. It is accompanied by ____
   book. ____ book tells you all about how to care for ____ doll.

3. BULLDOG DOZER is ____ construction set together with ____ bulldozer. ____ bulldozer
   keeps knocking down ____ construction you are making. Kids will love it!

TRYING IT

Think of a toy you would like to invent. Write a description of the toy. OR Think of a toy that you loved as a child. Describe it.

LANGUAGE NOTE
Be careful about using *a* and *the*.

_____

_____

_____

_____

_____

Grammar through listening is a processing approach that allows students to notice grammatical distinctions as they listen, and then helps them formulate grammatical rules based on what they have noticed.

Figure 10.3   *continued*

listen again, this time focussing their attention on the target grammatical feature (i.e. they are helped to notice it). Next, they use the data to try to arrive at an explicit understanding of the rule (e.g. the kinds of verbs that are not used in the present progressive tense). This provides a basis for an error-identification task, where they can check if they have understood the rule clearly. Finally, there is an opportunity for the learners to try to use the correct grammatical structure in their own sentences.

These materials . . . aim to teach grammar through input-processing by helping learners to attend to particular grammatical features; they train the skills of noticing. This contrasts with traditional approaches which aim to teach grammar through production practice of one kind or another. Second, the materials make use of oral texts on the grounds that learners need training in being able to notice grammatical features when they are listening. This is very difficult for learners, particularly if the features are redundant (i.e. are not essential for understanding the meaning). Third, the materials employ a grammar-discovery approach. Learners are shown how to analyze the data in order to arrive at an understanding of how a grammatical feature works. Fourthly, the materials provide practise in monitoring – the learners are asked to use their explicit knowledge to identify and correct errors of the kind that they typically make.

The main benefit of this style of listening instruction is in its alignment: it keeps development of listening ability and language acquisition in parallel. Learners perceive, rightly so, that they are working on both 'listening' and 'grammar' simultaneously.

10.5 Multimedia

Teaching principle: Multidimensional representations

When reading or listening in our L1 we do not understand the meaning of an utterance or a text just by understanding the meaning of its words. In fact we do not understand the text at all but rather our mental representation of it. For this representation to become meaningful and memorable we need to make use of all the resources of our mind. We need at least to:

- achieve sensory and affective experience of the text;
- connect the text to our previous experiences of language and of life;
- fill in the gaps in the text to achieve our own continuity and completion;
- relate the text to our own interests, views and needs.

In other words we need to achieve multi-dimensional representation of the text in order for us to give it meaning and for it to achieve a durable impression on our minds (Tomlinson, 1998).

Since the widespread use of video tape began in the 1980s, the use of video for listening instruction has been widely discussed among teachers. The most compelling reason for using video is its immediate possibilities for engagement: it can provide high-quality, authentic listening and viewing material for a range of teaching purposes. Now with the expanding use of DVD (digital video) and broadband digital broadcasts on the internet, it is hard to imagine not using video for some instructional purposes wherever the technology is available.

In the past, the often reported downside of using video is that the visual medium can be so compelling as input that the teacher and student ignore other aspects of learning. Teachers have often not known how to 'anchor' the video as a text that can be worked with for language learning. It now is recognised that use of video as learning material must follow general principles of listening instruction. Pre-viewing (pre-listening) activities are needed to focus learners' attention, viewing tasks are required to allow for selective viewing (selective listening), the input must be divided into chunks to allow for effective processing and maximal use as 'intake', there must be opportunities for clarification of meaning, and there must be practical follow-up activities. Recent teaching guides, such as those by Stempleski and Tomalin (1990) and Mendelsohn and Rubin (1995), have helped clarify appropriate methodologies for teachers to use.

In their teacher-training manual, Stempleski and Tomalin (1990) introduce the terms 'viewing comprehension' (the processing of linguistic and nonlinguistic input) and 'active viewing' (the integration of verbal and visual cues) to explore ways that video can be used for development of selective and global listening. They present a number of 'recipes' for using video in class settings, many of which focus on development of listening (e.g. video dictation). Figure 10.4 shows one activity.

One important consideration in video instruction is the use of **subtitles**. Although many teachers believe that use of subtitles prevents students from 'really listening', judicious use of subtitles can be very effective at engaging learners in the content and motivating them to get as much as possible out of each video they view.

Four subtitle variations are possible:

1. **traditional** (L2 audio, L1 captions)
2. **bimodal** (L2 audio, L2 captions)
3. **reverse** (L1 audio, L2 captions)
4. **unimodal** (L1 audio, L1 captions).

All variations can have some place in language learning, though the first three variations are obviously of most interest for developing listening. (L1 audio and L1 captions may be used occasionally for content verification purposes or for translation exercises.) Various researchers have

Prediction

Level   Beginners and above, children

Purpose   Active viewing, Discussion, Speaking, Vocabulary development

Sequence type   Any

Sequence length   1–5 minutes

Activity time   30 minutes

Preparation

Select a sequence from a TV news programme, drama or feature film, in which the situation is quickly and clearly established. Prepare a list of the following headings: TOPIC, SIGHTS, WORDS, SOUNDS, SMELLS. Make copies for all the students.

In class

1. Distribute copies of the list (or write it on the board). Tell the students that you are going to play the beginning of the sequence. Their task is to predict what the whole sequence will be like in terms of the headings in the list.
2. Play enough of the sequence to establish the topic.
3. In pairs the students discuss and write down the following under each heading.
    TOPIC   the subject of the sequence
    SIGHTS   things they expect to see
    WORDS   words they expect to hear
    SOUNDS   sounds they expect to hear
    SMELLS   things they might smell if they were there
4. Elicit from the students some of their ideas.
5. Play the rest of the sequence.

In their teacher training manual, Stempleski and Tomalin (1990) introduce the terms 'viewing comprehension' (the processing of linguistic and non-linguistic input) and 'active viewing' (the integration of verbal and visual cues) to explore ways that video can be used for development of selective and global listening. They present a number of 'recipes' for using video in class settings, many of which focus on development of listening (e.g. video dictation).

Figure 10.4   **Active viewing (Stempleski and Tomalin, 1990)**

experimented with differing use of modalities for presentations and various measures of comprehension and recall. In a study by Baltova (1998), L2 vocabulary learning was found to be superior with the bimodal treatment. Similarly, studies by Holobow *et al.* (1984) and McNeill (1998) found benefits for the use of both traditional and bimodal subtitles in aiding L2 learning.

Because the use of printed subtitles provides longer access to the input language, and because with subtitles speech is already parsed into individual words, learners who are literate in English nearly always exhibit greater understanding of content and retain more vocabulary from the input. However, many learners report that their interest in watching 'authentic' video (e.g. US television shows) is in large part motivation: they want to prove to themselves that they can 'handle the real thing'. As such, it makes sense to include some part of all video lessons with no subtitles.

Teaching principle: Modalities

Different modalities of presentation can be used for different purposes. Allowing learners to select modalities and design tasks and to experiment with different modalities may help them understand how better to develop their aural skills.

Teaching application: Preparing video guides

Tatsuki (1999) provides a useful example of the kind of video guide for particular movies that numerous teachers are developing for their own teaching. A video guide can act as a textbook, containing all of the skills exercises that are needed, but in the context of a video story that is of interest to the students.

In her study guide for *Raiders of the Lost Ark*, Tatsuki provides guided lesson plans for each scene of the movie. (A typical scene is three minutes long.) Because of her experience with multiple classes who have viewed the movie, she has identified '**hot spots**', areas of known listening problems for L2 viewers. By anticipating these 'hot spots', she is able to provide pre-viewing activities to help students activate the necessary expectations to understand the scene.

Teaching concept: Listening and new text types

Due to the expanding influence of the internet and computer technology generally, texts are becoming increasingly visual, multimodal, and interactive. The authors contend that texts are becoming 'incremental' and 'expansive': the user decides upon the ingredients and increments for both 'creating' and 'processing' a text.

Computer technology also allows for more 'user-determined events', more review and replay of selected parts of texts, as well as a 'shared now', in which text-users can mutually interact with texts and mutually create texts. All of these developments mean that it is becoming harder to define texts in terms of their 'informativity'. Literacy and 'oracy' now entail knowing how to manage new kinds of information. (adapted from Goodman and Graddol, 1996).

> **Teaching priniciple: New media**
>
> In considering new modes and new media which greatly extend the range and reach of experience for both teachers and learners, it is important not to lose sight of our focus on language and discourse, and the importance of fostering co-operative learning in an environment where, however distanced from each other physically, learners and teachers can still negotiate meanings, interact and support each other's learning (from Candlin and Mercer, 2000).

10.6 Strategy training

Some aspects of listening are under conscious control of the listener, while others are automatic and not under direct control. The conscious aspects of any goal-oriented behaviour are viewed in psychology as 'strategies', and it is widely-documented that expert performance in any behaviour involves planning and selection of appropriate strategies (Kasper and Kellerman, 1998).

The area of strategy training for second language learners has been very active since the early 1990s, starting with the work of O'Malley and Chamot (1990) and Oxford (1990), with much initial effort aimed at identifying and cataloguing the types of strategies that both successful and unsuccessful listeners use. The terms 'strategy' and 'learning strategy' themselves have been used in various senses in applied linguistics literature to refer to a range of goal-directed plans and behaviours and have encompassed all 'thoughts and actions that assist learning'. A number of categorisation distinctions have been used: direct vs indirect, cognitive vs affective, learning vs use, cognitive vs social, cognitive vs metacognitive (Chamot et al. 1999). The goal of finding distinctions is aimed at the critical objective of 'psychological validity': until the researcher has some certainty of what the experience of using the strategy is like and why someone is using a particular strategy, there can be no progress toward incorporating strategy training into pedagogy.

The most widely agreed-upon classes of language use strategies are 'social strategies' (e.g. asking someone for help), 'cognitive strategies' (e.g. guessing the meaning of an unknown word) and 'metacognitive strategies' (e.g. paying attention to the main points of a lecture), although the boundaries between these categories are not always clear.

For teaching purposes, two distinctions seem most important to make. First, if 'strategies' are decisions that the user (the learner) makes, the 'mental decision' or 'mental action' that the learner undertakes must be psychologically valid, that is, it must be clear to the learner when she is and when she is not engaging the strategy. Only psychologically valid strategies need to be considered for instruction. Second, strategies that are associated with improved or 'expert' performance are those that need to be identified, modelled and practised. Only 'success strategies' need to be taught. 'Success strategies' can be found through research of successful listeners – listeners who have made and are making progress in their listening ability (cf. Rost and Ross, 1991; Vandergrift, 1996; Fujiwara, 1989; Mendlesohn, 1998).

If these distinctions can be made, it is possible to teach strategies by way of indicating what the learner does (or should attempt to do) and what the teacher does to promote use of a particular strategy (see Table 10.1).

Within recent studies by Vandergrift (1996; 1998; 1999) and Rost (1999), there is broad agreement on the kinds of strategies that are frequently associated with successful listening. Five commonly recognised 'successful' strategies are: predicting information or ideas prior to listening, making inferences from incomplete information based on prior knowledge, monitoring one's own listening processes and relative success while listening, attempting to clarify areas of confusion and responding to what one has understood.

Teaching concept: Listening strategies of successful L2 listeners

These strategies are often practised by successful L2 listeners. By incorporating them into listening activities, the teacher gives all students an opportunity to practise them.

1. **Predicting**: Predicting information or ideas prior to listening.

2. **Inferencing**: Drawing inferences about complete information based on incomplete or inadequate information.

3. **Monitoring**: Monitoring one's own performance while listening, including assessing areas of uncertainty.

4. **Clarifying**: Formulating clarification questions about what information is needed to make a fuller interpretation.

5. **Responding**: Providing a personal, relevant response to the information or ideas presented.

6. **Evaluating**: Checking how well one has understood, and whether an initial problem posed has been solved.

The training paradigm that has been proposed by Rost and Ross (1991) for interactive listening and Vandergrift (1999) for transactional listening is that if learners are taught to emulate the strategies of more successful (or more proficient) language learners, those learners will accelerate their own progress.

Table 10.1   **Metacognitive strategies** (based on Vandergrift, 1996)

Strategy	What the learner does	What the teacher can do to promote this strategy
PLANNING		
Advanced organisation	Decide what the objectives of a specific listening task are. Why is it important to attend to this?	Write the topic on the board and ask learners why it might be important to listen to it.
Directed attention	Learners must pay attention to the main points in a listening task to get a general understanding of what is said.	In setting up a listening task ask learners what type of information they are likely to hear.
Selective attention	Learners pay attention to details in the listening task.	Before listeners listen a second time to a recording, set specific types of information for them to listen for.
Self-management	Learners have to manage their own motivation for a listening task.	Before setting up a listening task the teacher talks with the students in the L2 so that they become attuned to listening.
MONITORING		
Comprehension monitoring	Learners check their understanding of ideas, through asking confirmation questions.	Teacher sets up a task so that students have opportunities to ask for clarification and confirmation.
Auditory monitoring	Learners check their identification of what they hear.	Teacher sets up 'bottom–up' listening task to check for accurate perception of key words and grammatical structures.
Task monitoring	Learners check their completion of the task.	Teacher sets up task with intermediate steps so that students can tell that they are in the process of completing the task.
EVALUATION		
Performance evaluation	Learners judge how well they did on the task.	Teacher sets up task with tangible outcome that can be evaluated by learners.
Problem identification	Learners decide on what problems they still have with the text or task.	Teacher provides follow up to elicit problem areas.

Presentation of listening strategies by itself tends to be insufficient to ensure learner progress. In order for learners to take advantage of strategy training, they need awareness of the strategy, opportunities to see it demonstrated in actual discourse, understanding of its potential benefits, as well as targeted practice in using the strategy and experiencing its effects.

Teaching principle: Conditions for a listening strategy to be 'teachable'

1. The learner recognises a need to address 'confusion' or to compensate for incomplete information.
2. There is a recognisable point in the discourse in which a strategy (an alternate way of processing language or interacting) can be used.
3. The alternate way has a probable payoff in knowledge or affect that the learner seeks (e.g. to understand more of the listening extract).
4. The alternate way of processing can be practised again in an immediate context.
5. The new use of the alternate produces the demonstrable effect (on interaction, understanding, or learning).

10.7 Listening-awareness training

Key concept: Listening is a conscious activity under direct control of the listener

Effective listening involves a conscious shift in intentions while listening. This shift can be achieved through an understanding of typical distractions and ways of preparing for and overcoming them.

There is a considerable body of applied literature on 'effective listening'. This literature, largely intended for native speakers, though certainly applicable in principle to L2 speakers as well, tends to focus on the role of listening in close relationships and in professional encounters. Generally speaking, the applications tend to make four assumptions:

- all people have a basic psychological need to be understood
- effective listening creates understanding
- effective listening is the fundamental goal of communication in all professional and personal relationships

- listening attitudes and behaviour are intentional and can be changed through conscious decisions.

Most of the applications in this class are training-oriented 'how to' guides, aimed at teaching people how to become more *intentional* in their listening. Listening training typically covers a number of 'how to' points:

- how to prepare for listening
- how to focus selectively on information
- how to avoid distractions while listening
- how to be empathic
- how to become sensitised to non-verbal communication (gaze, posture, intonation)
- how to hear messages and paraphrase non-judgementally
- how to provide verbal and non-verbal feedback that will encourage the speaker to feel comfortable and reveal more
- how to ask questions.

Collectively, these attitudes and behaviours – preparing for listening, focusing selectively, avoiding distractions, showing empathy, etc. – are often referred to as '**active listening**'.

Effective listening applications often focus on determining the purpose for listening in a situation and adjusting one's attitudes to fit the purpose. Four types of listening are often distinguished.

- **Appreciative listening**: listening for pleasure, as to music, or a television show, or a comedy routine. This type of listening is for relaxation or for energising the listener.
- **Comprehensive or informational listening**: listening to gain knowledge, as to directions, a description, a person's position on a topic. This type of listening is intended to focus on information and to suspend judgement or evaluation.
- **Critical or deliberative listening**: listening to assess the value of a message or its validity, as to a persuasive speech or 'infomercial'. This type of listening is intended to lead to a decision on accepting or rejecting the value of a proposal.
- **Empathic or therapeutic listening**: listening to understand another person's feelings or point of view, as when a close friend needs a 'sounding board'. Empathic listening is said to facilitate problem-solving, foster development of a clearer perspective, and aid both the speaker and listener in restoring emotional balance.

Training in effective listening entails identifying one's goals in a listening situation and activating the appropriate skills and strategies for one's listening goals.

Teaching principle: Paraphrasing

Paraphrasing is an excellent technique for promoting listening. Almost always, the problem is not in the paraphrasing but in the listening skills of the person being paraphrased (Hank Washak, posting on newsgroup of International Listening Association *www.cios.org/www/:*).

Syntonic listening

Elgin's (1989) approach to '**syntonic listening**' is to raise the listener's awareness concerning not only the types of responses available, but to their positive or negative effect. (The purpose of 'syntonic listening' is to detect mismatches between communication styles of speaker–listener and to make adjustments to bring the styles more 'in tune' with each other.)

Five common listening styles

1. **Evaluating**
   Positive: That's a very kind thing to say.
   Negative: That's a ridiculous thing to say.

2. **Interpreting**
   Positive: You're only saying that because you're upset about your job.
   Negative: You're only saying that because you want me to feel sorry for you.

3. **Emotional**
   Positive: I'm sorry you feel that way. I wish I could help.
   Negative: It makes me feel terrible to hear you talk that way. I wish you'd keep it to yourself.

4. **Probing**
   Positive: Maybe it's not as bad as it seems. What did she actually say to you?
   Negative: Either give me a concrete example or just don't talk about it.

5. **Summarising**
   Positive: It seems to me that you're saying that you don't think she understood your proposal. Do I have that right?
   Negative: What you're saying is that you really screwed things up and that she knows it. That's what you're saying, right?

(Based on Elgin, 1989: 75–6)

Gaining Communication Competence

How to Become 'All Ears'

Following are seven steps to ensure you are a more effective listener.

Step One: Catch Yourself Exhibiting a Bad Habit

Recognition of a fault precedes correction of it. If you monitor your listening behaviour, you can catch yourself before you display an undesirable trait. That's the first step toward positive change.

Step Two: Substitute a Good Habit for a Bad Habit

Think about the new listening habits you would like to have. For example, if you are a daydreamer and mentally wander off while others speak to you, encourage yourself to exhibit greater attentiveness and concentration. Visualize yourself listening effectively when conversing. Imagine the positive impact your new behaviour will have on your relationships.

Step Three: Use Your Whole Body to Listen

Take steps to ensure that your physical mannerisms do not distract or confuse the person with whom you are interacting. Instead of leaning back with your arms crossed, fidgeting, playing with your hair or jewelry, gazing repeatedly at your watch, or otherwise signaling that you are not interested in what he or she is saying, make a commitment to convey a more positive listening demeanor. Display an attentive posture, make good eye contact, and exhibit appropriate facial expressions. In other words, get physically ready to listen. If you look more like an effective listener, you will be more apt to behave like one.

Step Four: Consistently Use Your Ears, Not Just Your Mouth

When you converse with another, you need to be able to shift naturally and frequently from a speaking mode to a listening mode. Rather than monopolizing the speaking role or spending your time planning what you will say once you get the floor, make a sincere effort when you're not speaking to focus on what the other person is saying to you. Rather than completing his or her statements because you 'know for sure' what he or she is going to say, let the person complete his or her own thoughts. Conversing with another compels us to develop not just a speaking presence, but also a listening attitude.

Step Five: Be Willing to See the Other Side

Because one of the greatest detriments to listening is an unwillingness to look at a situation from another's point of view, if you begin a conversation by telling yourself you are willing to see and feel from the other individual's perspective you increase your chances for more meaningful interaction. You may not end up agreeing with what you have heard, but you will be more likely to understand where the thoughts and feelings came from.

Step Six: Avoid the Tendencies to Distort Messages or Listen Assumptively

Every message delivered by one person to another exists in at least four different forms:

Form 1:   The message as it exists in the mind of the person speaking to you (his or her thoughts)

Figure 10.5   Conscious listening (Gamble and Gamble, 1998: 152–54)

Form 2:   The message as it is spoken (encoded by that person)

Form 3:   The message as it is interpreted by the listener (decoded by you)

Form 4:   The message as it is ultimately remembered by the listener (influenced by your personal selectivity or rejection biases)

When passed from person to person, messages become distorted. This happens because, first, we usually try to simplify the messages we hear as we process them. Second, because of our apprehensiveness, we may not want to admit that we didn't understand what some-one said to us; instead, we may try to make sense of what we were told on our own by mak-ing certain assumptions. Typically we do this by adding to, subtracting from, or otherwise altering what was said.

Step Seven: Participate Actively

Ask questions. Paraphrase. Listening is an active and responsive process, not a passive behaviour. It requires that you paraphrase – restate in your own words – what you have heard another say to you. Doing this lets you know whether you have correctly processed the words and feelings – the actual meaning – of another's message.

Keep in mind that developing yourself as an effective listener is a basic step in developing yourself as an effective communicator.

Figure 10.5   *Continued*

'Conscious listening'

The claims made for the benefits of effective listening in both business and personal relationship are often quite dramatic. Gamble and Gamble (1998), for instance, contend that effective listening will improve most relationships by decreasing stress, enhancing interpersonal knowledge, building trust, and improving decision-making, self-esteem of both parties, self-confidence and self-protection.

Based on an analysis of effective and ineffective listening attitudes and behaviours, Gamble and Gamble (1998) provide principles in the form of 'steps' to follow in order to become a better listener: (see Figure 10.5).

Applications such as this one are often targeted at young adults, fre-quently as part of communication courses in colleges and universities for learners who may never have previously analysed the listening process in much depth. The simplifications of communication principles and the focus on 'positive messages' are offered for the sake of accessibility, to allow for immediate application and to provide a framework for self-assessment.

More complex guides to effective listening, such as Nichols (1995), deal with the complexities of interactive listening and the inherent difficulties in understanding another person. Such guides avoid distilling listening principles into lists. Instead, they state principles, recognise the psycholog-ical dynamics in applying them to real situations, and discuss specific case studies in which the principles are applied.

10.8   Listening projects

Listening projects are extended activities that involve listening and other skills in an integrated way. They often extend over several class meetings and entail work outside the classroom as well.

White (1998) has outlined a number of stimulating listening projects, including preparing interviews for a class magazine in English, preparing a news broadcast with student reporters and newscasters collaborating on what to include in the broadcast, a music show in which students bring in CDs of their favourite songs and prepare activities to go with them, performing a short radio play (with sound effects), presenting an 'oral history' of their country, with visual aids.

The aim of listening projects is to involve listening in various modes. Most projects involve listening to recorded material in or out of class as *preparation* for their class activity. Many projects involve interviewing speakers (in the TL) outside of class and gathering and editing information. All projects involve student–student listening and interaction in preparing and rehearsing for the class performance or presentation.

As White notes, these kinds of activities forge links between the classroom and outside world. In this way 'students can use listening skills they have acquired in the classroom "for real"'.

10.9   Academic listening

An important area for listening instruction is transactional (one-way) listening, particularly in academic settings. The lecture, the main genre in academic settings, represents a clear listening target for many learners.

A useful starting point for thinking of lectures as vehicles of instruction is to realise that the genre of lecturing *is* communicative. According to Berlo (1960), the purpose of communication, generally, is to influence someone with intent. Rather than being mere presentations of excess quantities of information (that the listener is supposed to ingest), academic lectures are a prime example of a communicative situation in which a speaker aims to 'influence with intent'. The intention may be to raise awareness, to inform, and to change the audience's attitudes about ideas presented.

Listening to lectures is sometimes seen as a poor substitute for reading, but it has been shown that listening has distinct advantages over reading for certain kinds of learning. First, in listening contexts, it is generally easier to understand the speaker's emphasis and emotional affect toward various points or arguments, that is, how the lecturer 'feels about' the topic. It is also generally easier to understand the gist of what is being said (Lund, 1991; Brown, 1995). (At the same time, reading has a distinct advantage over listening in terms of remembering specific facts and details. This may be why we all feel compelled in lectures to take notes of facts and details we are likely to forget.)

Mason (1994) reports that even advanced L2 students experience pronounced difficulties in university lecture settings, particularly when the lecture deviates from the straightforward 'chalk and talk' pattern and includes audience participation. When questioned about the strategies they used to understand lectures, the students gave these responses:

- rely on previous background knowledge of the subject matter;
- compensate with concentrated study of reading materials;
- listen to or seek out native speaker peers;
- speak to professor or adviser about difficulties;
- seek outside help with subject matter in own language;
- use other classes with more familiar subjects to gain more confidence to speak out.

In an extended study of a single NNS student at a US university, Benson (1989) examined both the ethnographic features (settings, roles, preferences, expectations) of lectures the student attended and the student's approach

---

Sample application: Lecturing styles

In a classic study of learning in lecture-style formats, Brown (1978) surveyed lecturers and students about the most effective styles of lecturing. While there is not clear agreement on an ideal style, most learners report that effective lecturers have the following 'basic skills of lecturing':

1. **Explaining**: using examples and illustrations
2. **Orientation**: opening a lecture, introducing a topic or theme clearly
3. **Closure**: summarising themes and linking topics and themes
4. **Liveliness**: generating interest and enthusiasm, giving and holding attention
5. **Using audiovisual aids**: effectively using boards, overhead projector, slides, models
6. **Varying student activities**: allowing for different modes of working in the lecture
7. **Giving directions**: indicating how to carry out procedures or how to solve various kinds of problems
8. **Comparing**: comparing and contrasting ideas, giving advantages and disadvantages of various approaches, comparing different perspectives
9. **Narrating**: readings extracts from authentic sources to illustrate a point of view.

(Adapted from Brown, 1978: 47)

to a lecture (expectations for in-class behaviour, prior preparation, note-taking, supplementary reading, test-taking, discussion and collaboration with classmates). By viewing the lectures in the broadest terms, Benson was able to demonstrate how the comprehension processes of the listener are influenced by much more than the text of a lecture.

Recent research has examined in selected features of academic lecture texts: the **rate** and **pace** of delivery, use of **global** and **local macro-organisers**, supplementation with non-verbal information, transaction sequences, **asides**, definitions, and vocabulary elaborations (Flowerdew, 1994; Chaudron, 1994). This research has focused on how manipulation of these features (specifically, **simplification** or **elaboration**) affects comprehension and recall or note-taking of L2 learners. Results thus far are inconsistent. Not all modifications in the direction of 'simplification' of the lecture automatically result in better comprehension or recall.

Although some simplification and elaboration adjustments (specifically, increased pausing at natural pause points, use of visual organisers, vocabulary elaboration) do generally lead to better comprehension among L2 listeners, more consistent improvement results from cognitive focuses. Examples are presentations of background information (such as vocabulary) to listeners before the lecture (Chiang and Dunkel, 1992), attention to advance organisers (Benson, 1989), and training in note-taking strategies (Dunkel, 1988; Chaudron, 1995).

10.10   Content-based listening

Content-based listening is the use of content as the course focus, with the majority of content presented through listening via live presentations, discussions, recordings and video. Learners are instructed in listening strategies and are given structured tasks to help them learn to listen more effectively, but always under the umbrella of content-based teaching. Sometimes referred to as 'sheltered content', this approach is used for academic subject matter in many primary and secondary bilingual education contexts.

The sequence of instruction in these classes typically follows a logical sequence required by the subject matter, but adjunct-language focus lessons and individual tutoring are often used to support the content, hence the term 'sheltered content'. The focus in sheltered content classes is for the students to acquire information and skills *via* the second language, and in the process, develop their second-language skills – listening, speaking, reading and writing.

In a content-based approach, the activities of the language class are specific to the subject matter being taught, and activities are geared to stimulate students to think and learn through use of the target language. This approach lends itself to the integration of the four skills, and allows for truly 'authentic' listening. All listening, whether as lecture by the teacher or interaction with classmates is, in theory, geared to the students' needs to learn the subject matter.

The rationale for content-based language instruction is consistent with competency-based instruction. If the learners are eventually aiming for use of the target language for 'real purposes', and if the learners wish to be treated like 'real users' of the target language, content-based instruction or sheltered-content instruction appears to be the most efficient means of language learning (cf. Lambert and Tucker, 1972; Genessee, 1987).

Brinton et al. (1989) present three models of content instruction: theme-based, sheltered and adjunct. They discuss ways that these models can be adapted to all levels of proficiency, so that students even at beginning levels can benefit from the integrated, goal-oriented features of this style of language instruction.

10.11 Self-access listening

Since the 1960s there have been a number of key projects designed to promote ongoing adult education. One of the most notable of these is the Centre de Recherches et d'Applications en Langues (CRAPEL) at the University of Nancy. This centre remains an important focus for research on autonomous learning today, and an evolving model of what can be achieved in this area.

Quote 10.3 Benson on 'autonomy' and control

At the core of autonomy lies the idea of control. However, since there are several ways in which learners can take control of their learning, the idea of autonomy is necessarily complex, involving both attitudes and skills internal to the learner and situational factors conducive to their development...

The idea of autonomy involves five hypotheses:

1. Autonomy in learning is natural and available to all.
2. Autonomous learning is more effective than non-autonomous learning.
3. Autonomy is exhibited to different degrees by different individuals in different situations.
4. Learners who lack autonomy are capable of developing it given appropriate conditions and preparation.
5. The ways in which we organise teaching and learning exercise an important influence on the development of autonomy among our learners.

Benson (1989)

Sample application: Checklists for self-access centres

Although self-access centres are an essential tool for listening development, merely setting up one and stocking it with resources is hardly a guarantee that it will be successful.

Sturtridge (1997), Gardner and Miller (1999) and Benson (2000) all provide checklists of issues that must be considered if a self-access centre is to succeed. The following is an integrated list of their recommendations:

1.   Management of innovation

Curriculum managers, teachers and students all need to be consulted on the introduction of a self-access centre. Some teachers may see it as a threat to their jobs if the role of the centre is not properly discussed. As with any innovation, there needs to be a shared philosophy underlying any attempt to help teachers develop a new methodology or a new mode of working.

- Is there adequate consultation between centre management and teachers in the planning and use of the centre?
- Are activities in the centre integrated into the curriculum and the class timetable?
- Are the learners involved in the planning and management of the centre? Are they aware of its function and its role in the curriculum?

2.   Provision of a suitable location and facilities

Low-cost centres can be just as successful as high-cost centres. The key is in the planning and use of available resources. Centres must be in locations that are easy to reach for learners. Facilities must be continuously updated to maintain student interest.

- Is the centre easily accessible to the potential users?
- Is the centre sufficiently resourced and updated?
- Are available resources appropriately and imaginatively displayed?
- Does use of the centre encourage autonomy?

3.   Training and development of the staff

Successful centres have sound initial training programmes for all staff so that the goals and procedures are well understood. Centres often fail if all staff members do not become 'stakeholders'. Teachers need to become aware of their role in a self-access centre as facilitators; indeed they need to be trained to *stop teaching* students.

- Is training available to all members of the staff who are in contact with the centre?
- Does the centre have feedback mechanisms for staff comments and proposals?
- Are the staff involved in any research about the use of the centre?

4. Training and development of learners

Learners must be guided to consider their own working styles and strategies for learning. A successful centre will aim to make learner development an ongoing process.

- Is orientation and training available to all potential users of the centre?
- Is ongoing training available to regular users of the centre?
- Do learners have opportunities to explore all resources and develop autonomy?

5. Using the cultural strengths of learners

A successful centre must be able to acknowledge and utilise the strengths of learners who come from different cultural backgrounds and educational training. Ignoring learners' preferred styles can make them feel ill at ease and disinclined to use the centre. An example is that some learners may feel more comfortable working in groups, while others may prefer to work alone at rote learning.

- Does the centre accommodate different learning styles?

6. Suitable materials

Centres are accepted or rejected ultimately on the relevance of the materials they have to offer. Often organisers are obsessed with the quantity of materials provided, rather than the quality. Input materials may include audio (tapes or CDs), video (tapes or DVDs), internet sources and even 'live' input in the form of conversation partners.

Successful centres need task materials to accompany the input sources. Materials must be suitable for both 'explorers', those who like to learn on their own, and 'practisers', those who need guided exercises for learning.

- Are the materials in the centre suitably adapted for self-access use?
- Does the range and layout of materials facilitate exploration and exercise of choices?

(Adapted from Sturtridge, 1997: 68–74; Benson, 2000: 11–16)

In the model of autonomy developed at CRAPEL, individual learners and groups are able to plan, execute and evaluate their own learning programmes. At CRAPEL, this process is called **self-directed learning**. **Autonomy** refers to its ultimate goal. At the outset, the idea of autonomy in language learning was closely associated with three areas of practice: **self-access**, **learner training** and **individualisation**.

The first self-access language learning centres, at CRAPEL (Riley and Zoppis, 1985) were based on the idea of access. Access to a rich collection of authentic target-language materials was seen as offering learners the best opportunity for experimentation with self-directed learning. In recent years, in part due to the breakthroughs at CRAPEL, self-access centres have proliferated and the interest in '**resources-based learning**' has blossomed.

Autonomy and resource-based learning have also become important issues in technology-based learning, notably the field of computer-assisted language learning (CALL). Researchers on autonomy have emphasised that learners who engage in resource-based or technology-based learning do not necessarily become more autonomous as a result of their efforts. A great deal depends on the nature of the resources used and the use that is made of them (Benson and Voller, 1996; Benson, 2000).

The use of resource-based learning is essential in the case of listening development because it is widely recognised that learning to listen involves having access to *a massive amount* of aural input. Because so much L2 aural input (particularly in English) is available through television, radio, video and internet sources, the areas of self-access and self-instruction have become focal for listening development.

Sheerin (1989; 1997), has outlined activity support formats that will help learners get more from self-access listening sources than they might through '**naïve' listening**. She talks about different types of listening (**intensive vs extensive**), ways of finding suitable sources (short texts and long texts), the range of text types and genres that can be used (e.g. songs, books on tape), and types of exercises teachers can readily design to help students with self-access listening work (e.g. for shorter texts: cloze texts, scrambled pictures, texts with comprehension tasks, information transfer tasks; for longer texts: use of tape scripts for reference, summaries, comprehension questions, reactive listening).

To complete the functioning of a self-access centre, many organisers recommend the use of study plans, individual student contracts, periodic sessions with the centre coordinator, and evaluation forms.

Quote 10.4 Gardner and Miller on self-access language learning

Self-access is probably the most widely used and recognised term for an approach to encouraging autonomy. Self-access language learning is an approach to learning language, not an approach to teaching language. There are misconceptions in the literature about self-access. It is sometimes seen as a collection of materials and sometimes as a system for organising resources. We see it as an integration of a number of elements which combine to provide a unique learning environment. Each learner interacts with the environment in a unique way.

Gardner and Miller (1999: 9–11)

Chapter 11

Methods for assessing listening

Assessment is an integral part of instruction in that it suggests appropriate starting points for instructional design and allows for feedback on learner performance. This chapter provides an overview of issues related to the assessment of listening:

- types and specifications of listening tests
- factors that contribute to test difficulty and influence test performance
- uses of oral interviews and holistic rating scales.

11.1 Types of tests

Assessment is an important part of teaching, both as feedback to learners on their progress and as administration record-keeping. There is no question that assessment needs to be done regularly, consistently and fairly in any language course, including any listening course, because feedback is such a vital part of learning. The contentious issues concern not whether to assess learners, but rather *what* to assess and *how* to assess, and *what to do with* the results of assessment.

Most tests that teachers themselves produce and use are 'achievement tests', designed to measure simply whether students have mastered what is taught to an acceptable degree. Achievement tests are – and always should be – relatively easy to make, to administer, to score, and to use as direct feedback to the students. The reason that they should be easy to make is that the content and form should be derived directly from classroom material and tasks, or made from texts and tasks that are clearly parallel to classroom materials. If they are not, the tests will lack 'face validity' – they don't look like what the students have been studying – and 'content validity' – they don't have similar topics, they don't draw on the same knowledge base.

Achievement tests are always based on 'criteria', that is, the objectives that have been targeted for the class. To the extent that the criteria are clear and realistic, it is perfectly feasible that everyone passes every achievement test.

Testing concept: achievement testing

One way to ensure content validity in achievement testing is to have parallel forms of classroom tasks and activities. One form is used for teaching, another form is used for testing.

Placement tests, designed to place students in an appropriate programme of study, and proficiency tests, designed to determine how someone measures up against all other learners, are quite different. In order to be considered valid, these tests have to show a fair sampling of the types of behaviour that constitute the 'trait' being tested. In addition, placement and proficiency tests, in order to be fair to the test-takers, have to exhibit strong indicators of reliability, which can be established only through 'pre-testing the test' on suitable numbers of test-takers. That type of testing research is outside the scope of this chapter, though some issues of 'construct validity' will be addressed because it is so fundamental to the creation of all kinds of testing procedures.

11.2   Specifications

'What' is to be assessed – the construct – is the key issue in the testing of listening. Buck (1992), one of the leading figures in the testing of listening, has shown through factor analyses of proficiency tests that what is measured on most 'listening tests' is largely general language proficiency or general comprehension ability rather than a specific measure of listening ability. As Buck argues, quite sensibly, if we are trying to measure only general language proficiency and comprehension ability, we might as well *not* do it with listening since listening tests are much harder to construct and administer.

However, if we are trying to assess learners' listening ability, we need to focus on those aspects of proficiency and comprehension that are *unique* to listening. As has been outlined so far in this book, there are textual aspects and psychological (psycholinguistic and psychosocial) aspects that are unique to listening.

Textual aspects that are unique to listening, or certainly are more common in a listening mode, include the following:

Quote 11.1 Buck on listening

Listening comprehension is a process, a very complex process, and if we want to measure it, we must first understand how that process works. An understanding of what we are trying to measure is the starting point of test constructions. The thing we are trying to measure is called a construct, and our test will be useful and valid only if it measures the right construct.

Buck (2000: 1)

1. All **physical features** of spoken language that are *not* reflected in written language
   - **pause units** (short 2–3 second bursts of speech)
   - **hesitations**
   - **intonation**
   - **stress**
   - variable speeds
   - variable **accents**
   - **background sounds**

2. **Linguistic features** that are more common in spoken language
   - colloquial vocabulary and expressions
   - shorter, paratactically organised speech units
   - **false starts**
   - frequent use of **ellipsis**
   - frequent use of **unstated topics**
   - more **indexical expressions** (keyed to visible environmental features)
   - more two-party **negotiation of meaning** (less original clarity)

3. **Psychological features** unique to listening
   - negotiative mode: the possibility for (and sometimes the necessity of) interacting with speaker to clarify and expand meaning
   - constructive mode: the possibility of working out a meaning that fits the context, and is relevant to the listener and to the situation, incorporating visible contextual features
   - transformative mode: the possibility of interacting with, 'connecting' with, and influencing the speaker's ideas.

If we wish to test listening ability, and listening ability *only*, we need to be sure that the input to the test-takers and the activities of the test-takers include these features – as many as are feasible in the testing situation. If we do include these features, we can be *more* comfortable with the 'construct validity' of the listening test than if we do not include them,

> ### Testing concept: Listening tests vs general comprehension tests
>
> Listening as a skill shares 'traits' with other language skills, most notably the general skills of 'comprehension' and 'inference'. Listening also shares underlying factors with other language skills, including reading, that involve 'vocabulary knowledge' and 'grammar knowledge'. As a result, it is very difficult to test 'listening only'. It should be recognised that virtually any listening test will involve testing of other skills and traits, and that for most learners scores on their listening proficiency tests will correlate highly with scores on other tests.

or if we allow them to go uncontrolled. (It is theoretically not possible to be 100 per cent satisfied with the construct validity of *any* test.) And if we do not include these features or if we dilute them with other input and activity features that make listening more like reading, then we have to concede that we are testing an *integrated* set of skills that may include listening, but is not unique to listening (cf. Buck, 2000; Shohamy and Inbar, 1991).

If an assessment procedure aims to test listening as part of an integrated set of language skills (and there is certainly nothing wrong with doing that), the task is markedly easier. The issue is simply one of understanding what is – and is not – being assessed.

11.3 Forms of tests

A survey of current teaching and testing practices reveals several ways in which listening ability is assessed:

1. **Discrete item tests**
   - Multiple-choice questions following a listening text (scoring response right or wrong).
   - Open questions following presentation of a listening text (scoring questions on a scale of 'correctness' and 'completeness').
   - Standardised test scores (e.g. on TOEFL or TOEIC).
2. **Integrative tests**
   - Open summarising of a listening text (scoring on a scale of accuracy and inclusion of facts and ideas).
   - Cloze summarising of a text (scoring completions of blanks right or wrong).

- Dictation, complete or partial (scoring based on correct suppliance of missing words).

3. **Communicative tests**
   - Written communicative tasks involving listening (scoring on the basis of successful completion of a task, such as writing a complaint letter after hearing a description of a problem).
   - Oral or non-verbal tasks involving listening (scoring on the basis of successful completion of the task, such as following directions on a map).

4. **Interview tests**
   - Face-to-face performances with the teacher or another student (scoring based on a checklist of items, such as appropriate response to questions, appropriate use of clarification questions).
   - Extended oral interviews (scoring keyed to a scale of 'native-like' behaviours, such as the Foreign Service Institute scale).

5. **Self-assessment**
   - Learner rates self on given criteria, via questionnaire.
   - Learner provides holistic assessment of own abilities via oral or written journal entries.

6. **'Portfolio' assessment**
   - Learner is observed and evaluated periodically throughout course on behaviour in tasks and other class activities; observations may be audio or videotapes.
   - Portfolio may include any or all of the above types of objective and subjective measures.

Any of these methods of assessment can provide valid feedback to learners about their progress in listening. In order to serve as valid feedback or as a valid measure of learners' progress or ability, the test – its input and its tasks – has to be consistent with what is being taught as listening. Because of the well-known **washback effect** of testing – the focus of instruction tends to mirror the focus of tests – it is important for practising teachers to move towards the creation and use of valid listening tests.

Teaching principle: The washback effect

The focus of instruction tends to mirror the focus of tests: students come to expect that instruction should be similar to what they will be tested on. If teaching is not consistent with testing, or if instruction provided doesn't help them with test performance, students are dissatisfied. As a result, teachers begin 'teaching for the test', even if they believe the test itself is invalid.

11.4 Factors that influence test performance

Test format itself (multiple choice, summarisation, etc.) is no guarantee of a valid or invalid listening test. Regardless of the form of the test, the test writer must seek to control all the factors that influence listening test performance. Buck (1992) and Brindley (1998), in comprehensive surveys of institutional tests, have identified several factors that influence listening test performance:

1. **Nature of the input**: dialect, speech rate, length, background, propositional density, amount of redundancy.
2. **Nature of the assessment task**: use of visual context, amount of context given, clarity of instructions, availability of question preview, type of thinking processes involved.
3. **Individual listener factors**: memory, interest, background knowledge, motivation.

In order for assessment to become valid and useful, it is essential to define the 'construct', that is, the set of traits in the learner that we are seeking to observe, evaluate and provide feedback on.

All these factors affect the value of the test. Of the three, it is individual listener factors – memory, interest, background knowledge and motivation (to take the test) – that often receives the least attention. Concerning the factor of memory, for instance, it is important that we are testing 'ideal' memory of a text, and that we use a 'baseline' of test performance that is derived from the actual performance of real test-takers in an 'expert group'. ('Expert group' refers to people who have achieved the target proficiency.) Weir (1993; 2001) recommends that listening test items should be based only on those main points and details identified by native and non-native listening through **mind-mapping** and **note-taking**. Without these requirements, tests become divorced from the communicative contexts they are intended to reflect.

Testing principles: Improving construct validity

1. Successful performance on listening test items should be based only on 'expert performance' of the target group (e.g. adult native speakers), rather than determined by the listening text.
2. Listening test items should always aim to measure comprehension of the content first, not attention to irrelevant details.

11.5   Deconstructing tests

Because objectively scored discrete point tests are used so commonly in language education, it is important for teachers to 'deconstruct' these tests – analyse the structure and content of each item – in order to understand what is being tested and in what proportions on the test. The goal of this type of analysis is to discover what kinds of items actually distinguish good listeners from poor listeners, that is, *what kind of mental processes* good listeners are exhibiting that poorer listeners are not (cf. Vogely, 1995; Yepes, 2001).

Concept 11.1   **What is being tested?**

In an analysis of discrete point tests on the dialogue section of the TOEFL listening test, researchers found that five features were significant in discriminating among test takers.

1. The presence of infrequent oral vocabulary.
2. The sentence pattern of the utterances in the stimulus (i.e. the extract preceding the questions).
3. The presence of negatives in the stimulus.
4. The necessity of making an inference to answer the item.
5. The roles of speakers in the stimulus.

(Nissan, de Vincenzi and Tang, 1996)

In an analytic study of a listening test, Freedle and Kostin (1996) sought to analyse the structure and content of test items of one multiple-choice section of a listening test to reveal what skills are required of test takers in selecting the correct option on such items. They looked at test items and asked what elements each **response option** (the multiple choice options) had in common with the **stem** (what the students heard and/or read) and in what ways it was different from the stem. It was posited that the inferencing processes involved in determining these structural and content similarities and differences would be the underlying skills being tested by the item.

   The study focused on 100 test items taken from five Listening Comprehension sections of TOEFL. A scoring system using eight language measures was developed. A rater reliability study was performed to check if the raters agreed on the categorisation of each item.

   The eight categories that were revealed are:

Phonological and word level

1. A phonologically similar pair (stem: He looked sick . . . response option: He was thick . . .).

2. A pair of homonyms (stem: Too many people were present . . . response option: There were two people present . . .).

Word and phrase (lexical) level

3. Morphologically similar pair (stem: Her friend was . . . response option: She was friendly . . .).

4. Lexical synonymy (stem: He intended to leave . . . response option: He wanted to leave . . .).

5. Lexical inference (stem: They love bright colours . . . response option: They like red . . .).

6. Lexical repetition (stem: Those cars upset (= bothered) me. response option: That car upset (= upended) me.).

Sentence and clause level

7. Case (semantic role) of a noun or noun phrase in a sentence (stem: He cut the grass. response option: The grass was cut by him.).

Concept 11.2 **Creating tests**

Producers of standardised tests such as TOEFL have studied the following variables to find out which actually help discriminate systematically between better and poorer test takers, which is, after all, the goal of proficiency testing. When systematic factors are known, this helps test writers create test draft items that are likely to discriminate. The test items, of course, still need to be pre-tested with actual students before inclusion in a real test.

- One presentation of the passage (item stem or dialogue or lecture segment) vs. repeated presentation
- Length of the passage (shorter vs longer duration)
- Lower-level processing skills (verbatim recall) vs higher-level processing skills (inference)
- Ability to take notes while listening vs prevention of note-taking
- Length of written stem and responses (shorter vs longer)

It is surprising to note that only one of these factors (the length of written stem and responses) is a statistically significant differentiating factor in many discrete point listening tests.

(Cf. Henning, 1991; Hale and Courtney, 1991)

Suprasentential level

8. Logical inference (stem: She cut her finger . . . response option: She injured part of her hand.)

In a similar analysis of the lecture portion of the TOEFL listening test involving listening self-report of their test-taking procedures, Jamieson et al. (2000) analysed the model of 'information processing' (goal–process system) used by listeners during this portion of the test.

Stage 1: Listening to the stimulus

Goal: Listen to the stimulus (i.e. the two-minute mini-talk) and remember information in order to answer each question following the stimulus (fn1: ETS has since allowed the use of note-taking during the lecture).

Process: Represent in working memory information in the stimulus regarded as important.

Variables that may affect this process:
- stimulus variables: length of lecture, syntactic complexity, density of information, lexical difficulty
- listener variables: knowledge of the context of the task, knowledge of the language, attention, working memory capacity, background knowledge.

Stage 2: Listening to/reading each question

Goal: Understand the questions.

Process: Identify the given and requested information in the question and represent in working memory the requested information.

Variables that may affect this process:
- item variables: lexical difficulty, syntactic complexity, length
- listener variables: knowledge of the context of the task, knowledge of the language, attention, working memory capacity, background knowledge.

Stage 3: Searching for the correct answer

Goal: Retrieve information from stimulus that answers the question.

Process: Search working memory for informaiton in the stimulus that matches the information requested in the questions.

Variables that may affect this process:
- stimulus variables: length of lecture, syntactic complexity, density of information, lexical difficulty
- item variables: type of information, type of match, explicitness, main/ supporting idea redundancy
- listener variables: knowledge of the context of the task, knowledge of the language, attention, working memory capacity, background knowledge.

Stage 4: Identifying the correct answer

Goal: Select the correct answer from the options given.

Process: Identify an answer to the question by finding a match with the appropriate information from working memory and verifying that none of the other options is a better match.

Variables that may affect this process:
- stimulus variables: length of lecture, syntactic complexity, density of information, lexical difficulty
- item variables: type of information, type of match, explicitness, main/supporting idea redundancy, plausibility of distractors
- listener variables: knowledge of the context of the task, knowledge of the language, attention, working memory capacity, background knowledge.

11.6 Helping students prepare for tests

Students often experience anxiety in taking tests and as a result do not give their best performance. In order to help students do their best on standardised tests, it is useful to do four things: (1) familiarise the students with the format of the tests they will take, including all subsections of the test; (2) simulate test conditions with a full current-version test administered as the actual test will be (e.g. via computer if computer-based), with actual time constraints; (3) go over the test results with the students, pointing out strategies for maximising their performance; and (4) respond to any questions or concerns that students have about the test, scoring, and how the results are used. These steps tend to alleviate uncertainties that students have about standardised tests (see p. 179).

11.7 Oral interview tests

An essential element in assessing second language performance is evaluating a learner's ability in various settings in which goal-oriented oral communication is required (McNamara, 1998). Because these settings cannot often be readily replicated for testing purposes, evaluators often rely on some form of oral interview as a sample of the learner's oral and interaction ability. In an oral interview test (often called OPI, for Oral Proficiency Interview), the test candidate is placed in the role of the listener and is expected to respond (as quickly and completely as possible) to the interviewer's 'prompts', which are usually questions.

Helping students prepare for the computer-based TOEFL Test
(excerpted from a document created by the TOEFL programme
staff © 2000 Educational Testing Service)

Listening

What the section measures	Ability to understand conversations and talks in North American English
About the section	• section includes dialogues, short conversations, academic discussions and talks (mini-lectures) • points tested: main idea, supporting ideas, important details, inferences, order of a process, categorisation of topics/objects
Test-taking strategies for each section	Use visuals accompanying test questions effectively. Two types of visuals: (1) context-setting visuals: focus on what is said, not the visual (2) content-based visuals: may contain important content, therefore examinee should look at these visuals when listening

Skill-building ideas for the classroom	Practice listening skills
	Emphasise overall understanding, not analysis of sentences or word-by-word meaning
	• practice inferencing (drawing a conclusion from evidence or reasoning based on information presented)
	• listen to non-academic material, such as radio, TV and movies:
	  • develop own questions and have discussions about the material
	  • summarize the material orally or in writing
	  • become accustomed to colloquial English
	Familiarise students with different types of organisation (e.g. steps in a process, categorising of topics)
	• teach textual cues (order – now, next, etc.; opposing ideas – conversely, however, etc.)
	• teach oral cues (stress, intonation, pauses)
	• listen to short excerpts from academic material:
	  • listen for main ideas and important details with and without taking notes
	  • beginning-level students – write what they hear and connect those ideas to formulate sentences

- intermediate to advanced students – after listening to the material, break into groups and predict possible test questions
- advanced students – use notes to write short summaries
- very advanced – summarise the material orally
- exchange questions with other groups, and answer the questions
- make this into an enjoyable activity, such as a game-show

Although this provides an appropriate setting to test interactive speaking and listening, the notion of construct validity in these tests has been challenged. While the OPI ostensibly resembles 'natural conversation', it has been shown that such interviews lack the prototypical aspects of conversation, such as features of conversational involvement and symmetry.

Berwick and Ross (1996) have described oral interview tests more as a process of elicitation of specific output and compliance with routines than a 'normal' interactive conversation. Increasingly, interview tests are being conceptualised in terms of 'testing tasks', in which the tasks are closely associated with specific situations, goal-oriented, and involve active participation of the language user.

Berwick and Ross (1996) studied the features of accommodation and control used in oral interviews. The purpose of the study was to investigate the potential threats to validity of oral proficiency interview (OPI) testing through the use of arbitrarily constructed rating scales and the 'naïve' use of accommodation and control procedures used by the interviewer, particularly in the formation of interview questions.

The authors note that the interviewer–rater may not be aware of the constraints their own cultural background and expectations impose on the sample of speech produced by interviewees. Specifically, they point out that OPIs, as instances of cross-cultural interactions, often produce miscommunication due to misfits between politeness systems which are deployed to assert or maintain face (Brown and Levinson, 1978; Blum-Kulka, House and Kasper, 1989).

The authors employ a descriptive system for the accommodation and control features that are observed in the OPI (see Figure 11.1).

Because OPI have now been thoroughly analysed for similarities and dissimilarities with 'natural' discourse, it is widely suggested that alternate forms of oral assessment be used to supplement and triangulate the results from oral interviews (Ross, 1997b; Brindley, 1998; McNamara, 1998).

Accommodation

Feature	Definition
Display question	The interviewer asks for information which is already known to the interviewer or which the interviewer believes the interviewee ought to know.
Comprehension check	The interviewer checks on the interviewee's current understanding of the topic or of the interviewer's immediately preceding utterance.
Clarification request	The interviewer asks for a restatement of an immediately preceding utterance produced by the interviewee.
Or-question	The interviewer asks a question and immediately provides one or more options from which the interviewee may choose an answer.
Fronting	The interviewer provides one or more utterances to foreground a topic and set the stage for the interviewee's response.
Grammatical	The interviewer modifies the syntactic or simplification semantic structure of an utterance so as to facilitate comprehension.
Slowdown	The interviewer reduces the speed of an utterance.
Over-articulation	The interviewer exaggerates the pronunciation of words and phrases.
Other-expansion	The interviewer draws on the perceived meaning of the interviewee's utterance and elaborates on words or phrases within the utterance.
Lexical simplification	The interviewer chooses what is assumed to be a simpler form of a word or phrase which the interviewer believes the interviewee is unable to comprehend.

Control

Feature	Definition
Topic nomination	The interviewer proposes a new topic by foregrounding information not previously introduced in the discourse. This typically leads to a question which may be introduced by informative statements and which requires no link to previous topic development.
Topic abandonment	The interviewer unilaterally ends a current topic even though the interviewee may still show evidence of interest in further development.
Self-expansion	The interviewer extends and alters the content of the interviewer's immediately preceding utterance so as to accomplish interview objectives.
Propositional	The interviewer refocuses the interviewee's reformulation attention on a previously nominated topic or issue which has not produced enough language to confirm a rating for the interviewee.

Methods of manipulating the interview discourse structure, whether conscious or unconscious, can degrade the 'authenticity' of the interaction, and thereby jeopardise the validity of the interview test.

Figure 11.1   Features of accommodation and control in oral interviews (Berwick and Ross, 1996: 50–51)

11.8   Listening proficiency scales

A final consideration is holistic assessment, a way of reporting a listener's current stage of ability in a way that is comprehensive and comprehensible to you and the learner – and to anyone else who may utilise this assessment. Holistic assessments are typically scales, often at five levels, with 'plus' or 'minus' at each level creating fifteen discrete holistic ratings (e.g. 3–, 3, 3+). Each band on the scale consists of descriptors that depict some criterion on a target behaviour that the learner exhibits.

Proficiency scales can be very useful as part of a 'portfolio' assessment. Scales have a built-in feedback mechanism in order to suggest to the learner the kinds of skills needed to graduate to the next level.

A proficiency scale for listening has been established by the Centre for Applied Language Learning (CALL) in order to guide teaching and to serve as a basis for gauging progress. CALL serves various agencies that require second and foreign language training and was set up on a temporary basis to establish teaching and testing methods.

Figure 11.2 displays the preliminary result of their research. The proficiency level descriptions in the scale characterise 'comprehension of the spoken language'. Each of the six 'base levels' (coded 00, 10, 20, 30, 40 and 50) implies *control* of any *functions* and *accuracy standards* from the previous base levels. The 'plus level' designation (coded 0+, etc.) is assigned when proficiency substantially exceeds one base skill level and does not fully meet the criteria for the next 'base level'. The 'plus-level' descriptions are therefore supplementary to the 'base-level' descriptions.

A skill level is assigned to a person through a language examination or series of examinations or a series of long-term observations. Examiners assign a level on a variety of performance criteria exemplified in the descriptive statements. Therefore, the examples are intended to illustrate, but not to exhaustively describe, either the skills a person may possess or situations in which he or she may function effectively.

Statements describing accuracy refer to typical stages in the development of competence in the most commonly taught languages in formal training programmes. In other languages, emerging competence parallels these characterisations, but often with different details.

The term *native listener* refers to native speakers and listeners of a standard dialect. *Well-educated*, in the context of these proficiency descriptions, does not necessarily imply formal higher education. However, in cultures where formal higher education is common, the language-use abilities of persons who have had such education is considered the standard. That is, such a person meets contemporary expectations for the formal, careful style of the language, as well as a range of less formal varieties of the language.

11.9 Testing example: an achievement test

The following is an achievement test for several chapters in a listening course (Harsch and Wolfe-Quintero, 2000). It provides an overview of how the tests were developed, recommendations for adapting the tests and using the results, as well as samples of the actual items used.

Introduction to teachers

The *Impact Listening* tests are designed to be similar to standardised listening tests, such as the TOEFL and the TOEIC, which many students will need to take at some point. While the tasks in the *Impact Listening* coursebooks are designed to *teach* listening by helping students activate their knowledge and focus their attention, the *Impact Listening* tests are designed to *test* listening by checking whether students have heard particular parts of extracts precisely and have formed clear interpretations of what they have heard. While *teaching* listening does not need to focus on correct answers, *testing* listening does focus on correctness in order to provide an objective means of evaluating students and providing feedback.

There are two tests in this test pack. Test 1 is for units 1–10; Test 2 is for units 11–20. Each test has two parts. In Part 1, an extract from the Listening Task section for each unit is used as the basis of two test items. The students listen to the extract, then listen to two questions about the extract and select an answer provided on the answer key.

There are six types of questions used in Part 1. The questions are designed to check whether the students understand the following:

1. The context: who are the speakers? where are they? what are they doing? what is the relationship between the speakers?
2. The motivation of the speakers: why does one speaker say 'X'? what does the speaker want to do? why does the speaker do 'X'?
3. The key words that the speakers use: what expression does the speaker use?
4. Main ideas: where does the speaker want to go? why does the speaker do 'X'? what is happening in this conversation?
5. Paraphrases of meaning: what does the speaker mean by 'X'? what do we learn about the speaker?
6. Inferences about the meaning: what is the topic of this conversation? how does the speaker feel about 'X'? what do you think the speaker will do?

Questions vary in difficulty. 'Verbatim questions', questions that require students to remember specific words, are generally the easiest. 'Synthetic questions', questions that require students to piece together information and paraphrase ideas, are generally more difficult. 'Analytic questions',

Listening 0 (no proficiency)

No practical understanding of the spoken language. **Understanding is limited to occasional isolated words with essentially no ability to comprehend communication.** [=connected speech]

Listening 1 (elementary proficiency)

Sufficient comprehension to understand utterances about basic survival needs and minimum courtesy and travel requirements. **In areas of immediate need or on very familiar topics, can understand simple questions and answers, simple statements, and very simple face-to-face conversations** (=requests for information, and high frequency routines) in a standard dialect. These must often be delivered more clearly than normal at a rate slower than normal, with frequent repetitions or paraphrase (that is, by a native used to dealing with foreigners). Once learned, these sentences can be varied for similar level vocabulary and grammar and still be understood. **In the majority of utterances, misunderstandings arise due to overlooked or misunderstood syntax and other grammatical clues.** Comprehension vocabulary inadequate to understand anything but the most elementary needs. **Strong interference from the candidate's native language occurs.** Little precision in the information understood owing to tentative state of passive grammar and lack of vocabulary. Comprehension areas include basic needs such as: meals, lodging, transportation, time, and simple directions (including both route instructions and orders from customs officials, policemen, etc.). Understands main ideas. (Has been coded L-1)

Listening 2 (limited working proficiency)

Sufficient comprehension to **understand conversations on routine social demands and limited job requirements.** Able to understand face-to-face speech in a standard dialect, delivered at a normal rate with some repetition and rewording, by a native speaker not used to dealing with foreigners, about everyday topics, common personal and family news, well-known current events, and routine office matters through descriptions and narration about current, past and future events; can follow essential points of discussion or speech at an elementary level on topics in his/her special professional field. Only understands occasional words and phrases of statements made in unfavourable conditions; for example, through loudspeakers outdoors. Understands factual content. Native language causes less interference in listening comprehension. **Able to understand facts; i.e., the lines but not between or beyond the lines.** (Has been coded L-2 in some non-automated applications.)

Listening 3 (general professional proficiency)

Able to understand the essentials of all speech in a standard dialect including technical discussions within a special field. Has effective understanding of face-to-face speech, delivered with normal clarity and speed in a standard dialect, on general topics and areas of special interest; understands hypothesising and supported opinions. **Has broad enough vocabulary that rarely has to ask for paraphrasing or explanation. Can follow accurately the essentials of conversations** between educated native speakers, reasonably clear telephone calls, radio broadcasts, news stories similar to wire service reports, oral reports, some oral technical reports and public addresses on non-technical subjects; can understand without difficulty all forms of standard speech concerning a special professional field. Does not understand native speakers if they speak very quickly or use some slang or dialect. Can often **detect emotional overtones.** Can understand implications. (Has been coded L-3 in some nonautomated applications.)

Listening 4 (advanced professional proficiency)

Able to understand all forms and styles of speech pertinent to professional needs. Able to **understand fully** all speech with extensive and precise vocabulary, subtleties and nuances in all standard dialects on any subject relevant to professional needs within the range of his/her experience, including social conversations; all intelligible broadcasts and telephone calls; and many kinds of technical discussions and discourse. Understands language specifically tailored (including persuasion, representation, counselling, and negotiating) to different audiences. Able to understand the essentials of speech in some non-standard dialects. Has difficulty in understanding extreme dialect and slang, also in understanding speech in unfavourable conditions; for example, through bad loudspeakers outdoors. Can discern relationships among sophisticated listening materials in the context of broad experience. Can follow unpredictable turns of thought readily in, for example, informal and formal speeches covering editorial, conjectural, and literary material in any subject matter directed to the general listener.

Listening 5 (functionally native proficiency)

Comprehension equivalent to that of the well-educated native listener. Able to understand fully all forms and styles of speech intelligible to the well-educated native listener, **including a number of regional and illiterate dialects, highly colloquial speech, and conversations and discourse distorted by marked interference from other noise.** Able to understand how natives think as they create discourse. Able to understand extremely difficult and abstract speech.

Listening 0+ (memorised proficiency)	Listening 1+ (elementary proficiency, plus)	Listening 2+ (limited working proficiency, plus)	Listening 3+ (general professional proficiency, plus)	Listening 4+ (advanced professional proficiency, plus)
Sufficient comprehension to **understand a number of memorised utterances** in areas of immediate needs. **Slight increase in utterance length understood, but requires frequent long pauses between understood phrases and repeated requests on the listener's part for repetition. Understands with** reasonable accuracy only when this involves short memorised utterances or formulas. Utterances understood are relatively short in length. Misunderstandings arise due to **ignoring or inaccurately hearing sounds or word endings** (both inflectional and non-inflectional) [=little or no grammatical parsing], distorting the original meaning. **Can understand only with difficulty even when context strongly supports the utterance's meaning. Gets some main ideas.** (Has been coded L-0+.)	Sufficient comprehension to understand short conversations about all survival needs and limited social demands. Developing flexibility evident in understanding into a range of **circumstances beyond immediate survival needs.** Shows spontaneity in understanding by speed, although consistency of understanding uneven. **Limited vocabulary range necessitates repetition for understanding.** Understands more common time forms and most question forms, some word order patterns, but miscommunication still occurs with more complex patterns. **Cannot sustain understanding of coherent structures in longer utterances or in unfamiliar situations. Understanding of descriptions and the giving of precise information is limited.** Aware of basic cohesive features, e.g. pronouns, verb inflections, but many are unreliably understood, especially if less immediate in reference. **Understanding is largely limited to a series of short, discrete utterances.** Still has to ask for utterances to be repeated. Some ability to understand the facts. (Has been coded L-1+ in some non-automated applications.)	Sufficient comprehension to understand most routine social demands and most conversations on work requirements as well as some discussions on concrete topics related to particular interests and special fields of competence. **Often shows remarkable ability and ease of understanding, but under tension or pressure may break down. Candidate may display weakness or deficiency due to** inadequate vocabulary base or less than secure knowledge of grammar and syntax. Normally understands general vocabulary with some hesitant understanding of everyday vocabulary still evident. Can sometimes detect emotional overtones. Some ability to understand implications. (Has been coded L-2+ in some non-automated applications.)	Comprehends most of the content and intent of a variety of forms and styles of speech pertinent to professional needs, as well as general topics and social conversation. **Ability to comprehend many sociolinguistic and cultural references.** However, may miss some subtleties and nuances. Increased ability to comprehend unusually complex structures in lengthy utterances and to comprehend many distinctions in language tailored for different audiences. Increased ability to understand native speakers talking quickly, using non-standard dialect or slang; however, comprehension not complete. Can **discern** some relationships among sophisticated listening materials in the context of broad experience. Can **follow** some unpredictable turns of thought readily in, for example, informal and formal speeches covering editorial, conjectural, and literary material in subject matter areas directed to the general listener.	Increased ability to **understand extremely difficult and abstract speech** as well as ability to understand all forms and styles of speech pertinent to professional needs, including social conversations. Increased ability to comprehend native speakers using extreme non-standard dialects and slang, as well as to understand speech in unfavourable conditions. Strong sensitivity to sociolinguistic and cultural references. **Accuracy is close to that of the well-educated native listener but still not equivalent.**

Figure 11.2 Listening scales (CALL, 1999)

questions that require students to analyse the meaning and draw inferences, are generally the most difficult.

A mixture of questions is used in each test, and questions are meant to be challenging. The tests also require that students use short-term memory well. They must first listen to and understand a conversation extract, and then listen to questions about the conversation and select written answers. For most students, taking the test is more difficult than simply understanding the conversations because listening, reading and short-term memory are involved. Teachers should take this into account when interpreting the results of the tests.

In Part 2 of each test, students listen to extracts from the Real World Listening section and complete missing words and phrases. For each extract there are four blanks. Each blank is generally an entire phrase (noun phrase, verb phrase, or adjective phrase) rather than a single word. A mixture of phrase types is used in each test. This testing technique of using whole phonological phrases reinforces the idea that listening means hearing complete phrases and pause units rather than listening for individual words and sentences.

In each phrase, typically only one word is stressed and the other words are unstressed, as is characteristic of spoken English. For most students, just identifying the main word in each blank will be challenging enough. Before starting this part of the test, encourage students to guess all of the words, even if they have heard them only partially and are not entirely sure. This is what effective listeners do, and this style of testing will encourage students to listen in phonological phrases.

Use of the Impact Listening tests

Test 1 should be given to the class when the class has completed units 1–10. Test 2 should be given to the class when the class has completed units 11–20.

Administering the tests

1. At the beginning of class, hand out the test sheets, and if you are using the condensed answer sheet, hand these out as well. There should be one copy for each student.

   Set up your CD player and check that all students can hear easily.

2. Have all students complete the top part of the answer sheet with their name and class number.

3. Begin playing Part 1 of the test. Stop the CD after conversation 1, question 1. Be sure that all students understand the procedure. (You may wish to use questions 1 and 2 as examples.) Replay conversation 1 and

continue through question 20 without stopping. There is a five-second pause after each question. (See 'Alternate forms of the test' for variations.)

Begin playing Part 2 of the test. Stop the CD after conversation 1. Be sure that all students understand the procedure. (You may wish to use conversation 1 as an example.) Replay each conversation, so that students have an opportunity to hear each conversation in Part 2 two times. (See 'Alternate forms of the test' for variations.) Pause the tape for 10–15 seconds after the second playing to allow students to complete the blanks.

Total administration time is about 20 minutes.

4. Collect the test sheets and use the answer key for scoring. Or have students exchange papers, sign their own name at the bottom of the paper they have received, and correct the tests as a class. (See 'Scoring the tests' for a recommended procedure.)

5. Return scored tests sheets to the students and go over the test one more time for feedback.

Using the CD

The CD contains 30 track numbers to allow for easy administration of the tests. The track numbers allow you to replay individual tracks during administration of the tests or when checking the answers with the whole class.

If you do not have a CD player available, you may make a cassette copy of the CD for your own use.

Scoring the tests

The following scoring system is recommended for each test.

Part 1 of each test has 20 items. Only the answer given in the answer key should be considered correct.

Part 2 of each test has 20 blanks. For each *exactly* correct answer, one containing a verbatim version of what was said, two points should be given. For each *partially* correct answer, one containing a close version of the words in the blank, one point should be given. For each incorrect answer, one which does not demonstrate a clear understanding of the words in the blank, no points should be given.

Part 1 = 60 points (each correct answer receives three points credit)

Part 2 = 40 points (each completely correct fill-in receives two points credit)

Total = 100 points

You may 'weight' the scores differently by assigning more or fewer points to each item.

Alternate forms of the test

The most useful tests are those that 'fit' the students taking them. If all students do very well or very poorly, there is not much feedback for either the students or the teacher. When the *Impact Listening* tests are used as review tests, the most competent students should score in the 90–100 per cent range, and most students should score above 80 per cent.

Teachers may make the tests *more challenging* by doing one or more of the following.

1. For Part 1, do not use the multiple-choice answer sheet. Have the students listen to the questions and provide short written responses on a sheet of paper. This requires the students to formulate their own response, rather than select a response from the choices given.

Responses should be evaluated as correct if they provide an acceptable answer, not necessarily the exact answer provided on the multiple-choice form.

2. For Part 2, do not use the partially completed answer sheet. Have the students listen to the conversation and transcribe the entire conversation. Or provide an altered answer sheet, with additional parts whited out. For these variations, it is necessary to replay the conversation several times.

3. Play each conversation in Part 1 one time only and play each conversation in Part 2 two times only.

Teachers may make the tests *less challenging* by doing one or more of the following:

1. For Part 1, provide the oral questions in writing. Allow the students to read the questions before they listen to each conversation. This variation will allow students to listen selectively to the conversation in order to answer the questions. It will also allow them a better understanding of the questions before they make their choice of answers.

2. For Part 2, divide the blank lines into the exact number of words that fit into each missing part. Or parts of words, such as the beginning or the ending of a word, can be provided. These variations will provide prompts for the students in writing out their answers and will improve their performance.

3. Play each conversation in Part 1 two times and play each conversation in Part 3 three times.

Using the test scores

It is important to use test scores fairly. Because the test scores on the *Impact Listening* tests cannot be 'normed' over a large student population (as is done with tests such as the 'TOEFL'), it is not appropriate to use the test scores as a measure of overall proficiency.

The *Impact Listening* tests are designed to be review tests or 'achievement tests' that reward students for performing well in class and learning the skills and strategies being taught. Students who have completed all of the classroom tasks successfully and have become familiar with the self-study extracts should do well on the tests.

Students who perform well on the tests (who, for example, achieve a score of 80 per cent or higher) *and* do well on other assessment measures for the class should be evaluated with a successful grade for the class.

Helping students prepare for the tests

Reviewing material is an important part of learning, and listening skills in particular, can be consolidated by periodic review of audio extracts. As such, an important purpose of testing is helping students review.

Students can prepare for the tests by reviewing the units (1–10 or 11–20) that will be on the test. It is best to give the students' ample time, preferably a week, to prepare for a forthcoming review test.

In order to prepare at home, have students review the *Vocabulary Task* section of each unit by quizzing themselves on the blanks in each unit. Have them listen to the *Real World Listening* extracts on their self-study CD, once without referring to the script, and then a second time while looking at their completed self-study pages.

In order to prepare in class, you can review the Listening Task sections of all units, replaying the segments and asking the students to review their answers in their textbooks. Similarly, you can review the Real World Listening sections, focusing on the *Getting the Main Ideas* section.

Evaluating students' progress

Evaluating students' progress is an essential part of instruction. It helps you understand what your students have learned, as well as identify areas in which they need more work. Assessment also helps motivate most students to do their best in a class. Both formal and informal assessment should be done throughout the course. The two tests provided in this test pack can aid you in formally assessing your students' mastery of the listening material. Scores on these tests will provide you with an objective means of checking students' progress and ability in the course. Using this test pack along with other types of on-going informal assessment will help keep you informed of your students' needs.

There are a number of ways you can informally evaluate your students' progress. In order to provide more complete feedback to your students and to obtain more valid evaluations, it is recommended that you use more than one type of informal assessment. Using the following, on-going types of assessment along with the test pack will give you a fuller picture of your students' abilities and needs.

- **Classroom tasks** Participation and active learning are an important part of progress in oral communication (speaking and listening) classes. Give credit for all classroom tasks completed. If students complete the tasks in their books, they can get credit for doing that. If students interact with each other during task follow-ups and during the Interaction Links, they can get credit for that interaction. This is a kind of 'participation grade' that allows all students to receive credit for active learning during class.

- **Homework** Assign homework with the self-study CD and self-study pages in the back of the book. Students can do the tasks at home, in preparation for the next class. You can give the students credit for completing the homework, and then allow them to compare and correct their answers with their classmates in a small group. You can give credit for completion of the task, or for the number of correct answers.

- **Expansion activities** Students can also do expansion activities as written tasks at home. It is not necessary to correct students' writing, which can be very time-consuming and impossible with large classes. However, you can give students credit for doing the writing, and the writing will help them be more prepared for speaking activities that will follow in the class.

- **Dictation** Practice dictation tests can be done periodically using the *Impact Listening* extracts, to check students' progress and to give them practice in intensive listening. This will help you identify your students' listening problems and give you a means of evaluating them.

- **Classroom observations** As students engage in speaking activities, circulate and make observations. Take notes as you listen. After students have finished speaking, share your observations with the whole class. Use your observations to help you decide which areas of instruction to devote more time to.

Impact listening 3: Test 1

Name: _____   **Class:** _____

Part 1

Directions: **Listen to each conversation. Then listen to the questions. Answer the questions. Circle a, b, c, or d.**

Conversation 1

1. a. visited relatives
   b. went to graduate school
   c. worked for a high-tech company
   d. dreamed of an international lifestyle

2. a. Yes, completely.
   b. No. He wanted to go home.
   c. No. He had to work too hard.
   d. Yes, but sometimes he got homesick.

Conversation 2

3. a. He goes out dancing every night.
   b. He zips through his homework.
   c. He studies late every night.
   d. He has trouble sleeping.

4. a. She's worried about his health.
   b. She doesn't want him to go dancing.
   c. She's impressed by his ability in school.
   d. She wants him to take her dancing.

Conversation 3

5. a. He listens to what she says.
   b. He feels guilty.
   c. He is annoyed by what she does.
   d. He's curious about what she does.

6. a. She cleans his room.
   b. She uses his phone.
   c. She takes up too much space.
   d. She listens to his conversations.

Conversation 4

7. a. He cares a lot about fashion.
   b. He worries about money.
   c. He follows his friend's advice.
   d. He likes to wear cheap clothes.

8. a. He really likes designer clothes.
   b. He wishes he could afford $500 pants.
   c. He thinks his friend spends too much money on clothes.
   d. He wants to be more fashionable.

Conversation 5

9. a. He has to learn standard English.

   b. He can't speak English fluently.

   c. He has to study Chinese.

   d. He doesn't think the teacher will be good.

10. a. Because Mr Chen is a native speaker of English.

    b. Because Mr Chen can show them how to learn English.

    c. Because she's always right.

    d. Because Mr Chen is Chinese, too.

Conversation 6

11. a. He's single, and has never been married.

    b. He is currently married.

    c. He was married before.

    d. He doesn't say.

12. a. someone who likes quiet evenings together

    b. someone who likes dancing

    c. someone who likes bodybuilding

    d. someone he can trust

Conversation 7

13. a. She's having health problems.

    b. She works too much in the yard.

    c. She's retired.

    d. She feels her home is like a zoo.

14. a. The more people there are, the happier he is.

    b. He's glad Gloria is there to help.

    c. He doesn't care.

    d. It's OK, as long as they do the yard work.

Conversation 8

15. a. She likes the restaurants in Costa Rica better.

    b. She thinks American backpacks are safer.

    c. She thinks Costa Rica is more secure than the US.

    d. She thinks it's easier to have a lot of money in the US.

16. a. She likes the variety of restaurants.

    b. She doesn't worry about things being stolen.

    c. She worries about walking around with $20.

    d. She thinks that everything is too expensive.

Conversation 9

17. a. It does your driving for you.

    b. It fastens your seatbelt for you.

    c. It keeps you awake while you drive.

    d. It reads the newspaper to you.

18. a. study

    b. read

    c. do work

    d. drive

Conversation 10

19. a. He thinks it's a small amount of money, so he doesn't care.
    b. He thinks his friend has been gambling way too much.
    c. He wants his friend to play another game and win the money back.
    d. He's worried about something bad happening to his friend.

20. a. He wants to pay someone he owes money to.
    b. He wants to play cards again and win back what he lost.
    c. He's worried that he might get hurt if he doesn't have extra money.
    d. If he has enough money, he can stop gambling.

Part 2

Directions: **Listen to each conversation. Fill in the missing words.**

Conversation 1

TJ: You know I'm just a regular guy.

Cesar: No you're not.

TJ: Yes, I am. I've got parents and a bratty sister, just like you. I took piano lessons when I was little, and I go to church on Sundays. I like watching cartoons, and my mom (1)_____ the trash. And I worry about (2) _____. See? I'm just (3)_____.

Cesar: I don't think so. Nobody else I know is doing a Nike commercial. You've (4)_____, TJ.

TJ: Yeah, but the problem is my parents.

Conversation 2

Richard: You got the job? The management job? Oh, that's great!

Irma: No, I didn't say I got the management job. He (5)_____ in customer service, (6)_____.

Richard: Just customer service? But what about the management position? You were (7)_____. You can supervise people. You (8)_____.

Irma: I know. I showed him my resumé.

Conversation 3

Marty: And I wish Mom and Dad wouldn't try to solve everybody's problems.

Eddie: I don't think that will change. You know (9)_____ take care of everybody. She doesn't want to say no (10)_____ her.

Marty: But nobody ever asks me what I want!

Eddie: (11)_____ say what goes on in their house.
(12)_____ it is.

Marty: Yeah, you're right.

Conversation 4

Steve: I'm so (13)_____. I don't have time to sit down and eat.
(14)_____ too inflexible and they have too many rules.

Trish: Yeah, right, Steve, so you're going to (15)_____ to your way of doing things?

Steve: Yeah! There has to be more individual freedom (16)_____
_____ want.

Trish: Why don't you just relax and go with the flow?

Conversation 5

Doctor: You're pregnant.

Julie: No way!

Doctor: You're (17)_____ baby.

Julie: Are (18)_____? Ah, I need a cigarette.

Doctor: That's the (19)_____ need. You need to stop (20) _____.

Julie: But I can't stop smoking.

Doctor: For your baby's health, Julie, I'm afraid you have to.

(Photocopyable – *Impact Listening*, 3, ©Pearson Education 2001)

Impact Listening 3 tests: audio scripts

Test 1

Part 1

Directions: **Listen to each conversation. Then listen to the questions. Answer the questions by circling a, b, c, or d.**

Conversation 1 [Unit 1, Listening Task 1; CD 1, track 03]

A: Jim, I can't believe it – wow! I haven't seen you since we graduated high school! What have you been doing?

B: Well, after I went to college I went overseas for graduate school, and I had a great time. But finally I had to come home and get a real job in a high tech company.

A: Yeah, I remember you always wanted an international lifestyle.

B: Oh, I had a great time overseas, but I got homesick, too.

Question 1: What did Jim do overseas?
Question 2: Did Jim enjoy his time overseas?

Conversation 2 [Unit 2, Listening Task 1; CD 1, track 12]
A: Sam – how come you're so tired in class all the time? Another late night studying?
B: Are you kidding, Jennifer? I hardly study at all.
A: How can that be? You're the star student, the math ace.
B: No, I go out clubbing every night – I dance 'til the bars close, that's why I can't keep my eyes open.
A: Aren't you getting behind in work?
B: Nah, I just zip through my homework before dinner.
   Question 3: Why is Sam so tired?
   Question 4: What does Jennifer say about Sam?

Conversation 3 [Unit 3, Listening Task 3; CD 1, track 23]
A: Ahhhh! My mom is so annoying. She doesn't give me any space.
B: What do you mean?
A: I mean, I feel like she's spying on me all the time. Whenever I try to call someone on the phone, she hangs around listening to what I say.
B: She's probably just curious.
A: It's more than just curious. Even if I take the phone into my own bedroom, she'll suddenly come in, without knocking, and pretend to be looking for something, just to check up on me. I wish I could move out!
B: What a bummer.
   Question 5: How does the first speaker react to his mother?
   Question 6: What does his mother do?

Conversation 4 [Unit 4, Listening Task 2; CD 1, track 31]
A: Five hundred dollars for a pair of pants? You're crazy to spend that much on clothes.
B: Come on, man. These are the best. You just don't understand.
A: I understand that I can get a nice-looking pair of pants for around fifty bucks. You're paying $450 for the designer's name.
B: Maybe, but at least I never look like I'm wearing cheap clothes, unlike some people I know. Besides, these pants will never go out of style.
A: Okay, fine, suit yourself. It's your money.
   Question 7: Which best describes the speaker who is buying the pants?
   Question 8: Which best describes his friend?

Conversation 5 [Unit 5, Listening Task 4; CD 1, track 42]
A: I can't believe it! Our English teacher is Chinese.
B: Yeah, well, so are you! What's wrong with that?
A: But he's not a native speaker. I want a teacher who is American or British, so that I can learn standard English.
B: But, uh, Mr Chen can speak English fluently, and he knows things that native speakers don't know.
A: Yeah? Like what?

B: Like how to learn English. I'll bet he can show us how he did it, and that will make it easier for us, too.

A: Hmm. Maybe you're right.

Question 9: What is the first speaker unhappy about?

Question10: Why does the second speaker think Mr Chen can help her?

Conversation 6 [Unit 6, Listening Task 1; CD 1, track 48)

Hi! I'm Michael. I'm a 32 year-old white male, I'm divorced, and I want to try again with the right lady. I like bodybuilding, rock music, dancing, and I like to party. I'm looking for an attractive woman who likes the same things I do. And she's gotta be someone I can trust.

Question 11: What is Michael's marital status?

Question 12: What kind of woman does Michael want to avoid?

Conversation 7 [Unit 7, Listening Task 1; CD 1, track 57]

Hi, I'm Fred. About four years ago, Jeanne and I retired. We were looking forward to taking care of our yard. But just when we got the yard looking really nice, Jeanne's legs started causing her trouble. At first, I tried to take care of her and the yard all by myself, but it was just too much. So we asked our daughter Gloria to come back home to live with us, together with her family. Now it's like a zoo around here, but it's nice having Gloria here to help with Jeanne.

Question 13: What's wrong with Jeanne?

Question 14: How does Fred feel about Gloria's family moving in?

Conversation 8 [Unit 8, Listening Task 1; CD 1, track 66]

One of the things I really like about living in Costa Rica is that it's so safe. I mean, I can go walk around the streets with 50,000 pesetas in my wallet and I don't even worry about it. In American cities, I used to worry about walking around with twenty dollars in my wallet. And another thing is that sometimes I go into a restaurant and I can leave my backpack sitting at a table and I go up to order and I come back knowing that my backpack is going to be safe and no one's even touched it.

Question 15: What difference between Costa Rica and America does the speaker talk about?

Question 16: How does the speaker feel about living in Costa Rica?

Conversation 9 [Unit 9, Listening Task 1; CD 1, track 75]

How would you like to study for a test or read the newspaper while you drive? Well, now you can, thanks to Auto-Auto, the world's first automatic car. Just type in the address, fasten your seatbelt, and Auto-Auto does all the work for you. it will wake you up when you're almost there. Auto-Auto – be the first in your neighbourhood to have one.

Question 17: What does Auto-Auto do for you?

Question 18: Which of these things *doesn't* Auto-Auto let you do in the car?

Conversation 10 [Unit 10, Listening Task 2; CD 1, track 85]

A: Hey, Jason, do you think . . . could I borrow $100?

B: Are you crazy? What do you need that much money for?.

A: I lost two hundred in a card game last week, and all I had was a hundred. The guy I lost to told me I had to come up with the money. And tonight's the night. I don't know what he'll do to me if I don't have the money.

B: Okay, I guess I can loan you the money. I'd hate to see anything bad happen. Let's go to the cash machine.

A: Thanks, bud. You know, if you loan me an extra fifty or so, I can get in a game, and then I'll win it back.

B: Not a chance. You're lucky I'm loaning you the hundred. And I'll tell you something – this is the last time I'm gonna do it. You've been gambling way too much. You'd better kick the habit.

Question 19: Why does Jason agree to loan his friend $100?

Question 20: Why does the first speaker want to borrow *extra* money from Jason?

Part 2

Directions: Listen to each conversation. Fill in the missing words.

Conversation 1 [Unit 2, Real World Listening; CD 1, track 17]

TJ: I like watching cartoons, and my mom makes me take out the trash. And I worry about not having a girlfriend. See? I'm just like everybody else.

Cesar: I don't think so. Nobody else I know is doing a Nike commercial. You've got it made, TJ.

TJ: Yeah, but the problem is my parents.

Conversation 2 [Unit 5, Real World Listening; CD 1, track 44]

Irma: He hired me for a job in customer service, selling tours to Asia.

Richard: Just customer service? But what about the management position? You were perfect for that job. You can supervise people. You understand the business.

Irma: I know. I showed him my resumé.

Conversation 3 [Unit 7, Real World Listening; CD 1, track 62]

Eddie: I don't think that will change. You know your Mom wants to take care of everybody. She doesn't want to say no if anybody needs her.

Marty: But nobody ever asks me what I want!

Eddie: Kids never get to say what goes on in their house. That's the way it is.

Marty: Yeah, you're right.

Conversation 4 [Unit 8, Real World Listening; CD 1, track 71]

Steve: I'm so tired of this place. I don't have time to sit down and eat. People here are too inflexible and they have too many rules.

Trish: Yeah, right, Steve, so you're gonna convert everybody here to your way of doing things?

Steve: Yeah, . . .

Conversation 5 [Unit 10, Real World Listening; CD1, track 89]

Doctor: You're going to have a baby.

Julie: Are you kidding me? Ah, I need a cigarette.

Doctor: That's the last thing you need. You need to stop smoking, and immediately.

Julie: But I can't stop smoking.

Section

3 Researching listening

Chapter 12

Approaches to researching listening

Researching, with the emphasis on the '-ing' ending, is one of the most rewarding aspects of professional experience in teaching and applied linguistics. Far from the once stereotyped purpose of aiming to 'prove' something, teaching or applied linguistics research is simply the pursuit of knowledge in a defined, sustained and systematic way.

This section offers practical approaches to researching listening and suggests a number of specific research projects that can be carried out.

This chapter will . . .

- outline various purposes for researching listening;
- demonstrate ways of posing questions that are researchable.

12.1 Purposes for research

The first two sections of this book have explored the notion of listening, first in terms of defining what listening is, then in terms of 'best practices' for teaching listening. In this section, we expand the context by exploring areas of listening research. Though the type of research outlined in this section is relevant to the fields of psycholinguistics sociolinguistics and applied linguistics, the goal of the research outlined in this section is toward exploring issues and challenges that arise in educational and social contexts.

Ideally, teaching and researching share the common goal of finding principles and innovations that will support and enhance learning *for the researcher*. As Andre and Frost (1997) note, teachers and researchers in most fields share a unifying goal: 'We all search for the truth, we all push for intellectual innovation, we all share our truths and innovations with particular audiences, and we all wish to create environments that enhance learning.' This learning may, in turn, enhance the learning of those the researcher comes in contact with (particularly their students), but the primary goal is to deepen understanding in the researcher.

There are two vital links between teaching and research that this section develops. The first is that principles learned through research are understood more deeply and are likely to be applied with greater responsibility and commitment. We most often undertake research in an attempt to reconcile competing explanations of some phenomenon or to elaborate descriptions of that phenomenon. Mahoney (1997: 101), for instance, contends that once we have completed a cycle of research into a phenomenon, we have a greater commitment to incorporating that understanding into our work: 'As I assist students in the applications of principles learned through research, I also inevitably learn more . . . as we jointly push beyond commonly accepted answers and understanding.'

The second link is an equally practical one. In many professions, most researchers also teach and teachers are expected either to conduct research or to evaluate and apply research findings, in order to improve their teaching effectiveness.

One bridge between these two concerns, as Booth et al. (1995) point out, is 'action research'. In this kind of research the paradigm is that a problem or issue motivates research, not for its own sake but in order to help solve a practical problem and to promote educational change (cf. Kemmis and McTaggart, 1988 Allwright and Bailey, 1991). The researcher pursues issues whose solutions will have practical applications to teaching and learning problems, and potentially to educational change and progress.

The classic 'action research paradigm' is often perceived as a circle or spiral starting with a practical problem 'motivating' a research question, 'defining' a research problem, 'finding' a research answer, 'helping to solve' a practical problem. This paradigm has recently evolved into a looser 'practice-based research paradigm' which emphasises the direct involvement of the practitioner in identifying questions for investigation and means of carrying out the investigations with means available (cf. Burns, 1996).

12.2 Posing questions

Often the most challenging task any researcher or teacher-researcher faces is asking questions that *can be* answered through a direct form of enquiry. As Charles (1989) notes, the process of enquiry requires, above all, *improving the questions* we wish to ask before rushing to address them. In much educational and social research, improving questions entails:

1. posing a simpler *series of sub-questions* that might contribute to understanding a main question;
2. making the meaning of the questions as clear and focused as possible to ensure that each sub-question can be answered through enquiry and evidence;
3. arranging the sub-questions in a logical sequence;
4. making sure the answers to the sub-questions all contribute to addressing the main question.

Concept 12.1   **Ordering questions**

Charles (1989) has recommended a system of refining and ordering questions. Here is an example of a 'main question' from a language-education context:

→ How can teachers best hold the attention of students during oral communication activities?

Though interesting, this question, as posed, is not immediately answerable. Using Charles's suggestion, the enquiry would benefit from a series of sub-questions, such as:

- What do students actually do when they are 'paying attention'?
- What types of things naturally (i.e. not in classroom activities) hold these students' attention?
- Can teachers incorporate any of these 'natural' attention-holders into their lessons?

Each sub-question, in sequence, leads to manageable goals for research and helps address the larger issue.

Practical enquiries of this nature are of interest to both teachers and researchers. Paradoxically, it is often difficult for these two groups to communicate effectively. As Freeman and Johnson (1998) point out, teachers and researchers often differ in their beliefs about the 'knowledge base' for education.

While researchers in applied linguistics may view themselves as 'knowledge-generators' for teachers, the teachers may not view themselves in turn as 'knowledge-appliers', waiting to apply the latest knowledge in the field. Rather, they may see themselves as 'managers of learning', responsible for the practical issues of organising learners and delivering a multifaceted service to them.

The main types of knowledge that teachers will then be interested in are those that most directly assist them with *managing learning*, not those that may promise to *advance their understanding* of the teaching or learning process. This need to bridge the professional priorities and concerns of researchers and teachers leads to the notion that 'practical problems' in teaching concern not just application of or experimentation with new knowledge, but applications and experiments in the area of 'learning management'.

Most practice-based research begins not with our finding a topic is of theoretical interest to our profession, but rather with confronting a practical problem that has found *us*. Often, practice-based research then is undertaken out of necessity, to address a problem that must be resolved for practical and personal reasons. At other times, practice-based research is undertaken to deepen our understanding of an area of practice or to join colleagues in a mutual exploration of a common concern.

In the previous two sections of this work, various problems were identified in defining listening and in teaching listening. In the chapter that follows some of these problems are raised again, this time with an orientation toward how they might be investigated in a practice-based research paradigm.

Concept 12.2 **Personal considerations in formulating a research plan**

As a teacher or researcher embarks on a research plan, it is useful to ask a series of questions to help determine if the project is realistic:

- Is this topic researchable, given the time and resources I have, and the availability of data? If not, what aspects of the topic are researchable, given these constraints?

- Do I have a personal interest in the topic so that it will sustain me during the project? Is there a colleague who could join the study to make it more interesting?

- Will the results of the study be of interest to me? To others ? (Who?) Am I willing to share the results of my study?

- Does the study fill a void? Are there similar studies I should be aware of? Will this study replicate or extend or develop new ideas in the literature? Will the project contribute to my professional goals?

- Do I have a forum for sharing results? Am I familiar with the available means and standards for 'publishing' my results?

(Based on Cresswell, 1994)

Chapter 13

Listening research projects

This chapter sets basic frameworks for a range of action research projects types related to listening. It will outline . . .

projects with a sociolinguistic focus

- listening in daily life
- listening and social roles
- pragmatic analysis
- cross-cultural pragmatics
- developing pragmatic competence

projects with a psycholinguistic focus

- aural perception
- comprehension and memory

projects with a training focus

- listening in interaction
- benchmarking effective listening
- causes of misunderstanding
- listening to lectures
- strategy training

projects with a curriculum focus

- materials design and evaluation
- listening journals
- designing a self-access listening centre.

Each of the 15 project types in this chapter begins with a series of 'initial questions' that may be posed, then refined, in exploring the issue. An example study is given to provide an illustration of how the issue might be approached. This example, rather than suggesting a plan for a specific research project, is intended to show the kind of problems that may arise in investigating particular questions and to point out some tools that may be useful in conducting the project. The projects are presented here in no particular priority: each project is considered to be a worthwhile means of deepening an understanding of listening and providing insight into how listening can be taught more effectively.

Research projects, to be rewarding and worth sharing with colleagues, require commitment to planning, recording of actions and observations and a procedure for writing up or displaying the results. By formally carrying out the steps in a project, the foundation for documenting and sharing results will be readily established.

13.1   Listening in daily life

Initial questions

- How do people listen in their 'daily lives'?
- What different kinds of listening situations are they involved in?
- Do people 'listen differently' in their L2?

Psycholinguistic theories of language processing and sociolinguistic theories of language use often fall short in explaining what actually happens in 'daily life' situations involving spoken language comprehension. A study by Ruth Wodak (1996) examined 'important' everyday situations in which 'much depends on precise and relevant information being properly and accurately conveyed': people interpreting government guidelines, procedures in medical clinics and implications of radio news. We would assume that in situations like these people would attempt to use their maximum capacities for processing and remembering information. Wodak notes, however, that in each of the situations she observed, there were numerous examples of comprehension confusion and barriers to communication – and a less than ideal use of language. She calls these 'disorders of discourse', resulting from 'gaps between distinct and insufficiently coincident cognitive worlds' (1996: 2).

Studies of everyday language comprehension are a useful type of listening research in that they reveal the 'human nature' of understanding and misunderstanding. Frankly, much of the time we just don't seem to understand very well what is going on around us! What we understand from daily communication is constrained by our working memory, mismatches of schemata and our subjective world views. Our expectations about how much and how well we understand language, even in our L1, must be tempered by these constraints.

Research considerations: intermediate stages of understanding

Brown (1995) outlined the intermediate stages between understanding of what the newscaster has said and what a listener would have to do to produce a summary:

1. Interpret the language (and non-verbal images, if any) in the news item and construct a representation of these items in memory.
2. Construct an interpretation of the instructions (what does it mean to 'write a summary?').
3. Understand how to relate what is required by the task (giving a summary) to the language input – specifically, to decide how much information to include and how to present that information.
4. Produce the summary.

If a summary is considered inadequate, the reason may be that the listener had a problem at *any* one of these four stages, separately or in combination.

Project plan

1. Choose a 'real life' text, such as a radio or television or internet broadcast that your listener/learner often listens to.
2. If possible, also identify at least one 'official setting' that your learner is in on a regular basis. This could be a work situation or a public situation (e.g. shopping).
3. Ask your 'subject' to make audio recordings of these events.
4. Ask your subject to write a short report of the meaning or import of each event.
5. Go over both the recordings and the subject's reports by yourself. Form some questions that you can ask your subject about his or her report, to clarify and to expand their interpretations.
6. Meet with your subject. Go over the recordings and the report. Ask your questions.
7. What are your impressions of how your subject 'listens in everyday life'? Do you share any of Wodak's impressions? Does your subject share her impressions?

Wodak has studied a number of everyday language comprehension situations, including: therapist-client, judge-defendant, school committee member-member, doctor-patient, and news broadcaster-audience interactions. Her study of news broadcast comprehension (Wodak, 1996) reveals how subjective understanding is. In the following extract from the study, we see an original news broadcast, followed by three listeners' summaries of the extract.

Original broadcast text:

There has been a new development in the affair concerning the German company Flick. The government in Bond has a issued a decree to the concern according to which Flick is to pay back a tax rebate of about 3.2 billion Austrian shillings which is connected with the so-called party donations affair and the charge levelled against the Minister for Economic Affairs, Otto Graf Lambsdorff. A tax exemption status had been granted to the concern for investing in the American conglomerate Grace. Government spokesman Bonish declared that the prerequisite for such a dispensation, which had been assumed when the exemption was issued, had never existed. Shortly after the announcement, Flick instituted legal proceedings at the competent Administrative Court in Cologne. Minister for Economic Affairs Lambsdorff is accused of having accepted party donations form Flick and, in return, of having supported its tax exempt status in the cabinet.

Subject 1 recall interview (Interview 35:6)

A: Could you retell as exactly as possible, what -eh- what was just said? What was it all about?
B: Well, that Graf Lambsdorff, that he was bribed by Flick. And – eh – took money. And the like. And – eh – now that is – eh – eh – Flick wants to – refuses to –. That it made – eh – these donations. But they have gone into the matter.
A: Mhm – any details? Can you remember any?
B: Wel, I didn't really look out for details. Let's say just he said most important things.

Subject 2 recall interview (Interview 37:4)

A: Mhm – could you retell the report as precisely as possible? What was it all about?
B: Yes – it reports – that Flick – tried – eh – to save taxes by – eh – bribing – eh – politicians by financing a party. Eh – it was about 3.2 billion shillings. Which – eh – which were to be saved by Flick investing in the American company Grace. Ah – Graf Lambsdorff was accused. That he supported Flick in the government. – And –
A: Any other details?
B: Mhm – yes – that proceedings were institututed at the Admininstrative Court.

Subject 3 recall interview (Interview 31:5)

A: Could you retell the report as exactly as possible? What was it all about?
B: Yes – we've read and heard this and that. All about them up there – the big fish – then you remember.
A: Well – what was it all about?
B: Ah – parties and money – donations by –
A: And who did what?
B: Well, Flick – somehow, like – probably embezzled its donation money or something like that.
A: Mhm – mhm.
B: I don't listen so exact . . . You can't do anything about it anyway.

Wodak notes that the predisposition of each listener is defined in the light of their individual schema-oriented prior knowledge, their knowledge of their formal structure of the text, and their emotional attitude toward the news and its significance to their own lifestyle.

Figure 13.1   **Recalling news broadcasts (Wodak, 1996: 116–17)**

In a sense, 'expert comprehension', a term used by Kintsch (1998) to describe what an average, competent native speaker understands in a language-use situation, is often *much less* than an objective analysis of the information in the text would reveal. However, our understanding as a listener in a real context is also often *much more* than an objective analysis of the information in the text would reveal. Our interpretation is 'more' because we add conceptual knowledge to the text in understanding it and create a sense of relevance for the information.

13.2   Listening and social roles

Initial questions

- Do men and women approach listening differently?
- Do they approach different kinds of listening (e.g. listening for information, listening for entertainment) differently?
- If so, how does this affect involvement? How does it affect the kind of 'conversational work' that each does?

It is often claimed that men and women have different approaches to communication. Linguist Deborah Tannen has remarked:

> When men, upon hearing of the kind of work I do (sociolinguistic research), challenge me about my research methods, they are inviting me to give them information and show them my expertise – something I don't like to do outside the classroom and lecture hall, but something they themselves would likely be pleased to be provoked to do (Tannen 1990: 145).

Reports of gender differences appear in both sociolinguistic analyses (see, for example, Wodak, 1997; Kothoff and Wodak, 1998) and in anecdotes in the popular press.

One conjecture is that women listen to men more often than men listen to women because men consider listening at length to a woman to frame them as 'subordinate'. Fishman (1983) has characterised the 'work that women do' in conversation with men as clearly assymetrical: in many social conversations women end up doing more of the supporting moves (asking for clarification and expansion of ideas), backchannelling (showing or feigning interest, indicating comprehension) and responding (evaluating, linking to other topics) moves that keep the conversation going.

Concept 13.1 **Popular views of differences between women and men**

Study eyes brain use when listening

CHICAGO (AP) – Score one for exasperated women: New research suggests men really do listen with just half their brains.

In a study of 20 men and 20 women, brain scans showed that men when listening mostly used the left sides of their brains, the region long associated with understanding language. Women in the study, however, used both sides.

Other studies have suggested that women 'can handle listening to two conversations at once', said Dr Joseph T. Lurito, an assistant radiology professor at Indiana University School of Medicine. 'One of the reasons may be that they have more brain devoted to it.'

Lurito's findings, presented Tuesday at the Radiological Society of North America's annual meeting, don't necessarily mean women are better listeners.

It could be that 'it's harder for them', Lurito suggested, since they apparently need to use more of their brains than men to do the same task.

'I don't want a battle of the sexes', he said. 'I just want people to realise that men and women' may process language differently.

In the study, functional magnetic resonance imaging – or MRI – was used to measure brain activity by producing multidimensional images of blood flow to various parts of the brain.

Inside an MRI scanner, study participants wore headphones and listened to taped excerpts from John Grisham's novel *The Partner* while researchers watched blood-flow images of their brains, displayed on a nearby video screen.

Listening resulted in increased blood flow in the left temporal lobes of the men's brains. In women, both temporal lobes showed activity.

The findings tend to support previous suggestions that women's brains are 'either more bilaterally dominant' or more right-side dominant in doing certain tasks than men's, said Dr Edgar Kenton of the American Stroke Association, a neurologist at Thomas Jefferson University in Philadelphia.

Though preliminary, the study could help doctors treating stroke victims better understand how men's and women's brains differ, Kenton said.

It suggests that in a stroke affecting the brain's left side, women might recover language ability more quickly than men, though that remains to be proven, Kenton said.

(On the Net: International Society for
Magnetic Resonance in Medicine)

> **Project plan**
>
> 1. Identify a situation in which the 'roles' of individuals seem to determine how they participate in conversations: how they get the floor to speak, how they 'support' the speaker, etc. This could be a factor of gender, age, or status.
>
> 2. Tape record samples of conversations involving participants in these different roles. Listen to the recording to see if you can identify actual exchanges in which different behaviour by the participants takes place. Transcribe these sections.
>
> 3. Form a hypothesis that predicts the differential behaviours you have identified (e.g. Participant As will tend to respond with humour when asked a question about X). Show your hypothesis to a participant in these encounters (but not during an actual conversation they are participating in). What is their view of your hypothesis?

13.3 Pragmatic analysis

One of the first steps in exploring verbal communication is actually making the commitment to observe, record and analyse segments of actual conversation (and communicative writing).

Although nothing particular needs to be happening in a conversation to make it worth recording, it is often more interesting to use systematically occurring conversations, whether in social encounters (e.g. break-time in the student lounge) or in public encounters (e.g. passengers asking for information from a bus driver).

Recording natural conversations requires reasonably sensitive equipment with good quality built-in microphones. If you later identify any of the participants, you need their permission. And, of course, if you utilise the recorded material for any commercial purpose, you must obtain the explicit permission of all participants.

Transcribing recorded conversations is a very valuable analytic exercise in its own right because the act of transcribing slows down the communication process. This allows us to see the subtle coordinated signals at a 'microlevel' that make communication work on a 'macrolevel', both from the speaker and listener perspective.

The initial step in a transcription is to 'bracket' an event, say an encounter at an information booth in an airport. In this kind of event, it is easy to see the starting point (the person approaches the information booth) and the ending point (the person leaves the booth); it is also easy

Illustration

A pragmatic analysis of a conversation attempts to describe the key pragmatic variables: deixis (what is being referred to outside the conversation); intention (what the speaker's and listener's intentions are); implicit meaning (what shared background knowledge must be accessed in order to achieve understanding); strategic use (what strategies the speaker and listener employ to achieve meaning), and conversational meaning (what structures are developed in the interaction that promote or detract from the achievement of meaning).

In the following extract, an interviewee, an Indian male aged forty (*A*), approaches a teacher (*B*) at a language institute in England to request a language-proficiency certificate that he needs for a job. His request for 'an introduction' is apparently intended to allow the teacher at the centre to recognise his problem and respond to his request. The teacher's understanding of his request for 'an introduction' is apparently different.

A: you would me like to put on
    [*overlapping*]

B: oh no   no

A: there will be some of the things you would like to
                         [*overlapping*]

B: yes

A: write it down

B: that's right, that's right

A: but uh . . . anyway it's up to you

B: um . . . well . . . I . . . I Miss C.

A: first of all

B: hasn't said anything to me you see
     (pause)

A: I am very sorry if   she   hasn't spoken anything

B: (softly)   doesn't matter

A: on the telephone at least

B: doesn't matter

A: but uh . . . it was very important . . . uh thing for me

B: ye::s tell, tell me what it is you want
                                     um

A: Um, may I first of all request for the introduction please

B: Oh yes sorry

A: I am sorry
     (*pause*)

B: I am E.

A: Oh yes   (breathy)   I see . . . oh yes . . . very nice
B: and I am a teacher here at the Centre
A: very nice
                    [*overlapping*]
B: and we run
A: pleased to meet you (*laughs*)
                        [*overlapping*]
B: different courses
    (*A laughs*)
            yes, and you are Mr?
A: N.A.
B: N.A. yes, yes, I see (laughs) Okay, that's the introduction (*laughs*)
A: *would it be enough introduction?*

(Gumperz, 1983, p. 175)

We can see that the interaction is problematic in several pragmatic dimensions. A pragmatic analysis would seek to identify where in the interaction each of the pragmatic variables was not mutually understood.

Tool box   Discourse analysis codings

The linguistic descriptions of conversational data involve **codings** of a number of **paralinguistic** and **non-linguistic features** that influence what the language means to the participants. Here are the main codings for audio only:

[	overlapping utterances
=	a continuous utterance that has been interrupted
-	short, untimed pause within an utterance
((pause))	long, untimed pause within an utterance
((x seconds))	timed pause (pauses are timed only when they reveal a certain point)
((laugh))	non-verbal element or action
//. . .//	intonation unit boundary
p	'proclaiming' (falling) tone
r	'referring' (rising) tone
CAPs	tonic syllable
Bc	backchannel cue
{xxx}	attempted (but abandoned) utterance

Sample coding

Doctor: //p where do you FEEL this pain//

Patient: //p (4 sec.) around my HEAD//

Doctor: [r HEAD]

Patient: //p RIGHT//

For video transcriptions to be complete, additional codings are required, particularly for 'gaze direction' and any specific gestures of the head, shoulders, arms, or hands.

to describe the situation functionally (a person is seeking information about X). Most communicative situations are less easy to bracket, and some events can be bracketed in different ways. Once this is done, the transcriber simply transcribes *everything* that is perceptible on the tape, using a standard system of conventions

Once transcriptions are completed and organised according to events, they serve as valuable sources of information for teachers and researchers.

Project plan

1. Choose a recurring situation of interest, in which verbal communication takes place, for example, the opening 'small talk' section of your language classes. Obtain permission to conduct audio recordings. Code your recordings in writing so that you can find them and cue them up easily.

2. Listen to your recordings in juxtaposition. Make mental notes of areas of interest in the tapes.

3. Choose one recurring theme in the tapes and attempt to 'bracket' it in each extract in your recordings.

4. Transcribe this section of each recording. Plan to spend about 20 minutes of transcribing time for each one minute of audio tape.

5. Study your transcriptions. What do they reveal about language or conversation at a 'microlevel' that you had not previously been aware of?

13.4   Cross-cultural pragmatics

Studies of L2 users in conversational settings have helped us understand the dynamics of interactive listening and the ways in which L2 speakers participate in conversations – or alternatively may be denied full participation. Some of these issues have been researched at the discourse-analysis level, looking at how control and distribution of power is routinely carried out through the implicit rules of the interaction.

Research in cross-cultural pragmatics from the contrastive-linguistic tradition has been vital to our understanding of the dynamics of L2 listening in conversation. It has been shown that, in general, cultures differ stereotypically in their use of key conversation features: when to talk, how much to say, pacing and pausing in and between speaking turns, **'listenership cues'**, intonational emphasis, use of **formulaic expressions**, styles of cohesion, and indirectness (Tannen, 1984). The Cross-Cultural Speech Act Realisation Project (CCSARP) has documented examples of cultural differences in **directness–indirectness** in several languages for a number of speech acts, notably apologies, requests and promises. Knowledge of the cultural norms of the speaker is critical to listening success.

Most analyses of intercultural communication are based on a model of mismatch ('crosstalk') which derives from the cultural anthropological tradition (Gumperz, 1990). According to this mismatch view, conversations between speakers of different cultural backgrounds often become problematic because of contrasting discourse styles and a mismatched interpretation of **participant and activity frames**. If misunderstandings multiply due to mismatches of discourse styles, the speakers become entangled in a dangerous spiral of miscommunication that tends to reinforce the negative stereotype that people from the 'other' culture are uncooperative or rude or 'strange' (Auer, 1992). And, of course, an unpleasant byproduct of this cycle is that miscommunication then serves to 'reify' cultural differences (Sarangi, 1994).

An alternate point of view is that *inter*cultural interaction follows the same inter**subjective rules** as *intra*cultural interaction, with speakers and listeners seeking to find balanced, reciprocal participation. Discourse with participants from differing cultural backgrounds, particularly if one is a native speaker (NS) and one is a non-native speaker (NNS), is often mediated by the NS distorting – either amplifying or reducing – the responses from the NNS (Shea, 1995). This is often realised by the NS *not* incorporating the NNS's perspective into the conversation, due either to limited recognition of the information provided by the NNS or to a desire to avoid joint orientation to the conversation at hand. In conversations of this kind, the NNS is reduced to a 'passive listener' who simply affirms the talk of a 'superior', more 'knowledgeable' native speaker, with little opportunity to voice his or her own ideas and opinions.

Being reduced to a passive listener is one of the key problems that the NNS faces in interaction. The dissatisfaction that the NNS experiences in a passive listening role is often triggered initially by language understanding problems. However, understanding difficulties in conversation arise not only at the levels of phonological processing, grammatical parsing and word recognition. As has been discussed in Sections 1 and 2, these problems may also arise from informational packaging and from conceptual difficulty of the content. Other understanding problems that have been identified include understanding problems triggered by elliptical utterances (in which an item is omitted because it is assumed to be understood) and difficulty in assessing the point (or speaker's intent) of an utterance (Hinds, 1985). These problems can be cumulative in any interaction, leading to misunderstandings and breakdowns in communication, particularly if the NS partner does not recognise ways to repair problems cooperatively as they arise.

Bremer et al. (1996) have documented many of the social procedures that L2 listeners must come to use as they become more successful listeners and participants in conversations, including identification of topic shifts, providing backchannelling or listenership cues, participating in conversational routines (providing obligatory responses), shifting to topic-initiator role, and initiating queries and repair of communication problems. A clear conclusion of much research on L2 listening in conversation is that the listener needs to do a great deal of 'interactional work', including using clarification strategies, in addition to linguistic processing, in order to become a successful participant in TL conversation.

Project plan

1. Choose a language function (e.g. apologising, thanking) that is readily identifiable in two cultures (e.g. Japanese and Japanese–American) that you know or participate in.

2. Prepare an 'elicited response' type of questionnaire: 'What do you say when . . . ?' and/or a 'role-play' type of questionnaire: 'You're at the supermarket. The person behind you says, 'Hey. This is the express checkout. You have too many items. You have to go to the next checkout stand.' You say: . . .

3. Conduct your questionnaire with members of the two groups you are studying. With this methodology (non-experimental), it is OK to revise your questionnaire from subject to subject provided that you keep the questionnaire on the same topic (e.g. apologising).

4. Without 'rushing to find differences' (a common pitfall in cross-cultural research), describe your data in terms of the discourse moves and combinations of moves that your subjects use.

13.5 Developing pragmatic competence

Robbins (1996) showed that in cross-cultural dyads (American and Japanese students) addressing issues of 'uncertainty' and 'face' were vital in explain-

---

Initial questions

- How does a learner's motivation and attitude influence participation and learning in interaction?
- What role does 'risk-taking' have in learner improvement of communication ability?

---

ing the successful vs unsuccessful interactions and relationships between students from the different cultural backgrounds.

The study starts with an application of 'Uncertainty Theory' (Gudykunst, 1995) to cross-cultural communication. The general theory asserts that 'when strangers meet, their primary concern is one of **uncertainty reduction** or increasing predictability about the behaviour of both themselves and others in the interaction' (Robbins, 1996: 61). Uncertainty reduction can be carried out through asking questions or through self-disclosure, that is, revealing one's thoughts and feelings. The extent to which the social environment may prevent one or both of the participants from participating in questioning and self-disclosure will in part determine the nature and success of reciprocal listening in the interaction or relationship.

A second aspect of cross-cultural encounters concerns the notion of 'face' in management of self-expression and understanding. In many encounters, one party is decidedly superior to the other in terms of power or authority. The 'inferior' person, in addition to whatever communicative goal he or she might have, has the burden of not threatening the 'superior' person. In order to 'save face' (or to risk 'losing face'), very often the inferior party will say nothing, or as little as possible, and will avoid any excess 'trouble' for the superior person, such as asking for confirmation or clarification. The paradox for a learner of a language, of course, is that the learner must risk losing face constantly by seeking clarification, one of the key means to language improvement.

In order to explore these two sociolinguistic issues in a controlled context, Robbins (1996) conducted a longitudinal study of ten Japanese learners of English who were studying in the United States. The students participated in ongoing dyads as conversation partners with NS American university students. Robbins videotaped the conversation-partner sessions and later went over the taped sessions individually with each Japanese student. Robbins paused the tapes at prolonged silences or other 'marked expressions' at which it appeared the learner was struggling to understand something that had been said or was struggling to express an idea. Through various questioning probes, Robbins attempted to find out what the student 'needed' in the way of linguistic or pragmatic resources in order to continue the conversation.

Quote 13.1 Robbins on 'strategy shifts' and 'attitude shifts' in learners

The retrospective verbal reports (of the students) contained many NNS comments on the intercultural dimensions of this experience. They realised they were talking to a 'stranger' and were more nervous in Round 1 (the first part of the study) about speaking with a foreigner, but by the time of their conversations eight months later in Round 2, they said they felt more comfortable in speaking English only and interacting with foreigners. Attempting to translate precisely from Japanese caused problems in the beginning, but NNS found that after having more practice in speaking English they could say what they wanted to say, focusing more on the message than on the form of their contributions. A momentous improvement was seen in that some of the NNS developed the attitude that they did not need to be so worried about things they did not understand and could feel free to ask for clarification.... It goes without saying that intercultural partners who are enjoying their conversations will contribute more to mutual intercultural understanding than those who are nervous and self-conscious.

Robbins (1996: 216)

Project plan

1. Consider the types of encounters with NSs that your students have. Formulate a description of these encounters: Where do they take place? How long do they last? What are the outcomes? If possible, collect recordings or transcribe observations.

2. Interview the students, in their L1 if necessary, about their view of these situations. What kinds of apprehensions do they have? What kinds of social strategies do they use in encounters with NSs?

3. Set up a small-scale study based on Robbins' design. L2 learners are paired with NS conversational partners for at least two or three mandatory sessions.

4. Plan to monitor the NNSs' increase or decrease in comfort level in meeting with their conversation partner. Use interviews with the students periodically to find out their perceptions. If possible, video- or audiotape a session to play back with the student. Elicit comments from the student as they view or listen to the tape.

5. Interview students at the end of the sessions. Ask them to prepare a short report or presentation about their contacts with their conversation partner.

6. Make the student reports or interviews available to other teachers and students, making sure to include actual quotes from learners about their experience. Add your own annotations relating to the goals of the project.

Employing a framework for clarification strategies similar to those used in Bremer *et al.* (1996) and Rost and Ross (1991), Robbins also noted that the successful students – those who had built up continuing relationships with their voluntary conversation partners – had also made most progress in pragmatic competence. This was noted in increased use of 'questioning for information' (asking for unknown information, not yet expressed in the conversation) and 'self-disclosure' (offering not yet known information about oneself). (Robbins notes that the 'retrospective monitoring' of conversations – the use of ongoing clarification questions – often correlates negatively with proficiency.) In the words of one student, after developing a reciprocal relationship of self-disclosure with a NS, 'I felt I was finally out of the trap of just talking about things like 'how long have I been studying English', and so on . . . and so I wasn't as guarded as I used to be about speaking English, and I could try to express what I really wanted to say . . .'

13.6 speech-processing

> **Initial questions**
>
> - What speech elements does a learner actually attend to and perceive in connected speech?
> - Can these elements be put into a pattern that is implicational and developmental?
> - What do 'errors' in perception reveal about the nature of the listening process?

Ross (1997) presents a study of a listening-response test to a group of 20 L2 learners. In this study, the learners heard a short description of a picture, and then were to choose the correct picture from several possibilities. At the same time, they were asked to repeat the description into a lapel microphone. For example, one subject heard, 'This is a picture of two buses, parked side by side', and then repeated, 'picture two bus park side'. Based on an analysis of correct and incorrect choices, plus a transcription analysis through **implicational scaling**, Ross was able to outline what parts of the input the subjects were apparently *not hearing*, and estimate the kinds of inferences they were making, based on the incomplete information they had (i.e. based on the apparent gaps in information), to guess the correct picture.

Kim (1995) conducted a similar study of aural perception. After ruling out both dictation and elicited imitation (EI) (cf. Chaudron, 1998) as a suitable means of checking perception and comprehension, Kim used a picture-selection task, asking subjects (Korean learners of English) to say why they selected a certain picture after hearing a descriptive input.

Studies of this type focus on 'bottom–up processing', what the learner is actually *taking in* from the spoken input. Although it is well-known that L2 learners, like L1 users, can use 'top–down processing' (i.e. their expectations) to fill in for gaps in perception, it is important to find out what aspects of bottom–up processing can be developed through instruction, rather than only teaching learners how to compensate for problems in this area.

Having utilised two different forms of input (slow and normal), Kim was able to formulate an implicational scale (the relative frequency of complete vs incomplete responses from subjects in the study) for connected speech:

Phase 1 Pre-key word phase: The listener cannot identify key words that bear phonetic prominence in speech (e.g. reporting 'milk' or 'meal' for 'mail').

Phase 2 Key words: the listener identifies phonetically prominent words and forms associative relationships between them to understand (e.g. hearing 'mail', 'machine', and 'stamps').

Phase 3 Phrases: The listener encodes not only key words but also less prominent surrounding elements that form a small grammatical unit (e.g. hearing 'mail', 'put through a machine' and 'cancelling stamps').

Phase 4 Clauses: The listener encodes grammatical relationships between lexical words, identifying semantic relationships between arguments and predicates in a clause (e.g. hearing 'the mail is collected', 'taken to the post office', 'it is put through a machine').

Phase 5 Clause plus: The listener encodes not only almost all clauses in the input but also the relationships among them (e.g. hearing 'the mail goes through several steps before it is delivered').

Project plan

This project plan outlines an experiment intended to find out how learners use perception and parsing as they listen.

1. Identify or compose a text that has a clear theme and a set of facts. The text should be accessible to the students, but should have parts that are beyond the students' ability to comprehend fully. The text should be between one and three minutes long – long enough that the students cannot try to memorise it, but short enough to allow them to remember the main idea and some key facts without note-taking.

2. Prepare two versions of the text. One version is the full version. This will be used for the idea-reconstruction phase of the task. The other version has words gapped out. This version will be used to evaluate what specific perception and word-recognition problems your students are experiencing. Gap out words of a particular class. For example, you may gap out all of the function words in one paragraph and the content words in another paragraph.

3. For the first phase of the task, ask the students to listen without taking notes. You may read the passage aloud once or twice. Following this, ask the students to attempt to reconstruct the main ideas of the text in writing. If the students work in groups they will collectively remember more and 'push' each other to verbalise what they have understood. (This is the basic tenet of the 'dictogloss method' developed by Swain, 1985.)

4. For the second phase of the task, use the gapped version of the text, or simply have the students take dictation of selected portions of the text. Collect this version for compilation purposes. You can then distribute the full version of the text to the students as a follow-up.

5. Compile the students responses, using a baseline version of the text, and adding a mark for each full word that was recognised by the students. You can write the 'mishearings' below the baseline version. For example, if you have five students, you may have a compilation as follows:

```
X                 X
X  X              X          X                        X
X  X     X   X            X    X    X   X          X  X  X        X
X  X     X   X            X    X    X   X      X   X  X  X        X
```
It was smooth and fragrant and produced a consistent lather, but it wasn't Ivory.

―――――――――――――――――――――――――――――――

   Is smoo in flavour in produce that sister rather bottom was furry

6. From this implicational analysis, generalise about the kinds of word-recognition errors that your students are making most often. In what ways does your analysis fit with Kim's (1995) scheme outlined above? In what ways doesn't it fit?

Example: The 'Ivory Soap' story

Full version

The Origin of Ivory Soap

Harley Procter and his cousin, chemist James Gamble, came up with a special new soap in 1879. It was smooth and fragrant and produced a consistent lather, but it wasn't Ivory – it was called White Soap – and it didn't float.

One day in 1879, the man operating Procter & Gamble's soap-mixing machine forgot to turn it off when he went to lunch. On returning, he discovered that so much air had been whipped into the soap that it actually floated.

For some reason, the batch wasn't discarded – it was made into bars and shipped out with the other White Soap. Soon, to their surprise, P&G were getting letters demanding more of 'that soap that floats'. So they started putting extra air in every bar.

Now that they had a unique product, they needed a unique name. And they found it in the Bible. Procter was reading the 45th Psalm, which says: 'All thy garments smell of myrrh, and aloes and cassia, out of the ivory palaces . . .' when it hit him that ivory was just the word he was looking for.

In October 1879, the first bar of Ivory Soap was sold.

Dictation style 1: **verbatim reading, selected parts of the text gapped**

Origins of Ivory Soap

(1)   Harley Procter _____ cousin, chemist James Gamble, _____ a special new soap in 1879. _____ smooth and fragrant and produced a consistent lather, _____ Ivory – _____ White Soap – and _____ float.

(2)   One day in 1879, the man _____ Procter & Gamble's soap-mixing machine _____ to turn it off when he _____ to lunch. On _____ , he _____ that so much air _____ into the soap that it actually _____ .

(3)   For some _____ , the _____ wasn't discarded – it was made into _____ and shipped out with the other White Soap. Soon, to their _____ , P&G were getting _____ demanding more of 'that soap that floats'. So they started putting extra _____ in every _____ .

(4)   _____ , they needed a unique name. _____ in the Bible. Procter was reading the 45th Psalm – which says: 'All thy garments smell of myrrh, and aloes and cassia, _____ ivory palaces . . .' – _____ that ivory was just the word _____ .

In October 1879, _____ .

13.7   Comprehension and memory

Initial questions

- What do we remember after we listen to something?
- How does our memory change over time?
- How does our cultural background or personal background influence what we comprehend and what we remember?
- Do different 'comprehension probes' elicit different kinds of memory?

Example: Text recall

'*The War of the Ghosts*' was one of the texts used by Mandler and Johnson (1977) in their story experiments. Subjects were asked to read a passage involving an unknown cultural ritual and then were tested on their recall at various intervals. This experiment provided support for the notion that cultural background influences the ways we remember what we hear or read. We typically distort concepts and reconstruct events in order to make them fit with our own knowledge and expectations.

The War of the Ghosts

One night two young men from Egulac went down to the river to hunt seals, and while they were there it became foggy and calm. Then they heard war cries, and they thought: 'Maybe this is a war party.' They escaped to the shore and hid behind a log. Now canoes came up, and they heard the noise of paddles, and saw one canoe coming up to them. There were five men in the canoe, and they said:

'What do you think? We wish to take you along. We are going up the river to make war on the people.'

One of the young men said, 'I have no arrows.'

'Arrows are in the canoe,' they said.

'I will not go along. I might be killed. My relatives do not know where I have gone. But, you,' he said, turning to the other, 'may go with them.'

So one of the young men went, but the other returned home.

And the warrior went on up the river to a town on the other side of Kalama. The people came down to the water, and they began to fight, and many were killed. But presently the young man heard one of the warriors say, 'Quick, let us go home: the Indian has been hit.' Now he thought: 'Oh, they are ghosts.'

Because most listeners did not have an overall 'story structure' for this story, it was difficult to recall the sequence and significance of events. In addition, most subjects experienced problems interpreting key concepts: hunting seals, making war, having no arrows, returning home, being hit, ghosts.

Mandler and Johnson (1977) conducted a well-known experiment in which they presented subjects with stories and asked them to reconstruct the story at various intervals after they had read it. Some of these stories were very 'foreign' to the subjects: they involved characters and events and outcomes that were quite different from the stereotyped 'story schemas' that the subjects were familiar with. What they discovered is very consistent with schema theory: subjects tended to recall the story in terms of their own schema. When they retold the story, they left out key details that were unusual to them, they added other details to give the story more sense to them, and they distorted details to fit with their own way of looking at the world.

Project plan

1. Gather some stories or descriptions from other cultures, preferably with clear English translations. For example:

   A Babemba healing

   In the Babemba tribe of South Africa, when a person acts irresponsibly or unjustly, he is placed in the centre of the village, alone and unfettered. All work ceases, and every man, woman and child in the village gathers in a large circle around the accused individual.

   Then each person in the tribe, regardless of age, begins to talk out loud to the accused, one at a time, about all the good things the person in the centre of the circle has done in his lifetime. Every incident, every experience that can be recalled with any detail and accuracy is recounted. All his positive attributes, good deeds, strengths and kindnesses are recited carefully and at length. No one is permitted to fabricate, exaggerate or be facetious about his accomplishments or the positive aspects of his personality. The tribal ceremony often lasts several days and does not cease until everyone is drained of every positive comment he can muster about the person in question. At the end, the tribal circle is broken, a joyous celebration takes place, and the person symbolically and literally is welcomed back into the tribe.

2. Present the story – verbatim – to a group, either through listening or reading (different modalities can be used for a quasi-experimental study of effects of presentation mode on comprehension). You may want to repeat the story two or three times. (Avoid paraphrasing the story as this adds the speaker's own distortions!) The listeners should not take notes.

3. Ask each person to reconstruct the story, either in writing or orally. Record the recountings of the story.

4. Compare the original version of the story with the retellings. What is different? How do your findings relate to schema theory?

These processes are now known to be very typical of how comprehension and memory works. We use schemata – based on our past experience – to recreate narratives (and other genres) – in ways that are consistent with our ideas and beliefs.

Although there is little theoretical value in 'reproving' schema theory, there is often great value in utilising our understanding of the theory to experiment with comprehension and recall of 'unusual stories'. In looking at the reconstruction of a story, we would be interested in:

- what information is included vs what information is left out
- what information is added
- what information is distorted
- how the 'main idea' of the story is interpreted.

13.8 Listening in interaction

Initial questions

- What aspects of listening are interactive?
- How is interactive listening different from non-interactive listening?
- What is the role of listeners in interaction?
- How can I help learners to deal with interaction in better ways?

Cross-cultural communication involves all of the 'normal' issues of communication, but often has its own special flavour because of the wider differences concerning issues of 'face', politeness, power, communicative style and expected discourse structures. Any type of communication situation involving a non-native speaker and a native speaker or another non-native speaker are *de facto* instances of cross-cultural communication.

Studies of L2 listening in conversational settings have helped us understand the dynamics of interactive listening and the ways in which L2 speakers participate (or alternatively may be denied full participation) in conversations. Some of these issues have been researched at the discourse analysis level, looking at how control and distribution of power is routinely carried out through the structure (implicit rules) of the interaction.

Research in cross-cultural pragmatics has been relevant to our understanding of the dynamics of L2 listening in conversation. It has been shown that, in general, cultures differ in their use of key conversation features: when to talk, how much to say, pacing and pausing in and between speaking turns, 'listenership cues', intonational emphasis, use of formulaic expressions, styles of cohesion and indirectness (Tannen, 1984). The Cross-Cultural Speech Act Realisation Project (CCSARP) (Blum-Kulka et al., 1989) has documented examples of cultural differences in directness–indirectness in several languages for a number of speech acts, notably apologies, requests and promises. Clearly, knowledge of the cultural norms of the speaker influences listening success.

Other issues have been explored through conversational analysis of the problems L2 listeners experience. Understanding difficulties in conversation arise not only at the levels of phonological processing, grammatical parsing and word recognition. They may also arise from informational packaging and from conceptual difficulty of the content. Other understanding problems that have been identified include understanding problems triggered by elliptical utterances (in which an item is omitted because it is assumed to be understood) and difficulty in assessing the point (or speaker's intent) of an utterance. These problems can be cumulative in any interaction, leading to misunderstandings and breakdowns in communication.

Bremer et al. (1996) have documented many of the social procedures that L2 listeners must come to use as they become more successful listeners and participants in conversations, including identification of topic shifts, providing backchannelling or listenership cues, participating in conversational routines (providing obligatory responses), shifting to topic-initiator role and initiating queries and repair of communication problems. (See Table 9.2, p. 132.)

A clear conclusion of much research on L2 listening in conversation is that the listener needs to do a great deal of 'interactional work', including using clarification strategies, in addition to linguistic processing, in order to become a successful participant in TL conversation.

Project plan

1. Prepare a series of interactive tasks, such as information gaps (e.g. picture differences) or opinion gaps (e.g. students ask each other their views on certain given topics and record their answers as 'same' or 'different'). Group learners so that they have experience with different dyad partners (e.g. native non-native speaker, lower/higher proficiency-level learner, and with different tasks (descriptive instructive, narrative personal directions).

2. **Audio-record** the learners doing the various tasks. **Transcribe** the conversation. Code the 'problematic' exchanges in the interactions according to 'communicative outcome' (how the problem was dealt with). Based on the kind of communication task the learners are given, modify the coding scheme for 'effectiveness of outcomes' of Yule and Powers (1994):

Communicative outcome: an assessment category system

The system below applies to a directions-giving task in which the listener (receiver) has a partial map and must draw a path described by the speaker (sender) who has the fully completed map:

(a) **No problem** a problem exists but is not identified by either the sender or the receiver.

(b) **Non-negotiated solutions**
  - *Unacknowledged problem*: a problem is identified by the receiver but not acknowledged by the sender.
  - *Abandon responsibility*: a problem is identified by the receiver and acknowledged by the sender, but the sender does not take responsibility for solving the problem, either by saying they will skip it, leave it, or forget it, or by telling the receiver to (interpret however he/she wants).
  - Arbitrary solution: a problem is identified by the receiver and acknowledged by the sender who then makes an arbitrary decision about some defining features of the location or path. The key element here is not accuracy, but the arbitrariness of the decision which does not attempt to take the receiver's world into account or to make the receiver's world match the sender's.

(c) **Negotiated solutions**
  - *Receiver's world solution*: a problem is identified and acknowledged by the sender who then tries to find out what is in the receiver's world and uses that information to instruct the receiver, based on the receiver's perspective.

13.9 Benchmarking effective listening

Initial questions

- What is 'high-quality' communication?
- How does this standard of quality differ by setting and roles of the participants?
- What role does listening (listening attitudes, listening behaviour) play in assessing this quality?
- Can 'benchmarks' be identified for listening in a specific setting?
- If so, can these benchmarks be taught?
- How does benchmarking differ in different kinds of social and professional encounters?

The quality of communication in most situations is influenced by conscious monitoring and selection of strategies by the participants. In a variety of situations, including air traffic control booths, doctor–patient encounters, counsellor–student and parent–child relationships, the quality of communication affects both the transactional outcomes and the affective and relational outcomes of the interaction. The notion of **benchmarking** was developed in communication theory as a way of identifying patterns within an interaction that contribute toward qualitative outcomes.

Benchmarking effective listening can be conducted in any specific context, such as doctor–patient or salesperson–client interactions. A study of benchmarking can examine questions including: On what factors do speakers base their assessment of the listener's effectiveness? Which factors are most important? When does the speaker assess the listener? Does the speaker's prior experience with the listener impact on the speaker's assessment of the listener's effectiveness?

Sample study

A classic study by Rhodes (1987) illustrates how bench-marking can be applied to various communicative dyads. In this study, subjects (students at a US university) took part in four dyadic discussions that were set up to be similar to typical classroom discussion in undergraduate classes. Participants had a different partner for each discussion and each discussion was on a different 'policy' topic (US foreign interventions, farming subsidies, drunk driving and alcohol abuse). Each dyad had two observers, who at the end of each discussion rated each participant's effectiveness as a listener using a **semantic differential scale**.

This scale consisted of the following pairs of contrasts, to be rated on a seven-point scale:

[1] – [2] – [3] – [4] – [5] – [6] – [7]
Responsive – unresponsive
Open-minded – close-minded
Patient – impatient
Interested – uninterested
Attentive – inattentive
Relaxed– tense
Trusting – suspicious
Warm – cool
Accepting – rejecting
Sincere – insincere
Direct – indirect

Friendly – unfriendly
Permissive – domineering
Involved – detached
Personal – impersonal
Considerate – inconsiderate
Sensitive – insensitive
Receptive – unreceptive
Calm – nervous
Sympathetic – unsympathetic
Thoughtful – thoughtless
Tolerant – intolerant
Encouraging – discouraging
Mature – immature.

In addition to the ratings from the observers, each participant also rated his or her partner on the same scale at the end of each discussion. In this way, each participant received 12 listening-effectiveness ratings.

Based on the rating averages, subjects in the top quartile were placed in an 'effective listener' group; subjects in the low quartile were placed in the 'ineffective listener' group. In the second stage of the study, each dyad took part in a similar 15-minute discussion.

Subjects were instructed to attempt to exchange enough information with each of their partners to determine each other's position on given topics (e.g. child-rearing practices in America). At the end of each discussion, participants completed questionnaires outlining their own position on the topic and their understanding of their partner's position.

Three hypotheses were tested in this experiment:

1. Effective listeners would exhibit more conversational behaviours judged to be 'effective'.

2. There would be more instances of 'negentropic' tendencies (i.e. seeking feedback and demonstrating progress toward the agreed goal) in dyads among 'effective listeners'.

3. Goal achievement (i.e., accurate statements about the partner's position on the topic) would be higher among 'effective listeners'.

All three hypotheses were supported in the analysis of the results, supporting the notion that effective listeners consciously exhibit attitudes and actions that engender 'effective' communication. (Of course, it can be argued that the two phases of the experiment were designed specifically to support these hypotheses.) The direct application of this study, and others based on this model, is in demonstrating discourse patterns that contribute to effective listening. Because these patterns are largely under the conscious control of the participants, effective patterns can be practised and used in dyadic interaction.

Project plan

1. Read over the procedures for the Rhodes (1987) study. Look at the semantic differentials and select those positive traits that seem most descriptive of 'effective' listeners in topic-oriented discussions. Add additional differentials.

2. Attempt to replicate the study, with students in your own classes. Tell your students that you will be doing a communication study with them and you will share the results at the end of the study (i.e. after two or three rounds of discussions). Choose appropriate topics, or have the students select topics that will sustain 5–10 minute discussions. (For reliability of your study, all student groups should use the same selected topics.)

3. Go over the ratings that your students received as listeners/participants. Do you receive symmetrical results, as in the Rhodes study? If not, what do you think the reasons are? If so, what do you think the reasons are?

4. At the *end* of the study, share the results with the class. What are their views of the value of the study?

13.10   Causes of misunderstanding

Initial questions

It has been said that 'Misunderstandings are always co-constructed.'

- In what sense is this statement true?
- In what sense is it not true?
- What are the causes of misunderstanding in your learner(s)?
- What misunderstandings do you experience in your L2?
- Are there ways to treat misunderstandings?
- Are there ways to prevent them?

Misunderstandings (and partial understandings) are much more common in discourse than most of us realise. We typically don't notice a misunderstanding unless there is an adverse effect on us, and only then might we attempt to repair it and try again for better understanding.

When we are in the position of an L2 listener, we often do notice more misunderstandings because of their adverse effects: we may not get what we want, if only in the way of response from our interlocutors. In L2 situations, understanding difficulties in conversation arise not only because of the L2 listener's incomplete command of the language code, but also from a number of other sources.

Examining these understanding problems has been a productive application of linguistic, psycholinguistic and pragmatic approaches. Studies by Hinds (1985), Esch (1992), Rost (1990), Bremer et al. (1996), and D. Long (1990) have contributed to the growing portrait of understanding problems in L2 discourse.

L2 listening problems are typically associated with multiple rather than single causes. The following causes have been noted:

Lexical

- ambiguity
- substitution of an item
- inaccessible lexical items
- mishearing of a lexical item
- false cognates

Grammatical

- ellipsis
- difficult construction

Conceptual

- mismatch of schema
- inadequate elaboration
- false assumption of shared knowledge
- indirectness (difficulty in assessing the point of an utterance)
- information packaging
- unfamiliar content
- unfamiliar routine.

Conceptual difficulties arise when contextual sources such as the immediate situation or world knowledge are limited, and the listener must come to depend solely upon linguistic information. In such cases, most often represented by abstract topics being introduced that are out of the 'here and now' context, the L2 listener is at a double disadvantage. First, he or she cannot draw upon contextual information or readily available background knowledge to understand the discourse. Second, the language of abstract topics tends to feature a high proportion of low-frequency vocabulary and subordinate syntactic structures. This double disadvantage makes it difficult to assess exactly what has contributed to an understanding problem, beyond the obvious 'conceptual difficulty' of the topic.

A practical contribution of research on misunderstanding is its demonstration that all misunderstandings are co-constructed, rather than the responsibility of the minority speaker. However, the reality is that the 'minority speaker' is often saddled both with the blame for misunderstandings and the responsibility for sorting them out. While both the speaker and the listener need to be prepared to do 'interactional work' in order to achieve understanding, NNSs usually take on the responsibility for using **clarification** and **confirmation strategies** in order to achieve understanding with their NS counterparts.

Other issues have been explored through conversational analysis of the uptake problems L2 listeners experience. Understanding difficulties in conversation arise not only at the levels of phonological processing, parsing and word recognition – that is, from the L2 listener's incomplete command of the language code. In addition, they arise from 'informational packaging' within the conversation and also from 'conceptual difficulty' of the content (Esch, 1994). Other understanding problems that have been identified by Hinds (1985) and others are: understanding problems triggered by mishearing a single lexical element (word or phrase), understanding problems triggered by complex utterances, elliptical utterances (in which an item is omitted because it is assumed to be understood), unfamiliar content in utterance, and difficulty in assessing the point (or speaker's intent) of an utterance. These problems can be cumulative in any interaction, leading to misunderstandings and breakdowns in communication.

Project plan

Collect a body of misunderstandings involving yourself as a non-native speaker of a language, or of a volunteer or group of volunteer NNS. Alternatively, you can observe the misunderstandings that take place around you.

Record each misunderstanding on a card set up like this:

date

event

participants

verbal element (transcribe as accurately and completely as possible)

physical elements present

other notes:

Try to record the data as soon as possible after it happens in order to reflect the facts as closely as possible.

Possible follow-ups: Once a body of typical understanding problems is collected and analysed, it raises the question of whether a specific 'mini-course' of teaching ways of identifying and dealing with these problems might be helpful to learners. A proposal by Bremer et al. (1996: 237) suggests that a programme of instruction might include:

1. a focus on the use of explicit responses to understanding problems e.g. metalinguistic comments (such as 'I'm not sure I understand this') and the use of partial repetition to distinguish the non-understood elements;

2. a strong encouragement to formulate hypothesis, to develop high-inferencing capacities in the struggle for understanding;

3. awareness raising of the strategic use of different responses to an understanding problem that fits the local context;

4. awareness of issues of face in conveying problems of understanding and in mitigating face-threats to gate-keepers;

5. encouragement to take intiatives in topics as a way of reducing some frame and schema difficulties in understanding.

VanLier (1995) has also suggested the value of using language-awareness sessions to raise and discuss explicit causes of understanding problems.

13.11 Listening to lectures

Initial questions

- How do listeners come to understand academic lectures?
- What do listeners understand in academic lectures?
- What problems do L2 listeners have in academic lectures?
- How do listeners rate lecturers?
- How does preparation, note-taking, class participation and review influence lecture understanding?
- What are valid tests of lecture comprehension?

Academic lectures have been a salient area for L2 listening research, in part because the listeners are so clearly embedded in a one-way information flow, and in an 'audience/addressee' mode rather than a 'participant' mode. It is easier to make long-term, systematic observations in these settings and it is possible to manipulate certain variables in the situation such as mode of presentation, modification of input, type of pre-listening and post-listening tasks and assessment.

In lecture settings, which are still the dominant form of secondary and tertiary classroom education, the listener is expected to 'absorb' information from the lecturer. The listener needs to attend selectively to information and record, organise and, most importantly, integrate that information cumulatively with other information gained over a long period of time. The listener is eventually required to recall that information, in some integrated form, usually for purposes of assessment.

A good deal of research has been conducted on selected features of academic lectures, such as rate and pace of delivery (Griffiths, 1991), use of global and local macro-organisers (DeCarrico and Nattinger 1988), vocabulary elaborations (Fahmy and Bilton, 1989), definitions (Flowerdew, 1992) and their effects on learner comprehension. The purpose of these studies has been to show, in controlled experiments, the relative effects of various simplifications (e.g. a slower rate of speech) on comprehension (as measured by follow-up tests, such as cloze tests). Although these experiments do help the researchers, and teachers who read this research, understand the nature of lecture comprehension, they ultimately cannot produce definitive findings about the 'value' of a given manipulation of a lecture text since so many other content variables (cf. Brown's [1995] treatment of 'cognitive difficulty') and learner variables come into play.

Although some simplification and elaboration adjustments in lectures (specifically, increased pausing at natural pause points, use of visual organisers, vocabulary elaboration) often lead to better comprehension among L2 listeners, more consistent improvement results from cognitive adjustments. Examples of cognitive adjustment are presentations of background information (such as vocabulary) to listeners prior to the lecture (Chiang and Dunkel, 1992), use of other pre-listening tasks (Bhatia, 1983), attention to advance organisers (Benson, 1989), training in effective note-taking, summarising, and review practices (Rost, 1990), and previews of the final assessment procedures (Chiang and Dunkel, 1992).

Rather than replicating any of these experimental studies, a useful action research project in this area is to survey learners on areas in the lecture in which they experience difficulties. One way to do this is to have students evaluate the lecturer in terms of his or her 'weaknesses' in delivering a lecture. An experimental format, based on Brown and Bakhtar (1983), is to present a series of statements about the lecturer, and ask the students to rate simply 'true' or 'false'.

Brown and Bahktar's original questionnaire used 18 statements, but more or less could be used.

1. I do not organise my lecture clearly.
2. I do not stress the major points of the lecture clearly.
3. I forget to provide examples and illustrations.
4. I don't start and finish on time.
5. I am nervous and anxious during the lecture.
6. I do not provide a clear opening when I begin.

7. I have difficulty getting to the point I want to make.

8. I say too much too quickly.

9. I have difficulty timing my lecture.

10. I use too much technical language.

11. I tend to make too much use of humour.

12. I assume too much knowledge on the part of students.

13. I am frequently not happy with my own knowledge of the topic I am lecturing on.

14. I forget to provide a summary of my lecture at the end of the lecture.

15. I do not link the sections of my lecture clearly.

16. I do not clearly indicate when I am making an aside as opposed to a major point.

17. I do not leave sufficient time for students to copy diagrams and notes.

18. I do not clearly indicate reservations or doubts about the points I am putting forward.

(Incidentally, in Brown and Bahktar's studies (8) *I say too much too quickly*, and (12) *I assume too much knowledge on the part of students*, are by far the most common student 'complaints'.)

Based on what students indicate as a 'weakness' in the lecturer, whether or not it can be substantiated by the lecturer's actual behaviour, the teacher/researcher gains insight into what features of 'simplification' (of the lecture text or style of delivery) or 'easification' (preparation of concepts prior to the lecture) are most important to address.

Project plan

1. Prepare a survey for students about the lectures or lecturers they are currently in contact with. If possible, have students complete the survey as soon as possible following a lecture. (Also, if you can, record the lectures on video or audio tape for later reference.)

2. Collate questionnaires for at least three lecturers. Record student ratings of 'weaknesses', or 'difficulties' they are experiencing. Are there consistencies in the ratings for the same students? For the same lecturers?

3. Based on what you learn from the surveys, consider changes in the style of lecturing, or ways of preparing students for lectures. Also consider sharing your findings with the lecturers. Are there ways of approaching lectures that could be modified in order to maximise student learning?

13.12 Strategy training

> **Initial questions**
> - What are listening strategies?
> - Are L1 and L2 listening strategies different?
> - What strategies do listeners use while listening in their L2?

One important area of L2 listening research is development of strategy use. Strategy development is important for listening training because strategies are conscious means by which learners can guide and evaluate their own comprehension and responses. It is also known that listening strategies can help students work with more difficult material (Vandergrift, 1999).

Listening strategies are defined as conscious plans to manage incoming speech, particularly when the listener knows that he or she must compensate for incomplete input or partial understanding. When confronted with a difficulty, the listener may use either a **psycholinguistic strategy** (what communication strategy pioneer Claus Faerch (1984) called 'an unseen action in the head') or a **behavioural strategy** (a 'visible action in the world').

Strategy use has been studied through **retrospection** (asking the listener how he or she solved various problems while listening), through **on-line tasks** (particularly with 'problem texts' that force a listener to utilise a strategy for understanding), or through reflection (with paused listening activities, asking the listener what he or she is attending to at a particular moment).

In an early study of listening strategies (with the use of 'talk aloud' protocols), Kasper (1984) found that non-native listeners tended to form an initial interpretation of a topic (a 'frame') and then stick to it, trying to fit incoming words and propositions into that frame, while native listeners were better at recognising when they had made a mistake about the topic and were prepared to initiate a new frame.

A study by Rost and Ross (1991) presented listeners with paused texts (delivered in a one-to-one setting) and had them ask clarification questions. The researchers found that more proficient listeners tended to use more 'hypothesis-testing' (asking about specific information in the story) rather than 'lexical push-downs' (asking about word meanings) and 'global reprises' (asking for general repetition). However, they also discovered that after training sessions, listeners at all levels could ask more hypothesis-testing questions and that their comprehension (measured by written summaries) improved as a result.

Vandergrift (1996) reports on an extensive study involving retrospective self-report, in which learners report in an interview the techniques they used to comprehend recorded L2 (French) texts and their teacher while in class, as well as any out-of-class listening in French. Elaborating on O'Malley and Chamot's (1990) strategy classifications, Vandergrift found explicit examples of learner use of both metacognitive strategies such as planning and monitoring (e.g. 'I read over what we have to do first'), cognitive strategies such as linguistic inferencing and elaborating (e.g. 'I used other words in the sentence and guessed'), and socio-affective strategies such as questioning for clarification and self-encouragement (e.g. 'I ask the teacher to repeat'; 'I tell myself everyone else is probably having the same problem'). He found a greater (reported) use of metacognitive strategies at higher proficiency levels. Based on these findings, Vandergrift (1996) proposes a pedagogy for encouraging use of metacognitive strategies at *all* levels of proficiency: a recommendation consistent with that of O'Malley, Chamot and Kupper (1989).

Concept 13.2   **Listening strategies**

Working with English-speaking students learning French, Vandergrift (1996) has profiled novice and intermediate students in terms of their thinking processes, as reflected in their think-aloud protocols. Based on these profiles, Vandergrift provides some pedagogic suggestions to help learners foster successful 'thinking processes' while listening.

metacognitive: planning – advance organisers, directed attention, selective attention, self-management, monitoring – comprehension monitoring, auditory monitoring, evaluating.

cognitive: inferencing, voice and paralinguistic cues inferencing, kinesic inferencing, extra-linguistic inferencing, between parts inferencing; elaboration – personal elaboration, world elaboration, academic elaboration, translation, transfer, repetition, resourcing, note-taking, deduction, imagery.

socio-affective: questioning for clarification, cooperation, lowering anxiety, self-encouragement, 'taking emotional temperature'

Project plan: Listener reports of strategy use

Listening is impossible to observe directly, so researchers must utilise indirect means of accessing the listening process. One method, developed by Kasper (1984) for L2 use, and elaborated by Vandergrift (1997; 1998) for listening is the **'think aloud protocol'**.

Subjects are asked to listen to an audio extract or view a video extract. The extract is paused at pre-set points, usually corresponding to idea units or transitions in the text, or to plausible chunking units for short-term memory (approximately 20–30 seconds). At each pause point, the subject is asked to verbalise what he or she is thinking, or produce some other 'protocol' that can be analysed later.

The subject's report is based on a combination of factors influencing comprehension of the text and interpretation of what is important to respond to. These will include **text factors** such as phonology, lexis and syntax, and **extratextual features** (paralinguistic or non-linguistic factors), such as tone of voice or body language. They will also include **listener factors** such as 'intratextual perceptions' (speculations about the information in the text), prior knowledge, and 'metacognition' (speculations about one's thinking processes).

1. Preparation: Observe both the successful and unsuccessful listeners in a class. What are the 'thinking processes' of successful vs unsuccessful listeners? Try to identify observable correlates of these thinking processes. Do you believe that thinking processes or strategies can be taught or must they develop naturally as proficiency increases?

2. Identify a pre-recorded audio or video text, such as a lecture segment. Alternatively, you can pre-record your own tape for this purpose. Prepare a 'unit' of text to present to your students. This could be two to five minutes in length, depending on the difficulty of the text and level of the students. Prepare several pauses for the student(s) to introspect.

3. Identify the prompt or 'probe' that you will use to elicit the students' reaction or response. If a student is unsure of what to say or how to continue, you can use 'non-cueing probes' to encourage the student to report what he or she was thinking: 'What are you thinking now?' 'What didn't you understand?' 'How did you figure that out?' Non-cueing probes do not mention anything specific in the text, so as to avoid the question –answer–feedback cycle common in instructional settings.

4. Play the tape for the students. For this (or any) methodology to have validity, the system you use must be replicable. If you wish to examine and compare the listeners' protocols in detail, you will need to administer this procedure in a controlled way: with one student at a time, pausing only at the pre-set points, using the same probes, etc. However, if you wish only to get a feel for this kind of research and its potential applications, you can use the methodology with a larger group, having the subjects write, rather than verbalise, their responses. Or it could be done in a language lab-type setting with individual microphones and tape recorders.

5. Analyse the data. Prior to the experiment, prepare a simple coding system that has some validity in terms of the listening skills and strategies the students are developing. For example, you might have three categories: (1) asks a question (2) summarises (3) 'passes' (says nothing).

6. After you have recorded the students' responses, transcribe them. Code the responses with your coding scheme. If possible, ask a colleague to code the responses with you. This can be done together, so that you can discuss discrepancies. Or it can be done separately, so that you can judge the reliability of your coding scheme. If necessary, revise the scheme and review all of the protocols with the revised system. Both methods will improve the reliability of the coding system.

7. Formulate some generalisations about what kinds of reactions or responses constitute effective or ineffective 'listening strategies'.

8. Write up the results of your project. Include short sections for: Background to the study; Procedures; Results; Applications for learning; Appendix (of sample protocols).

9. Ask a colleague who did not participate in the study to read your report and comment. Or prepare a short presentation for a faculty meeting.

13.13 Materials design and evaluation

Initial questions:
- What is the role of input in listening instruction?
- What is the role of tasks?
- On what basis do you choose input and tasks for your classes?

Teaching materials for listening consist of some form of input and some form of a task or a sequence of tasks. Tasks play an important part in language pedagogy. Candlin (1987) defines a task as a 'problem-posing, social, and interdependent activity which involves the application of existing knowledge to attain a goal'. This definition allows instructional planners and teachers to conceptualise units of instruction that involve problem-solving and social dimensions and that build in applications of knowledge toward an outcome.

When selecting or evaluating materials for language learning, it is useful to have some formal criteria, based on principles of effective instruction, to apply to all materials being considered. Here is an example.

Materials evaluation

- Does it teach what you want to teach?
- What classroom procedures will you be using when you employ these materials?
- Is the material at the right level for your students?
- Are the procedures easy to figure out – for you? For the students?
- Are there appropriate visuals – charts, illustrations, etc., to engage students and guide learning?
- Is it reasonably up to date?
- Are the exercises varied? (Too varied?)
- What kind of supplementation will be necessary?
- Does the material allow for learners at multiple levels to use it?
- Is the material readily available?
- Is it reasonably priced for the students?
- What kind of supplementation will be needed in class and out of class?

(Adapted from Skierso, 1998)

Project plan

1. Survey the materials currently used in your programme for teaching listening. Develop a questionnaire like that of Skierso (1998).
2. If possible, have at least two reviewers for each book or set of materials (or web learning site, etc.).
3. Discuss the responses to the surveys. How does the survey assist you in making decisions about the utility of materials?
4. If you can design your own materials, what will be the top priorities for you?

13.14   Listening journals

Because a major aspect of language development involves the learner coming to manage increasing amounts and complexity of oral input, learning to attend to input is a major area of interest in language education.

Diary studies are a useful project for understanding learner awareness. Schmidt (1995: 45) summarised the advice gleaned from his own diary study relating to his learning Portuguese as follows:

Initial questions

- If you could slow down the listening process, what more could you learn?
- What are some ways of 'slowing down' the listening process?
- What is the value of self-reflection in language learning?

- Pay attention to input.
- Pay particular attention to whatever aspects of the input (phonology, morphology, pragmatics, discourse, etc.) that you are concerned to learn. (Nothing comes free!)
- Look for clues as to why target language speakers say what they say. Compare what you say with what target speakers say in similar contexts. Build and test hypotheses when you can.
- If you cannot find a general principle to explain how something works, concentrate on noticing how specific instances are used in specific contexts.

Fujiwara (1990) reports that a semester-long 'listening diary' homework project helped transform her students attitudes about listening. In this project students had access to recorded materials for home study and guided procedures for completing their diary entries which were read by the instructor but not evaluated. Fujiwara's students reported that they

- learned new listening strategies and adopted for their own continued use those that they found most helpful;
- became aware of what and how to learn;
- improved their ability to evaluate their strengths and weaknesses as listeners in the foreign language;
- began to set learning goals for themselves;
- developed a more positive attitude toward learning through listening.

In addition to the function of adding and sharpening learning strategies, however, keeping a journal can be a way for a learner to begin to notice specific features of input that can be used for learning and acquisition (Goh, 1997).

Having reviewed research on subliminal, implicit and incidental learning, Schmidt (1990) claimed that

> nothing in the target language input becomes intake for language learning other than what learners consciously notice, that there is no such thing as learning a second language subliminally. Incidental learning – learning without consciously trying to learn – is certainly possible when task demands focus attention on relevant features of the input . . . Incidental learning in

another sense, picking up target language forms from input when they do not carry information crucial to the task, appears unlikely for adults (Schmidt, 1990: 129).

Using his own diary study as evidence (learning Portuguese in Brazil), Schmidt argued that *conscious* processing of new grammatical forms in input has a central role in language learning. According to Schmidt, the rules of languages are not acquired in a subconscious manner.

Project plan

1. Using yourself as a language learner of a second language, or using a volunteer learner of English as second language, plan a long-term journal project. The means of keeping the journal can be written (notebook or computer file) or audio (audio cassette or audio computer file). The theme of the entries can be generally related to learning the language, or to oral situations in particular.

2. Check that you (or the learner) are making regular entries into the journal, even if it appears there is nothing to say!

3. At the end of a given period (say two weeks) go back over the journal entries. What kind of 'affective data' (information about the learner's attitudes and feelings) is there? What kind of 'learning strategy' data is there? What kind of 'noticing' or 'usage' data is there? Does the process of making entries seem to help the learner (you) plan better for language learning? Does it help the learner notice more about language use?

4. You may wish to add variations to the journal procedure.
   • Have the learner listen to a (video or audio) taped recording (of a programme or conversation) and after listening, make a journal entry about the experience of listening to the programme.
   • Have the learner make entries specific to one area of learning, such as participating in conversations.
   Do the variations add anything to the value of the process?

13.15 Designing a self-access listening centre

Initial questions

• What role does self-access play in developing listening skills?
• What are the relative strengths and weaknesses of self-access learning centres?
• What would the ideal self-access centre be like? Would your students use it?

Self-access listening centres are an important resource for language teaching. Here are some principles that successful centres have followed:

- have an ample amount of oral material, on a variety of topics, in different modalities;
- prepare exercises to accompany at least some of the materials;
- require learner logs or journals to report what they have listened to and their reactions to it;
- keep tape scripts available for reference for at least some of the material;
- provide a means of ongoing teacher support for learners who use the listening centre;
- give guidance to students on how to use the centre;
- give advice for long-term learning strategies.

On this last point, Rubin and Thompson (1998) offer L2 learners support for development of learning styles and strategies. For non-interactive listening, they provide general practice suggestions: listen regularly, choose appropriate materials, find the right level of difficulty, choose materials that you will enjoy. In non-interactive listening, such as in self-access centres, the most common problem noted is 'I'm not getting anything out

---

Project plan

1. Identify a group of learners who will benefit from a self-access listening centre. Survey them on what they would like the centre to include.
2. Gather available resources that can be used to start the centre. For a group of 25 learners who will use the centre occasionally, you can 'start small', with perhaps a few music CDs, a dozen videos, five or six recorded interviews. You can add materials as needed.
3. Develop written tasks to go with each 'input'. These can be open-ended. Again, you can revise them on an ongoing basis.
4. Develop some form of learner logs. Learners should record what they listened to and their evaluation of it.
5. At the end of a given period, prepare a 'top ten' list. What programmes did the learners use most? Which received the highest evaluations? Why?
6. Post your top ten lists in the self-access centre. Elicit comments from the students.
7. After a period of time, prepare some tips for other teachers on developing a self-access centre. See the illustration box on p. 244 for an example.

of it [i.e., the L2 television, movies and videos].' Rubin and Thompson offer practical support: Use visual cues, use background knowledge, use information, determine the genre of the segment, listen to familiar elements, jot down repeated words and phrases.

Illustration box: Ideas for adaptation to a self-access video centre

Transcripts Generally, I use screenplays – or preferably

Transcripts – together with the movie, to help students grasp the language, which is often idiomatic (*Clueless*, for instance). You can find lists of published scripts at the larger internet booksellers. A search on the web for screenplays will also reveal a number of sites that have full texts, notably DrewUs Script-o-rama.

Caption decoder (provides captioning at the bottom of the screen) This reinforces listening with reading.

Comprehension questions These help focus students' attention on specific aspects of a film or video. I usually have students work on these in a small group discussion format.

Dictations or modified dictations help develop listening ability.

Vocabulary round-tables Invite students to identify new words and expressions in the script, try to come up with their meanings and share their word lists with other students.

Sequencing activities Write out one-sentence summaries of the key events in the film. Either cut them into pieces or put them on a page in random order. Have students rearrange or number them to reconstruct the chronological story of the film.

Acting out Have students select a small portion of the film and act it out with fellow students. I would suggest recommending specific scenes which would lend themselves to this.

Student-developed quizzes Have students come up with their own questions about the film and then face off in teams in a quiz-show format.

Sportscasting Turn down the sound. Students in pairs take turns describing the action on the screen.

Recommended films In addition to *When Harry Met Sally* and *Clueless*, the films that I have had the most success with are *Butch Cassidy and the Sundance Kid*, *Dead Poets Society*, *The Graduate*, *The Princess Bride* and *A River Runs Through It*.

(Joseph McVeigh, Middlebury College, Middlebury, Vermont)

13.16   Sample action research report

Many teachers who engage in informal action research will want to write up their results in a simple way. A sample action research report follows. The footnotes refer to annotations made for this book: they provide comments on the reasoning for the research study and decisions on how to report the study. The bracketed notes in the text are added here to highlight the functions of each section for the writer of a short research report.

Departmental Research Report
English Language Program (ELP)
University of California, Berkeley
Dr Michael Rost

Teachable communication strategies

[*This first section briefly states the purpose of the study, the context and key principles on which the project is based.*]

This departmental study, carried out in the ELP between March and August 1996, was intended to identify a core of 'teachable' communication strategies for L2 learners that might help unify our Oral Communication Skills (OSC) curriculum. In addition, the study was intended to contribute to the 'typology and teachability' research paradigm in second language acquisition developed by Rost and Ross (1991). A cluster of strategies was identified, presented and practised with a group of 48 students. Subsequently, each strategy was rated by the students in terms of perceived utility and utility scores were compiled and ranked so as to identify a hierarchy of utility for teachers and researchers.[1]

Methodology

[*This section presents the methodology so that the reader can easily visualise the steps in order to follow your discussion and so that colleagues can replicate the study if they wish. Using explicit steps, particularly when they correspond to time frames or to key decision points, help readers appreciate the planning of the study variables or observations and thus appreciate any results or recommendations you may share.*]

---

[1] This action research reports adopts a non-specialist perspective because it is likely to be read by both teachers and administrators. The opening statement of the background, purpose and procedures of the study must be clear and concise. The introductory section aims to situate the study in the present context (the English Language Programme and specifically the oral communications curriculum) and also show its relevance to larger enquiries in the field.

The methodology of the study consisted of four steps.[2]

Step 1: Recording of 'uncoached conversations' and analysis of conversational problems

Twelve dyads at level 53 (intermediate) were audio-recorded during information exchange tasks and portions of the conversations perceived as 'typical' were transcribed (see Appendix).

The following conversational problems, well-known anecdotally, were confirmed:[3]

- lack of idea clarity
- lack of topic links
- lack of coordination between speakers
- lack of comprehensibility (volume, pronunciation, intonation)
- lack of specific vocabulary
- grammar control problems.

Step 2: Selection of 'discourse strategies' to improve each area

The following strategy areas, adapted from Bremer et al. (1996), Rost and Ross (1991), and Bialystok (1990), were proposed as likely to be helpful in improving the problematic areas of S-S and S-T discourse.[4]

- clarification of problematic utterances
- explicit extension and linking of topics
- coordination of speaking turns and information flow
- social coordination to improve affect and attitude.

Step 3: Formulate criteria and typology for strategy training

[*This is the part of the study that most teachers are interested in because it presents specific ideas for the classroom. Even though most teachers, in teacher rooms and teacher conferences, will want a copy of this part of the study only, it is important to contextualize your teaching ideas and create parameters for when and how your ideas work.*]

---

[2] Methodology for action research is simply the steps or stages that must be carried out to complete the intended cycle of research. Note that the procedures were designed to be carried out in a manageable time-frame and with available resources. It is important that the time-frames for planning, conducting, writing, and reporting the research be manageable in order to secure a degree of success with the project.

[3] For the purposes of reporting the research, only the most salient aspects need to be mentioned in this report.

[4] Based on input available to us and on our intuitions about what variables would be suitable for this action research project, these are the areas we defined. Especially in a group research project, it is important to have a small number of agreed-upon topics or variables to investigate.

Based on Rost and Ross (1991), a strategy is considered teachable if these conditions are satisfied:[5]

1. The learner recognises a need to address 'confusion' (or compensate for incomplete information).
2. There is a recognisable point in the discourse in which a strategy (an alternate way of processing language or interacting) can be used.
3. The alternate way has a probable payoff in knowledge or affect that the learner seeks.

---

1. Check your understanding.
   {'What do you mean . . . ?'}

2. Ask about words you don't know.
   {'What does ____ mean?'}

3. Paraphrase
   {'Do you mean . . . ?'}

4. Start and end the conversation smoothly
   {Let's go over this . . . Thanks for the information . . . }

5. Change topics when necessary
   {OK, let's go on to . . . }

6. Change turn direction when necessary
   {Now, can you tell me . . . ?}

7. Ask for reasons and examples.
   {'Why do you think so?'}

8. Ask follow-up questions.
   {'What happened after that?'}

9. Initiate new topics.
   {'Yes, but what do you think about . . . ?'}

10. Show interest in your partner.
    {'Oh, really . . .'}

11. Comment on what your partner says.
    {'That's interesting . . .'}

12. Use 'open' body postures to promote contact.
    {eye contact, non-use of paper, materials during interaction}

---

[5] It is useful here to cite a few published sources that were used in guiding the study.

4. The alternate way of processing can be practised again in an immediate context.

5. The new use of the alternate produces the demonstrable effect on interaction, understanding, or learning.

Specific strategies were formulated that were thought to meet these conditions and address the discourse difficulties noted in Step 1.[6] These strategies are (with demonstrable 'strategy token'):

Step 4: Creation of instructional design for strategy training

The instructional design that was selected for this experimental training was the following:[7]

- Teacher presents one strategy per class, randomly ordered, over 12 class sessions. The presentation consists of a demonstration, with sample behaviours or linguistic expressions.

- Teacher utilises a familiar conversational format, pair discussion of short readings with 'interaction questions'. The pair discussions would rotate so the students had an opportunity to interact with at least three classmates on each reading–discussion task.

- Teacher intervenes during the pair discussions to point out where the focus strategy can be used.

- Teacher reviews the strategy at the end of each session, and periodically reviews the strategies presented to that point.

- In the final class meeting, teacher reviews the body of 12 strategies and asks students, independently, to rate each strategy in terms of its usefulness for them personally.

Step 5: Compilation of rankings and presentation to other teachers.

The rankings of 24 students were compiled. The following results were attained.[8] These are grouped by relative order, within four communication constructs: clarification, coordination, expansion and social.

[Although presentation of results can utilise statistical information, there is no justification for presenting statistics (here chi-square measures of frequency) since

---

[6] Many practising teachers feel that the action research actually starts here, with the selection of specific teaching intervention points. However, for the sake of validity, it is important to have the proper context built up before the selection of teaching points is made.

[7] Instructional design recommendations are the most common application of action research in language education. Instructional design should specify materials, procedures and outcomes.

[8] The actual numbers are available, but as they have no real significance to the ranking and the intended purpose of the study, they are not included in the report. A true experimental design, which sets up hypotheses to be tested, would include the appropriate numerical tables and statistics.

the study was not set up as an experimental study with hypotheses to confirm or negate.]

1. Clarification

- Check your understanding.
  {'What do you mean . . . ?'}
- Ask about words you don't know.
  {'What does ____ mean?'}
- Paraphrase
  {'Do you mean . . . ?'}

2. Coordination

- Start and end the conversation smoothly
  {Let's go over this . . . thanks for the information . . . }
- Change topics when necessary
  {OK, let's go on to . . . }
- Change turn direction when necessary
  {Now, can you tell me . . . ?}

3. Expansion

- Ask for reasons and examples.
  {'Why do you think so?'}
- Ask follow up questions.
  {'What happened after that?'}
- Initiate new topics.
  {'Yes, but what do you think about . . . ?'}

4. Social

- Show interest in your partner.
  {'Oh, really . . . '}
- Comment on what your partner says.
  {'That's interesting . . . '}

Implications

[*This section can present simply statements of your own intentions on how to use the findings or the understanding you have gained from your study. Unless the study is set up with an explicit experimental design, statements of cause and effect cannot be made. Note, however, that an action research study like this can form the basis of a quasi-experimental study.*]

This framework will serve as a basis for continuing research in the ELP and for curriculum development of the Oral Communication Skills sequence within the programme.[9] Further analysis of the results, e.g. by correlation of rankings to TOEFL scores, or nationality, is possible, depending on future research and teaching needs.

References[10]

Bialystok, E. (1990) *Communication strategies: a psychological analysis of second-language use.* Oxford: Basil Blackwell.

Bremer, K., Roberts, C., Vasseur, M., Simonot, M. and Broeder, P. (1996) *Achieving understanding: discourse in intercultural encounters.* Harlow: Longman.

Rost, M. and Ross, S. (1991) Learner strategies in interaction. *Language Learning,* 41: 235–73.

Appendix (sample extracts from Step 1)[11]

Extract 1

S1 (Taiwan, male, aged twenty-two); *S2* (Spain, female, aged twenty-one)

> *S1*: [*memorised question from discussion sheet*] Do you think it is possible to stay in love a long time?
> *S2*: I don't know is possible[12] . . . fall in love . . . in every . . . I don't know . . .'cause they think . . . the emotion is very different . . . because if you stay with a person in the older life . . . it is different . . .
> *S1*: Yes, different love . . . maybe long marry is different love . . .
> *S2*: You say marry . . . you don't say fall in love forever . . .
> *S1*: No . . . but sometimes you stay a long time one person . . . and you don't say fall in love . . .
> *S2*: Yes, exactly.

Extract 2

T–S interaction: task focus

T–S interactions (often marked by confused expectations). *T* (American, male, aged twenty-nine); *S* (Japanese female, aged twenty-one). *S* had written about the influence her parents had on her. Following is the planned 'discussion' of her paper.

---

[9] Conclusions or implications tie the results back to the original question or concern, which is the basic cycle of action research.

[10] It is advisable to use only a few key references and to cite only sources that are readily available to the public.

[11] Selected extracts that were part of the data collected give the reader a flavour of the study.

[12] When transcribing learner data it is important to preserve the actual features, even if they are ungrammatical.

T: You say that your mother had a greater influence on you than your father?

S: [*seven seconds silence*] Mother?

T: Right, your mother. You say here she's 'bright-eyed'. That's interesting. Can you explain that a bit?

S: [*five seconds*] My mother?

T: Yes. What do you mean when you say, 'She's bright-eyed'?

S: [*five seconds*]

T: [*showing paper*] Here, in your paper. You say, 'She's so bright-eyed and wonders many things.'

S: Yes, my mother.

T: Can you give me an example?

S: Example of my mother?

T: Yeah. Yeah. Give me an example. What's your mother like?

S: Oh, she likes many things.

IV Exploring listening

Resources and references

Sections I, II and III have discussed ways of defining, teaching and researching listening. This final section of the book provides lists of resources and references that will be helpful to readers who wish to explore specific topics further. Updates to this section are given regularly on the series website (see Introduction).

Chapter 14 will provide...

- sources of listening material, audio only and multimedia;
- guides for evaluating resources;
- an annotated list of recommended teaching resources and reference materials in the area of listening;
- a list of teaching journals and discussion groups relevant to the teaching of listening;
- sample discussions relevant to teaching and researching listening;
- sources for learning more about current research.

14.1 Sources of listening material

An extensive body of resources for teaching and researching listening is available at a reasonable cost, and often free of charge. Authentic English materials in fiction and nonfiction, in music and other performing arts, is readily available on audio tape, audio CD, CD-ROM, video tape and DVD formats. Further resources, of an almost limitless variety, are available by broadcast via commercial television, cable, and satellite. Multimedia materials, as well as broadcasts, have expanded geometrically over the internet.

In addition to authentic materials, pedagogic materials – designed explicitly for language teaching – are available from individuals, language schools, internet providers, as well as the established language education publishers.

Because it is literally impossible to catalogue all available resources, particularly since these resources are expanding and being updated daily, this section offers a small sampling of resources and resource ideas. This section also suggests some of the sources that can be explored to identify even further resources for teaching and researching listening.

14.1.1   Audio tapes, CDs and CD-ROMs

British Library Education Service This organisation produces a magazine called *Sources*, which includes sound recordings of feature articles. <www.bl.uk/index.html>

Pacifica Foundation *www.pacifica.org* Offers tape recordings and transcripts of interviews with a variety of interesting and unorthodox guests.

Talking Tapes Direct (PO Box 190, Peterborough PE2 6UW, UK; Tel. ((+44) (0) 1773 230645; Fax (+44) (0) 1773 238966) Features audio recordings of programs originally broadcast on radio and television.

education.guardian.co.uk A wide collection of educational CD-ROMs organised by topic and professional interest.

www.educate.com.au This company offers a wide range of educational videos, grouped by interest area and age.

www./ivcs/ivoc/ca An example of an institutional publisher (University of Victoria) offering business education materials on CD-ROM.

www.libraryvideo.com This instructional media company offers an extensive selection of educational CD-ROMs for children to young adults.

www.lyrics.ch Contains lyrics for many songs. Useful for teaching purposes.

www.nflrc.hawaii.edu/ithompson/flmedia/skill_frame_1.htm Criteria for use in evaluating listening material on CD-ROM from Thompson, 2000.

www.musiceducationonline.org   Provides a catalogue of music CDs as well as useful links to music sites.

14.1.2   Television and video

Commercial, cable, satellite and public television offer virtually unlimited resources for finding input in English and many other major languages.

The key to using television broadcasts for language learning is in selection of appropriately interesting and valuable sources and in providing suitable tasks that allow learners to evaluate their understanding. Some approaches for making television more suitable for instruction are:

'chunking' the programme into short segments, allowing for previewing of vocabulary and tasks, using subtitles and replaying sections of a broadcast or programme if pre-recorded.

Public television

BBC World Service Television (broadcasts of worldwide news.) *www.bbc.co.uk/worldservice* (mailing addresses can also be included)

Behind the News (Australia)

www.broadcast.com
www.real.com
www.bbc.co.uk/worldservice (BBC radio)
www.radio.cbc.ca/index.html (Canadian Broadcasting Company radio)
www.cnn.com
www.msnbc.com
www.abcnews.com
brinkley.realaudio.com/content/npr.html (NPR online)

CNN (blocks of news pre-packaged with synopses and activity booklets are available.) *http://cnn.com*

ITN World News and Central News (videos of various news programmes with activity workbooks, published by Oxford University Press) *www.itn.co.uk*

Voice of America (variety of interview, documentary and news programmes) *www.voa.gov*

Commercial television

In a recent survey of 300 students in an intensive English programme in the United States (Rost, 1999) found that the following commercial programmes were reported by students to be most valuable to them for their language learning:

news: CNN, ABC Evening News

cartoons: 'The Simpsons', 'South Park'

situation comedies: 'Friends', 'Mad About You', 'Seinfeld'

documentaries: 'Animal Planet', 'Discovery', 'NOVA'

dramas: 'Party of Five', 'The X-Files', 'Real World'

interview shows: Jay Leno, David Letterman, Jerry Springer

legal shows: Judge Judy.

Similar surveys in other countries are likely turn up similar 'pop' shows that serve a useful purpose for sharing local resources.

Concept 14.1 A grading system for using television commercials for listening comprehension practice

Teachers can enhance the listening ability of EFL learners by providing them with interesting authentic materials. Television commercials in particular are good sources of material, provided that they are selected carefully. The aim of this project was to develop a scale for grading TV commercials in terms of their difficulty as listening comprehension material.

To develop this scale, many factors which affect listening comprehension were considered. These factors covered text, speaker, presentation and listener characteristics. Based on these factors, a 20-item grading scale was developed and used to assess and rank in order of difficulty ten US TV commercials. Special attention was given to those factors which would be likely to hinder intermediate-level Japanese junior college students who are learning English Japan. The ten commercials were then shown to this target group, and the predicted difficult was compared with the actual difficulty. This was measured by a five-question task sheet and a questionnaire.

The results showed that there was a good match between the predicted and actual difficulty, but there were also some anomalies. Possible reasons for these anomalies were considered: for example, not giving weight to certain factors and unevenness in the difficulty of the tasks. Overall, the project showed that this grading scale might be a helpful tool for teachers who wish to use authentic TV commercials for teaching listening comprehension.

(Posting on Internet teacher discussion group)

Commercial video

A number of websites are now available as resources for commercial video, providing scripts and notes that may be useful for teaching.

http://movieweb.com/movie/movie.html Includes direct links to production companies, lists of top movies and a list of all movies available on MovieWeb.

http://us.imdb.com/ Gives plot lines along with comments from viewers and user-vote tabulations on their favourite movies

http://www.geocities.com/classicmoviescripts/scripts Provides scripts and guides for classic movies.

14.1.3 Captioning

Many television programmes and videos (on video tape and DVD) provide captioning. Learners often find captioning to be a useful resource for making video more useful as a learning resource.

Quote 14.1 Testimonial on the virtues of using captioning

Here in Korea, I encourage my students to purchase a caption machine, which allows them to see the spoken English in English. In the USA, I think all tvs are now equipped with a 'switch' that allows the same effect.

One adult friend/student said, after about two months, she could hear the English without reading the English! She was as surprised and delighted as I was. She also found herself getting quite addicted to 'Guiding Light'.

I tape some NPR 'All Things Considered' and use them in class. If the student is reading the news, hearing the news is easier because much of the content will be familiar.

I've also started to suggest that my students make 'tape-journals' in which they record a few minutes each day, and at the end of the week, review what they have said.

Teacher in teaching discussion group

One teacher's review of research on the educational use of English-captioned materials is available at: *www.robson.org/capfaq/kikuchi.txt*.

14.1.4   Internet sources

There are numerous sites on the internet that provide authentic listening material that can be utilized for language learning. Material on virtually any topic can be found. The problem, as with all media materials, is knowing how to select what is of value and to guide learners in making effective use of them. Sites that are oriented toward 'authentic' uses – for reference, educational, community, commercial, or entertainment purposes – will not guide language learners in how to take advantage of them for learning purposes.

Various teachers and researchers have offered guidelines on how to take advantage of the web for language learning. Two laudable efforts are from J. Nelson *www.ialc.wsu.edu/eslint/thesis/thesisindex.html* and J. Graus *<heep://home.plex.nl/~jgraus>*.

These guides point to the need for:

(1) identifying accessible materials of suitable interest and relevance for learners

(2) finding materials at an appropriate level of difficulty

(3) creating tasks for the learners before, while, and after they work with the materials

(4) providing interactivity and feedback to the learners

Example of authentic sources include the following well-known URLs:

www.bbc.co/uk/worldservice/BBC_English/progs.htm
BBC Enlgish: Radio programs with Internet Pages:

Listening online
www.clet.ait.ac.th/sall.htm

PBS online
www.pbs.org

Yahoo! Radio Programs
www.yahoo.com/News and Media

Voice of America Internet Audio
www.voa.gov/programs/audio/realaudio

In addition to the growing use of authentic sites for language learning, there has been an explosion of internet sites specifically for teaching English, many including audio and video material and tasks.

Following is a partial list of sites. Listening extracts on these sites are playable by means of additional software, such as RealPlayer® or Shockwave®.

Sample ELT Publisher sites (offering a combination of free and fee-based courses):

www.englishsuccess.com English Success (Longman), contains a variety of multimedia courses at different levels.

www.globalenglish.com Global English, offers several general English and business English courses.

www.EnglishListening.com The English Listening Lounge, contains a variety of short authentic extracts and tasks.

www.peakenglish.com Peak English, offers various online courses for general and business purposes.

14.2 Teaching resources

14.2.1 Online teaching resources

Guides and links for online teaching are provided here because many present interesting possibilities for expanding the use of listening in language learning and in content instruction.

- The NODE site provides resources for instructional design related to online courses *http://node.on.ca/tfl/design*

- Subject-matter teaching
  The IMS project is an attempt to develop an international specification and database for online courses (*http://www.imsproject.org*)

Other sources of information about learning networks:

Cisco Educational Archive *www.cearch.org*

Consortium for School Networking *www.cosn.org*

3Com Education site *www.3com.com/edu*

Internet2 *www.internet2.org*

Internet Society *www.isoc.org*

The 'Web Teacher' *www.webteacher.org*

WWW   Virtual   Library: Networking *src.doc.ic.ac.uk/bySubject/ Networking.html*

Journals (abstracting journals)

Applied Linguistics www3.oup.co.uk/applij

Centre for Information on Language Teaching and Research *www.clit.org.uk* (Provides online publications and services related to language teaching and research, including reviews of current books.)

Computer Mediated Communication Magazine www.december.com/cmc/mag/

Discourse and Society www.sagepub.co.uk

ELT Journal www3.oup.co.uk/eltj

ERIC Digests (1118 22nd Street N.W., Washington D.C.) *www.ed.gov/ databases* (Abstracts of numerous articles on language research and language teaching.)

ESL Journal www.eslmag.com   (A useful online journal of teaching ideas and resources.)

Foreign Language Teaching Forum www.cortland.edu/flteach/flteach-res.html (A useful resource site for teachers, includes abstracts of articles on teaching ideas.)

Human Communication Research (Journal of the International Communication Association) *www.sagepub.co.uk/journals*

International Review of Applied Linguistics www.oup.co.uk/iral

Journal of Communication www3.oup.co/uk/jnlcom/

Journal of Pragmatics (Journal of the International Listening Association) *www.cios.org/www/il*

Language Teaching uk.cambridge.org/journals/> (An international journal that keeps readers informed on the latest findings in research that is relevant to language education. Each issue is a collection of over 150 abstracts.)

LLBA (Linguistics and Language Behaviour Abstracts) library.dialogue.com/ bluesheets/ (A valuable resource on the latest developments in linguistics and various related disciplines.)

National Council of Teachers of English *www.ncte.org* (Publishers of several journals of L1 English teachers, which include articles of relevance to L2 teachers as well.)

College English

English Journal

Language Arts

Primary Voices

Research in the Teaching of English

School Talk

System www.elsevier.nl

TESOL Quarterly www.tesol.edu/pubs

Triangle: Educational Action Research www.triangle.com/ear

14.2.3   Books on L2 teaching

The following list provides accessible resources for teachers who seek to apply listening theory to teaching and testing. These recommended works cover crucial aspects of listening pedagogy. For instance:

- selecting appropriate input sources: deciding on authentic sources or prepared sources, on audio or video, or 'live' (teacher, student, or guests)
- grading materials; chunking input into appropriate segments for presentation: dividing the input into segments that allow for maximal attention and learning
- providing tasks and activity cycles for learners to engage in: focusing on listening skills and strategies to be developed in the activity
- integrating listening with other language skills, course activities and work on acquisition of grammar and vocabulary
- developing strategies ways of explicitly employing strategy instruction into language learning
- providing assessment: feedback to learners on their relative success in listening.

Chamot, A., Barnhardt, S., Beard, P., El-Dinary and Robbins, G. (1999) *The learning strategies handbook*. New York: Longman (This volume outlines the Cognitive Academic Language Learning Approach [CALLA] and shows how the model [planning–monitoring–problem-solving– evaluating] can be applied to language instruction, including listening development.)

Flowerdew, J. (1994) *Academic listening: research perspectives*. Cambridge: Cambridge University Press (A comprehensive collection of research of L2 users listening to lecturers, carefully annotated by the editor. A vital handbook for any teacher responsible for training students for university listening. Accessible research studies on various aspects of academic listening: the listening process [expectations (Tauroza and Allison), notetaking (Chaudron, Loschky, Cook), recall (Dunkel and Davis), summarising (Rost)], academic discourse [topic structure (Hanson), discourse patterns in different disciplines (Dudley-Evans), macrostructure and microstructure features of lectures (Young)], ethnographies (student perspectives on learning (Benson), student and lecturer perceptions of comprehension strategies (Mason), student perspectives on notetaking (King), and pedagogic applications [analysis of an academic purposes test, the 'Test of Listening for Academic Purposes (T-LAP)' (Hansen and Jensen), guidelines for training lecturers (Lynch)].)

Lynch, A. (1996) *Communication in the classroom*. Oxford: Oxford University Press (In this very functional guide, Lynch discusses communication inside and outside the classroom, research on input and interaction, and classroom applications for teaching listening and speaking.)

Mendelsohn, D. and Rubin, J. (eds) (1995) *A guide for the teaching of second language listening*. San Diego CA: Dominie Press (A varied collection of articles by top people in the area of listening pedagogy, this volume offers the right mix of theoretical background and practical suggestions. Includes articles on dimensions of difficulty in listening comprehension [Brown], interactive listening strategies [Lynch], academic listening [Chaudron], principles of classroom teaching ['How to become a good listening teacher'] [Buck], learning strategies [Chamot], assessment [Thompson], pronunciation and listening [Gilbert], listening strategies [Mendelsohn], video [Rubin], instructional models [Morley].)

Morley, J. (1984) *Listening and language learning in ESL: developing self-study activities for listening comprehension*. Orlando: HBJ (A vital source of ideas for selective listening tasks, this book discusses the use of authentic sources for listening and the design of manageable tasks for learners at all levels.)

Nunan, D. and Miller, L. (eds) (1995) *New ways in teaching listening*. Washington DC: TESOL (A collection of favourite listening activities from teachers around the world, this volume offers numerous specific ideas (coded by student level) and boundless inspiration for the classroom teacher. Organised into six parts: Developing Cognitive Strategies [listening for the main idea, listening for details, predicting], Developing Listening with Other Skills [listening and speaking, listening and pronunciation, listening and vocabulary], Listening to Authentic Materials, Using Technology [phone, language lab recorders, answer machines, recorded messages from public sources, information lines, radio, TV, video, even a 'vibrotactile aid'], Listening for Academic Purposes, Listening for fun.)

Richards, J.C. (1990) *The language teaching matrix*. Oxford: Oxford University Press (This widely used work has a substantive chapter on teaching listening, with a focus on designing classroom materials for listening. Richards outlines the notions of top–down and bottom–up listening and presents a comprehensible view of exercise types in a quadrant framework involving a function [transaction-interactional] dimension and a processing [top–down vs. bottom–up] dimension.)

Rost, M. (1991) *Listening in action*. London: Prentice Hall (One of the original 'recipe books' and recognised as a pioneering work for teacher training, *Listening in Action* provides an outline and rationale for four types of listening activities, tasks and exercises: intensive listening, global listening, selective listening and interactive listening.)

Rubin, J. and Thompson, I. (1998) *How to be a more successful language learner*. Boston: Heinle & Heinle (This volume offers practical advice for teachers and students on the known principles of second language learning. It contains helpful chapters on the communication process, on listening, and on strategy use.)

Underwood, M. (1989) *Teaching listening*. Harlow: Longman (One of the pioneers in advancing listening in the language curriculum, Underwood helpfully outlines listening activities in three stages: pre-listening, while-listening, and post-listening. She also discusses criteria for selecting and adapting authentic recorded material.

White, G. (1998) *Listening*. Oxford: Oxford University Press (A superb resource and training book for teachers, this provides practical guidance for teachers on all aspects of L2 listening instruction. White discusses what it means to become a good listener, and covers the essential areas of making listening materials and using published materials, as well as listening in real life. She also provides a helpful list of resources.)

14.2.4 Teacher discussion groups

TESL Discussion Group *Listserve@cunyvm.cuny.vm*   Organised at City University of New York, this group offers free membership for teachers. Allows access to 50,000+ teachers, around the world (over 44 countries at last count), subdivided into various interest groups. By tracking 'threads' of various topics, a participant (or 'lurker') can follow discussions of topics that are relevant to his or her current teaching practice. Ongoing discussions often include topics related to listening, such as 'Dictation', 'Selection of audio tapes', 'Is it ethical to use video in the classroom?' and 'How do I teach "frozen listening students"?' Contributions are typically personal, lively and helpful – even if not always well-informed. The spirit of the list is in creating collaborative conversations and problem-solving forums for teachers.

The International Listening Association (ILA) *www.listen.org*   This is a professional organisation whose members are dedicated to learning more about the impact of listening on all human activity. Members include professionals from such areas as education (a lot of college instructors of 'communication' courses), business, health care, government and law. This diversity provides opportunities to examine the rich and complex nature of listening from a wide range of perspectives. Annual conventions and regional conferences are organised to share expertise, to support listening research efforts and to promote the practice and teaching of effective listening.

Sample bulletin board postings

Reply-To: listen-2@ecnet.net
Sender: owner-listen-2@ecnet.net
Subject: Re: Limits on listening effectiveness
MIME-Version: 1.0
X-PRIORITY: 3 (Normal)

P . . . here:

My own take on listening in conflict situations is yet another view. I really don't like saying that people listen LESS. I come from a communications theory background and there, the axiom is that 'nothing never happens'. Therefore I wouldn't ever say (except casually) there is less listening in situation A than in situation B.

In my theory, all listening, like all perception, is selective. What I mean is that we are always responding to SOMETHING.

That's why it doesn't really work (in a conflict situation) to say

'You aren't listening!!!!!!'

I like talking about it this way: What happens is that the angrier people get, the more they listen to the relationship implications of the conversation and the less they listen to content. The more they respond to tone and intention, and the less they respond to substance. The angrier, the more they respond to feelings and the less to fact.

So if you and I are in some kind of conflict and it heats up, escalates, we start being more upset with the WAY we are being talked to, begin to focus on that instead of the issue.

that's why the way out is to focus on interests, not positions, and to separate the personal from the problem.

The trouble is that we get emotionally hijacked. It's hard to ignore the attitude and focus on the logic. Different brain parts are involved.

But I think the LISTENING stays the same except in the highest stages of conflict, in which people intentionally shut out messages from the other.

The Belove model (from Dreikurs) says that conflict escalates through four levels: (1) focus on different needs; (2) focus on power differentials; (3) focus on entitlements to retribution and punishment; (4) focus on cutting off communication.

Further, each higher stage is a comment on the lower stages and the progress back usually involves reworking issues at each level.

>Something very interesting in one of the computer trade magazines this week. Maybe some of you have seen this too. IBM researchers 'are looking to "sonification" as a way to use sound as a computer interface so users can absorb more data without adding to what users often complain is already too much visual clutter on their desktops' (*Info World*). 'The thinking is humans can use their ears to interpret sound in the same way that they use their eyes to recognize and process visuals.' For example a process being monitored (a stock, or input from an instrument) could increase in sound as it increased. An example cited in the article that I am familiar with is how you shift (manual) a car when the sound (and I would say feel) is right. We could learn to do this with other processes – actually, I think we monitor conversations as this sound level and make changes in our conversation in accordance with changes in vocal cues.

What do you think?

Isn't change in vocal sound one of the components we use to establish footing in frames as we interact with others?

14.2.5   ELT textbooks

A wide range of ELT textbooks focusing on listening is available commercially, and titles of interest emerge continuously. Only a few are mentioned here. Most teaching of listening is done in the larger context of language learning or content learning. The key to effective listening instruction is in developing conscious plans and strategies for listening with whatever material is used.

Conversational listening

Harsch, K., Wolfe-Quinteros, K., Robbins, J.G., McNeill, A., Kisslinger, E. (2000) *Impact Listening*. Harlow: Longman (This series of three titles focuses on development of listening strategies [predicting, guessing from context, responding to the content, clarifying], and features authentic conversation extracts. Each unit also features a 'focus on form' section to promote noticing of grammatical features.)

Helgesen, M. and Brown, S. (1995) *Active listening*. Cambridge: Cambridge University Press (A series of three books, *Active listening* incorporates principles of personalised activities and opportunities for students to talk about themselves following the short listening tasks.)

Nunan, D. (1998) *Listen in*. Singapore: Thompson (A series of three books, *Listen in* provides task chains, allowing learners to build upon vocabulary and ideas in previous tasks.

Richards, J. (1996) *Tactics in listening*. Oxford: Oxford University Press (This series of three books utilises short selective listening tasks, based on unit themes – common functions and topics. The tasks are highly visual and usually involve picture selection or choosing among short verbal responses.

Academic listening

Lebauer, R. (1999) *Learning to listen, listening to learn*. New York: Longman (Based on real lectures, this course introduces students to authentic listening and learning in an academic setting.)

Solorzano, H., Frazier, L., Kisslinger, E., Beglar, D., Murray, N. (2001) *Contempory Topics* (vols 1, 2, 3) 2nd edn. New York: Longman (For high-beginning to advanced students, this series provides solid coverage of pre-academic listening skills.)

14.2.6   Books on L1 listening

Borisoff, D. and Purdy, M. (1991) *Listening in everyday life: a personal and professional approach*. Lanham MD: University Press of America (This volume examines the role of listening in both personal and professional settings.)

Bostrom, R. (ed.) (1990) *Listening behaviour: measurement and application*. New York: Guilford Press (Bostrom and the contributors to this volume examine the way that oral messages are perceived, processed, remembered, and understood. Their focus is the Kentucky Comprehensive Listening Test, a test utilising memory models. The test distinguishes among short-term memory, short-term memory with rehearsal, and intermediate-term retention of oral input.)

Brownell, J. (1996) *Listening: attitudes, principles, and skills*. New York: Allyn & Bacon (This work provides a psycholinguistic outline of the listening process, including perception, comprehension, interpretation and memory. It focuses on the importance of listener evaluation of the speaker and listener response, and shows how effective listening builds social relationships and increases student confidence.

Burley-Allen, M. (1995) *Listening: the forgotten skill.* New York: Wiley (This book reviews the need for listening as a communication skill in professional settings, citing data that listening comprises over 40 per cent of most work in management.)

Cairo, J. (1989) *The power of effective listening.* New York: Simon & Schuster. (audio) (Motivational presentation on how to become a more effective listener.)

Glickstein, L. (1998) *Be heard now.* New York: Dell (This book on public speaking and self-expression is based on principles of listening to the audience as a way of guiding one's own presentation. Glickstein uses the provocative principle of 'speak into the available listening' to help speakers allay 'stage fright'. Additional information at *www.speakingcircles.com*)

Nichols, M. (1995) *The lost art of listening: how learning to listen can improve relationships.* New York: Guilford Press (Written by a family therapist, this guide explores the psychological basis of listening.)

Nichols, R. and Stevens, L. (1957) *Are you listening?* New York: McGraw Hill (This is perhaps the first 'how to' guide for applying conscious listening principles to everyday life.)

Sproston, C. and Sutcliffe, G. (1990) *20 training workshops for listening skills.* Philadelphia: Ashgate.

Stone, D., Patton, B. and Heen, S. (1999) *Difficult conversations.* New York: Viking Penguin (Written by members of the Harvard Negotiation Project, this book discusses how to deal with difficult conversations from a 'learning stance'.)

Wolvin, A. and Coakley, C. (1992) *Listening,* 4th edn. Dubuque: IA: Brown (Oriented towards college-age readers, this is a very readable survey of the 'active listening' process.)

Wolvin, A. and Coakley, C. (1992) *Listening* (4th edn). Dubuque IA: Brown (This classic work, frequently updated, provides a broad overview of listening in social and academic environments. It outlines reasons for success and failure with listening, and demonstrates means of practising listening as a skill in a variety of social and school settings.)

14.2.7 Alternative approaches to listening

Campbell, D. (1997) *The Mozart Effect: tapping the power of music to heal the body, strengthen the mind and unlock the creative spirit.* St Louis, MO: MMB Music (A well-documented approach for activating imagination and intelligence via music and sound.)

Fiumara, G.C. (1995) *The other side of language: a philosophy of listening*. London: Routledge (Fiumara synthesises the work of Wittgenstein, Heidegger and Gadamer, among others, to argue for the replacement of 'warring monologues' with 'genuine dialogue', and the type of listening which necessarily accompanies it.)

Gardner, K. (1990) *Sounding the inner landscape*. Rockport, MA: Element Books (Framed as a study of 'music as medicine', this remarkable book provides a very accessible introduction to the broad auditory topics of rhythm, melody and harmonics.)

Ury, W.L. (1991) *Getting past no*. New York: Bantam Books (An approach to successful personal, political, and business negotiations based on principles of active and proactive listening.)

Tomatis Language Centres The purposes of the Tomatis Language Centres, founded by the French physician Albert Tomatis, include retraining the ear by a series of guided exercises for regulating aural–neural metabolism; treatment for neural disorders and auditory-feedback disorders (such as stuttering); learning foreign languages and learning to sing (Alfred A. Tomatis, Sound Listening and Learning Center, Phoenix, AZ 85016).

14.3 Guides for researching listening

As discussed in Section III, research can follow different paradigms: experimental, ethnographic, or 'action'. This volume has forwarded the approach of action research, as it is the style of research with the greatest 'ecological validity' for most educational contexts: it can be accomplished within the time-frames and human resources available. The books listed below, however, cover all three research perspectives.

Andre, R. and Frost, P. (eds) (1997) *Researchers hooked on teaching: noted scholars discuss the synergies of teaching and research*. Thousand Oaks, CA: Sage (A refreshing view on how teaching and researching intersect, this collection of articles covers issues relevant to teaching and research in social sciences; it includes articles such as 'Struggling with balance', 'If it's not teaching and researching, what is it?' and 'Scholarship as a career of learning through researching and teaching'.)

Booth, W., Colomb, G. and Williams, J. (1995) *The craft of research*. Chicago, IL: University of Chicago Press (A rigorous guide for organising research and communicating one's intent, this book focuses on how to connect with the reader and how to focus on topics and questions of significance. There is an excellent section on making and supporting claims.)

Borg, W. and Gall, M. (1989) *Educational research: an introduction*. New York: Longman (A short introductory course, this gives helpful advice on reviewing literature, has careful introduction to sampling and measurement and outlines statistical tools for the analysis of quantitative data.)

Burns, A. (1999) *Collaborative research*. Cambridge: Cambridge University Press (An up-to-date guide to conducting research with colleagues, including methods of collaborative design, data collection and analysis, and reporting.)

Charles, C.M. (1988) *Introduction to educational research*. New York: Longman (A clear, introductory outline of the main types of educational research [historical, descriptive, correlational, causal, experimental]; helpful discussion of steps in beginning research, considerations and cautions in selecting topics, refining topics and stating problems clearly.)

Chaudron, C. (1988) *Second language classroom: research on teaching and learning*. Cambridge: Cambridge University Press (A classic work on the topic, this book reviews classroom research methods and four main traditions in research: psychometric; interaction analysis; discourse analysis; ethnographic analysis; clear discussion of the notions of reliability and validity; thorough review of classroom research concerns.)

Cresswell, J. (1994) *Research design: qualitative and quantitative approaches*. Thousand Oaks, CA: Sage (A helpful guide for stating the purpose of a study and choosing the right paradigm for research, this book compares qualitative and quantitative approaches in a research context and shows how one can adopt combined qualitative and quantitative designs.)

Schacter, J. and Gass, S. (eds) (1996) *Second language classroom research: issues and opportunities*. Mahwah, NJ: Erlbaum (This book explores the idea that classroom research must be interesting and justifiable from linguistic, psychological and SLA perspectives, and also be pedagogically appropriate. It discusses issues of researchers working with teachers, 'classroom fieldwork', ethics and advocacy [attempting to help the subjects].)

Seliger, H. and Shohamy, E. (1989) *Second language research methods*. Oxford: Oxford University Press (A comprehensive sourcebook for educators, this situates second language research in social science framework, focuses on different sources of knowledge, presents plans for research design, qualitative and descriptive research, correlational and multivariate research, case-studies, group studies, tests, surveys, questionnaires, self-reports, observations and quantitative research. It also explains control groups, factorial designs and separate sample designs.)

Wallace, M. (1998) *Action research for language teachers*. Cambridge: Cambridge University Press (This is an inspiring introduction to action research, written from the perspective of the teacher: how will this help me? Provides guidance for field-notes, journals, verbal reports, questionnaires, observation techniques and evaluating teaching materials.)

14.4 Natural language processing research

The following sites have public access sections on speech recognition technologies:

Bell Labs *www.bell-labs.com/projects*

Commercial speech recognition site *www.tiac.net* (This site provides updates on companies dealing with speech recognition, and provides summaries of new products and services.)

Machine Listening Group. The MIT Media Lab *http://sound.media.mit.edu* (This group is conducting research on audio technologies that will be needed for future interactive media applications.)

Macquarie University, Speech Hearing and Language Research Centre *www.shlrc.mq.edu.au* (Outlines current research on speech, psycholinguistics, speech pathology, as well as material for online courses.)

MIT Spoken Language Systems Laboratory *www.sls.lcs.mit.edu*

University of Colorado at Boulder: Speech Recognition Research Centre *www.colorado.edu.slhs/*

Glossary

accent A regional variation in speech patterns.

accentuated input Input that is modified to facilitate comprehension (also called **modified input**).

accommodation Mental act of understanding that involves changing the cognitive structure to make sense of the environment.

acculturation The degree to which a learner adopts the customs and norms of the target language group.

acoustic snapshot Spectral representation of spoken input, usable by a computer for identifying sounds.

acoustic variability The variation in the sound quality of different phonemes due to speaker and situation variability.

activation Increased electrical activity in a part of the brain, caused by neural transmissions to that area.

activation space Conceptual framework of concepts in long-term memory from which schema are activated.

active information Any information currently in short-term memory.

active listening Generic term for a series of behaviours and attitudes by a listener to prepare for listening, focus on the speaker, and provide feedback.

activity frame Part of the speaking context, the activities that the speaker and listener are engaged in.

Affective Filter Hypothesis Hypothesis proposed by Burt and Dulay suggesting that learning experiences that help students lessen their anxiety will generally be beneficial.

affective involvement The perception of status between the speakers in an interaction and the effect of this perception on the interaction.

alertness A state of readiness to deal with incoming input.

allophonic variation A variation of a sound prototype that is still recognisable as an example of the sound.

anchored instruction A type of instruction proposed by Bransford in which a 'problem' text serves as a 'macro-context' for teaching.

appropriate response NLP term for production of a linguistic response that is suitable for the user's purpose.

articulatory causes The movements of the articulatory apparatus (diaphragm, lungs, throat, lips, tongue, nose) that cause speech.

assimilation (cognitive psychology) Mental act of understanding that involves the interpretation of events in terms of existing cognitive structure.

assimilation (phonology) A sound variation of phoneme due to nasalisation, labialisation, palatalisation, glottalisation, voicing, devoicing, or lengthening, which results from two sounds being pronounced in sequence.

attention Cognitive system that exerts conscious control of mental resources for processing input.

auditory cortex The part of the brain that initially processes incoming sound and passes speech for further processing.

auditory nerve Eighth cranial nerve, consisting of multiple fibres, that connects the cochlea, or inner ear, to the auditory cortex of the brain (sometimes called cochlear nerve).

authentic language Language that is targeted at the listener for genuine purposes and needs, not specifically for language-learning purposes.

backchannelling A type of listener response that signals one is following the speaker's discourse.

background sound Any nonlinguistic sound that co-occurs with speech and influences the discourse.

baton signals Hand and head movements made by a speaker to indicate emphasis and prosodic cadence.

behavioural strategy An observable action by the listener to improve comprehension or alter the course of the conversation.

bench-marking Defining criteria against which participant patterns of behaviour will be modelled and assessed.

bottom–up processing A form of language processing that bases inferences on perceptual cues taken from the incoming language boundaries.

categorical perception The acquired ability to discriminate and categorise the possible speech sounds of one's native language.

challenge A response by a listener that disputes the speaker's right to make the preceding move or that disputes an assumption underlying the speaker's assertion.

child-directed speech (CDS) Form of speech characteristically directed to children to help them learn to understand language.

claim An assertion that the speaker wishes the listener to accept.

clarification strategy Asking a question or indicating a query about the meaning of something that was said.

cognitive structure A pattern of physical or mental action that underlies specific acts of intelligence.

cognitive transfer Shifting of a learned skill or competence from one domain (such as first language use) to another domain (such as second language use).

common ground A mutual acknowledgement by speaker and listener of shared assumptions needed to participate in the discourse.

communication pattern An aspect of the systems theory of communication, a communication pattern is the observable, recurring sequence of behaviour, both verbal and non-verbal, of the participants.

communicative language teaching An approach to language teaching that emphasises acquisition of functional behaviours necessary to use the target language for communication.

communicative state An aspect of the systems theory of communication, a communicative state is the result of the actions, verbal and non-verbal, of the participants.

compensatory strategy A way of trying to understand input that has linguistic characteristics unfamiliar to the listener.

compound bilingualism A hypothetical form of bilingual competence in which the person adds a second language mental lexicon after the first language lexicon has been acquired.

comprehensible input Language that a listener is able to understand even though it contains some linguistic elements that are unfamiliar.

Comprehensible Output Hypothesis Proposal by Swain which claims that the effort of composing new utterances for comprehension by a listener is required for language to develop.

conceptual redeployment Learning process by which the regular use of a domain of experience or comprehension comes to be used for the first time in a new domain.

confirmation check Direct or indirect means of confirming than the listener understands the current topic or information in a conversation.

confirmation strategy Asking a question or indicating a query about the extent to which the listener has understood what was just said.

constatives Those aspects of the speaker's speech that have 'truth value'.

content words Noun, verb, adjective, adverb that carry the primary meaning of an utterance.

context of situation The variables of speakers, purposes, setting, relevant objects and prior action that affect interpretation of meaning.

contextualised language routine An event involving language in which the spoken language occurs with other related behaviours.

continuous perception The acquired ability to hear speech as a continuous sequence of discrete sounds.

contrasts A perceived difference in sound quality (frequency, tone or duration) between two sounds.

controlled process Any process that requires attention.

conversational adjustment A means of modifying conversational input, such as using a 'here-and-now orientation', that may make the language easier to understand.

coordinate bilingualism Hypothetical form of bilingual competence in which the person organises his or her mental lexicon in an integrated way.

criterion referencing Type of instruction in which instructional goals are derived from 'end stage' performances that learners are targeting.

deception The deliberate confusion of speech and non-verbal signals to misguide the listener.

declarative knowledge Knowledge about the rules and conventions of a language.

detection Cognitive recognition and registration of a particular stimulus; detection makes a stimulus available for ongoing processing.

dichotic listening Listening through one ear only.

directional changes in perception Five complementary processes (enhancement, attenuation, sharpening, broadening, realignment) by which a child learns the sounds of its first language.

directional gaze Eye movement and focusing used by a speaker to direct the listener to create relevance.

dispreferred response Responding to a discourse move in a way not intended or expected by the speaker.

distal mode An orientation in the nervous system to allow attention to memories, or abstract or imaginary references.

dual coding A presumed type of storage of knowledge in long-term memory that has separate access by L1 and L2 cues.

duration The time that a sound endures, measured in milliseconds (ms).

echoic memory The sensory aspect of short-term memory that holds an after-image of an experience for several seconds.

elaborative simplification A kind of discourse simplification in which the speaker seeks to enrich or expand the input.

elision Omission of individual phonemes that results from simplifying a cluster of sounds for easier pronunciation.

ellipsis The omission of elements in speech that are presumed to be known or recoverable by the listener.

engagement The decision by the listener to interpret the speaker's speech.

equality position The starting point for an interaction in which both speaker and listener acknowledge common ground.

excitation pattern The system of movements of neural cells inside the cochlea that create the perception of a particular sound.

extensive listening Listening to a text for general meaning.

extratextual features Paralinguistic features such as tone of voice and non-linguistic feature such as body language that affect the difficulty of a listening task.

face-saving A politeness strategy that allows the party perceived to have the superior position not to lose that authority or status.

face-threatening Acting to demote the status of an interlocutor.

false start An utterance that is initiated and then abandoned by a speaker.

flouting a maxim Deliberately misusing a conversational maxim in order to create a particular nuance of meaning.

formulaic expression A fixed expression that occurs often in discourse.

frequency Measurement of vibrations, expressed as hertz (Hz). The relationship between the fundamental frequency (f_0) of a sound and its other audible harmonic frequencies (f_1, f_2, f_3,) determines the identity of a sound.

function words Prepositions, article and particles that are attached to content words, and are interpretable only with content words.

given information Information assumed to be known or easily recalled by the listener.

goal-directed communication An aspect of the systems theory of communication, goal-directed communication is the assumption that all behaviour in a group is intentional, that it is related to a desired outcome.

grounds Supporting facts or ideas that lead the listener to accept the speaker's claim.

guide signals Systematic gestures and movements of any part of the body by the speaker, such as extending one's arms or leaning forward, to focus meaning.

hearing Physiological system that allows for reception and conversion of sound waves that surround the listener.

hesitation A pause in conversation while the speaker decides what to say next.

$i + 1$ Term used by Krashen to characterise input that was at 'one level' above the listener's current ability to understand.

illocution What the speaker does by saying something.

immediate mode An orientation in the nervous system to allow attention to present stimulation.

implicational scaling Research technique of ordering instances of an observed behaviour in order to assess the order in which behaviours are acquired or exhibited by a group of subjects.

inactive information Any information known by the listener but not currently active in short-term memory.

indexical expression An expression in the discourse (such as 'over there') that refers to environmental features and can be understood only if 'indexed' to the specific situation.

indirectness A common discourse strategy of stating an intention in a way that avoids a direct confrontation with or a direct response from the listener.

inferencing (making inferences) The process of solving a problem or interpreting a text from incomplete information.

initiating act An intention by a speaker, realised by verbal and non-verbal means, to open up a discourse exchange, usually in order to achieve a specific communicative purpose.

inner ear The part of the ear encased in the skull, consisting of the cochlea and connecting nerves, that converts sound to electrical impulses.

Input Hypothesis Hypothesis proposed by Krashen which claims that humans acquire language in one and only one way, by understanding messages.

intensity (phonology) The loudness of a sound, measured in decibels (dB).

intensive listening Listening to a text closely to monitor the specific language used.

intention (discourse analysis) The speaker's purpose in delivering an utterance.

Interaction Hypothesis Hypothesis proposed by Long and colleagues which claims that the learner triggers language acquisition through interactional adjustments.

interpretive community A structured or unstructured group of people who share common values, belief and experience.

intersubjective rules The means by which the speaker and listener negotiate reciprocal participation in a conversation.

intonation The use of tone variations to affect meaning in speech.

intonation unit Unit of speech, defined by the presence of one primary intonational prominence.

involvement A decision to attend to a stimulus with the purpose of finding or constructing meaning.

irony The act of creating a contrast between literal meaning and intended meaning.

kinesic signals The body movements, including eye and head movements, the speaker makes while speaking.

learning strategy A mental or behavioural device that a learner employs for the purpose of long-term learning.

learning-by-selection The means by which a child narrows the number of possible inputs to its language acquisition system.

lexical segmentation Processes of recognising words in the stream of speech.

lexical segmentation strategy A means of identifying words in the stream of speech.

limited capacity system A cognitive system, such as attention, that has bounded resources, constrained by time or capacity.

linguistic environment The speakers of the target language and their speech to the L2 learners which provides linguistic and interactional input for a learner of a language.

linguistic intentions The particular sounds that the speaker is intending to produce.

listener factors Features internal to the listener (such as readiness and prior knowledge) that affect the difficulty of a listening task.

listenership cues Feedback provided by the listener to signal participation and understanding.

listening Mental process of constructing meaning from spoken input.

listening first methodology An approach to language teaching that provides massive amounts of listening input at the early stages, with no expectations for production.

listening strategy A decision by the listener to make a cognitive or behaviour change in order to understand something that is said.

locution The act of saying something.

long-term memory (LTM) Total store of information, idea and experiences that are accessible to a person.

macro-organiser A speaking device by which the speaker signals to the audience the rhetorical organisation of the upcoming discourse segment.

maxim of manner One of Grice's conversational maxims. (Avoid obscurity of expression. Avoid ambiguity.)

maxim of quality One of Grice's conversational maxims. (Do not say what you believe to be false. Do not say something for which you have inadequate evidence.)

maxim of quantity One of Grice's conversational maxims. (Make your contribution to the conversation as informative as is required.)

maxim of relation One of Grice's conversational maxims. (Be relevant. Say only those things that are relevant to the situation.)

mental representation Cognitive formulation of the current discourse in relation to what the listener already knows.

metrical segmentation strategy Means of identifying words in the stream of speech that utilises metrical principles (such as 'every strong syllable is likely to be the onset of a new content word').

mind-mapping Technique of outlining a person's understanding of a topic through linked words and phrases.

misunderstanding A significant mismatch between the speaker's and listener's mental representation of a discourse.

modified input Input that is modified to facilitate comprehension (also called **accentuated input**).

monitoring The conscious observation of communication and cognitive processes.

naïve listening Pedagogic term referring to a learner listening without a set task or purpose.

natural approach An approach to language teaching that emphasises providing the learner with input necessary for learning.

natural language processing (NLP) Field of study that explores computer processing of and understanding of language produced by humans.

negotiation for meaning The interactional work that speaker and listener undertake to achieve mutual understanding.

neural net Model of computer language processing that performs simultaneous calculations at phonetic, lexical and syntactic layers of input.

new information Information assumed to be unknown or not easily recalled by the listener.

non-understanding Inability of the listener to activate any schema to understand the discourse.

note-taking Writing down key words, ideas and notations while listening.

on-line task Teaching and research technique of asking a person to perform a task while listening.

oral approach Approach to language teaching that emphasises extensive use of speaking and listening only.

orientation Alignment of attention to particular stimuli in the environment.

parsing Analysing speech into semantic groups of words and relationships between the groups.

participant frame Part of the speaking context, the roles that the speaker and listener assume.

pause unit Unit of speech, defined by the presence of a pause at both the beginning and end of the unit.

paused task A type of pedagogic task in which a prepared input is paused at a particular juncture for student activity or feedback.

perceived social distance The perception by the listener of his or her role in an interaction and rights to seek understanding.

perceptual constancy The ability to tolerate variability in speaker or speed and still identify sounds accurately.

performatives Those aspects of the speaker's speech that are intended to have an effect on the listener.

perlocution What happens to the listener as a result of a speaker saying something.

phonological loop A feature of short-term memory that allows for a sensory impression to be 'replayed' for a short period of time, probably 2–3 seconds in duration.

phonological tagging The means of accessing knowledge in a bilingual's long-term memory.

phonotactic knowledge Knowledge of the phonological constraints of a language.

preferred response Responding to a discourse move in a way intended and expected by the speaker.

pre-listening Pedagogic phase of a listening activity that occurs prior to learners listening to a set input.

procedural knowledge Demonstrable knowledge of how to employ a language in specific contexts of use.

prominence The perceived location of a stress peak in an utterance.

propositional model Mental representation of the relationship between the content words in an utterance.

prototype Mental model of a sound that serves as a reference for identifying variations.

psychoacoustic effects Impressions caused by the frequency, timbre and duration of sound waves that reach the ear.

psychoacoustic elements The four elements, frequency, tone, duration, and intensity that determine the characteristics of a sound.

psychological strategy An unobservable decision by the listener on how to process a given input.

psychological distance The perceived difficulty by a learner of coming to be a member of a target group or speaker of the target language.

reasoning Process of interpreting a text on logical grounds.

recast Form of feedback to the speaker in which the original message is recast, often with linguistic corrections.

receiver apprehension Anxiety experienced by the listener that interferes with listening performance.

reduction Centring of vowels, weakening of consonants that results from a phoneme being in an unstressed syllable.

Reform Movement Trend in the early 1900s to base second language learning on theories of child language acquisition.

representation A mental model, held in short-term memory and used for interpretation of discourse.

resources-based learning An approach to curriculum design that emphasises the use of learning resources (such as multimedia and community resources).

response options Set of items in a test from which the test taker must select the appropriate response.

restrictive simplification A kind of discourse simplification in which the speaker attempts to control or highlight features of phonology, lexis, syntax and discourse structures.

retrospection Research technique of asking a subject what he or she has just been thinking.

route Sequence or path of experiences through which someone comes to acquire a language.

sarcasm Act of creating implications in a speaking turn that are intended to deride the listener.

schema Mental representation of a recurring pattern of knowledge or related concepts. (plural: **schemas** or **schemata**)

segmentation Way of identifying the location of word boundaries.

selective attention Commitment of attention to a particular stream of information or connected train of thought.

semantic analysis **NLP** term for computer modelling of the intended meaning of a speaker.

semantic contingency A characteristic of child-directed speech that allows the child to understand language based on situational and personal cues.

semantic differential scale A rating scale that requires subjects to evaluate an input in terms of opposing criteria (such as easy–difficult).

semantic relation Means by which two or more words or groups of words are related logically.

short-term memory (STM) The activated neural connections in long-term memory that are being used for comprehension.

single coding A presumed type of storage of knowledge in long-term memory that may be accessed by either L1 or L2 cues.

situational model Type of learning that integrates prior knowledge with information learned from a text.

social accommodation Movement of an interlocutor towards the discourse and behaviour standards of another interlocutor.

social distance Perceived difficulty by a learner of understanding and adapting to the norms of a target group.

speech recognition NLP term for decoding of speech into the exact words produced by a speaker.

spiral learning Type of instruction proposed by Bruner that is designed and sequenced to facilitate noticing and inferencing.

Spoken Language System (SLS) Generic name of a computer system that processes spoken language.

statistical recogniser Part of a computer's speech recognition system that calculates probabilities of speech strings in the spoken input.

stem The given part of the test item that the test taker must understand before providing a response.

stress A change in intensity (length and loudness) to signal meaning in speech.

structural relation Means by which two or more words are related in the grammar.

superior position Apparent claim by one party in an interaction to possess needed information or authority or higher social status.

syntonic listening Style of listening in which the listener adjusts to the communicative style of the speaker.

teaching principle Axiom of instruction that is generalisable across various learner needs, goals, constraints and learning styles.

template matching recogniser Part of a computer's speech recognition system that matches acoustic snapshots with pre-existing sound templates.

text factors Aspects of the text itself (such as word choice and speed of delivery) that affect the difficulty of a listening task.

textbase model Type of learning from a text that utilises the text information only and is not integrated into long-term memory.

think-aloud protocol Research technique of allowing a subject to 'think aloud' while performing a task.

tone Pattern of sound waves created by a vibration; the purity or complexity of this pattern determines the clarity of a sound.

top–down processing Form of language processing that bases inferences on expectations and predictable generalisations cued by the incoming language.

topic shift Change in the subject matter of the discourse.

trochaically timed language A language, such as English, whose prosody is marked primarily by metrical feet consisting of one long or stressed syllable followed by one short or unstressed syllable.

Uncertainty Management Theory A theory of communication that predicts the amount of openness the speaker and listener will exhibit towards each other.

uncertainty reduction In **Uncertainty Management Theory** a strategy of the listener to reduce uncertainty in the conversation through self-disclosure or asking questions.

unstated topic A topic in the discourse that is understood by the speaker and listener although it is not explicitly stated.

uptaking Acknowledging the validity and appropriateness of a discourse move by a speaker.

variation The problem of recognising words that are uttered with deviations from the ideal form.

violating a maxim (discourse analysis) Deliberately violating a conversational maxim in order to deceive a listener or to save face.

washback effect The tendency in an educational setting for teaching goals to mirror outside testing goals.

working memory Another term for short-term memory, that is, the activated neural connections in long-term memory that are being used for comprehension.

References

Allwright, R. and Bailey, K. (1991) *Focus on the language classroom: an introduction to classroom research for language teachers*. Cambridge: Cambridge University Press.

Anderson, R. (1996) The primacy aspect of first and second language acquistion: the pidgin–creole connection. In W. Ritchie and T. Bhatia (eds), *Handbook of second language acquisition*. San Diego, CA: Academic Press.

Anderson, R. and Shirai, Y. (1994) Discourse motivations for some cognitive acquisition principles. *Studies in second language acquisition*, 16: 133–56.

Andre, R. and Frost, P. (eds) (1997) *Researchers hooked on teaching*. London: Sage.

Aniero, S. (1990) The influence of receiver apprehension among Puerto Rican college students (PhD thesis, New York University). *Dissertation Abstracts International*, 50: 2300A.

Aslin, R. (1981) Experimental differences and sensitive periods in perceptual development: A unified model. In R. Aslin, J. Alberts and M. Petersen (eds), *Development of perception: psychobiological perspectives*. New York: Academic Press.

Aslin, R., Jusczyk, P. and Pisoni, D. (1998) Speech and auditory processing during infancy: constraints on and precursors to language. In R. Seigler (ed.), *Mussen's handbook of child psychology*. New York: Wiley.

Auer, P. (1992) Introduction: John Gumperz's approach to contextualization. In P. Auer and A. DiLuzio (eds), *The contextualization of language*. Amsterdam: John Benjamins.

Austin, J.H. (1962) *How to do things with words*. Oxford: Oxford University Press.

Austin, J.H. (1998) *Zen and the brain*. Cambridge, MA: MIT Press.

Ausubel, D. (1978) In defense of advance organizers: a reply to the critics. *Review of Educational Research*, 48: 251–7.

Baddeley, A. (1986) *Working memory*. Oxford: Oxford University Press.

Baltova, I. (1998) Vocabulary teaching with subtitled video (handout). American Association of Applied Linguistics, Vancouver.

Bartlett, C. (1932) *Remembering*. Cambridge: Cambridge University Press.

Bates, E. and MacWhinney, B. (1989) Functionalism and the competition model. In E. Bates and B. MacWhinney (eds), *The crosslinguistic study of sentence processing*. New York: Cambridge University Press.

285

Beach, C. (1991) The interpretation of prosodic patterns at points of syntactic structure ambiguity: evidence for cue trading relations. *Journal of Memory and Language*, 30: 644–63.

Beach, W. (2000) Inviting collaboration in stories. *Language in Society*, 29: 379–407.

Beebe, L. (1985) Input: choosing the right stuff. In S. Gass and C. Madden (eds), *Input in second language acquisition*. New York: Newbury House.

Benson, M. (1989) The academic listening task: a case study. *TESOL Quarterly*, 23(3): 421–45.

Benson, P. and Voller, P. (eds) (1996) *Autonomy and independence in language learning*. Harlow: Longman.

Berlo, D. (1960) *The process of communication*. New York: Holt.

Berwick, R. and Ross, S. (1996) Cross-cultural pragmatics in oral proficiency interview strategies. In M. Milanovic and N. Saville (eds), *Performance testing, cognition and assessment*. Cambridge: Cambridge University Press.

Bhatia, V. (1983) Simplification vs easification: the case of legal texts. *Applied Linguistics*, 4: 42–54.

Bialystock, E. (1990) *Communication strategies: a psycholinguistic analysis of second language use*. Oxford: Basil Blackwell.

Birdwhistell, R. (1970) *Kinesics and context: essays in body motion communication*. Philadelphia, PA: University of Pennsylvania Press.

Bisanz, G., LaPorte, R., Vesonder, G. and Voss, J. (1981) Contextual prerequisites for understanding: some investigations of comprehension and recall. *Journal of Verbal Learning and Verbal Behaviour*, 17: 3337–57.

Bloomfield, L. (1942) *Outline guide for the practical study of foreign languages*. Baltimore, MD: Linguistic Society of America.

Blum-Kulka, J. House, and G. Kasper (eds) (1989) The CCSARP coding manual (Appendix). In *Cross-cultural pragmatics: requests and apologies*. Norwood, NJ: Ablex.

Bobrow, D. and Winograd, T. (1977) An overview of KRL: a knowledge-representation system. *Cognitive Science*, 1: 3–46.

Booth, W., Colomb, G. and Williams, J. (1995) *The craft of research*. Chicago, IL: University of Chicago Press.

Borg, W. and Gall, M. (1989) *Educational research*. Harlow: Longman.

Bostrom, R. (1990) *Listening behaviour: measurement and application*. New York: Guilford Press.

Bostrom, R. and Waldhart, E. (1988) Memory models and the measurement of listening. *Communication Education*, 37: 1–13.

Braidi, S. (1998) *The acquisition of second language syntax*. London: Arnold.

Bransford, J. (1990) Anchored instruction: why we need it and how technology can help. In D. Nix and R. Sprio (eds), Cognition, education and multimedia. Hillsdale, NJ: Erlbaum.

Bransford, J. and Stein, B. (1993) *The ideal problem-solver* (2nd edn). New York: Freeman.

Brazil, D. (1985) The communicative value of intonation (Discourse Analysis monographs, No. 8). Birmingham: University of Birmingham.

Brazil, D. (1995) *A grammar of speech*. Oxford: Oxford University Press.

Bremer, K., Roberts, C., Vasseur, M., Simonot, M., Broeder, P. (1996) *Achieving understanding: discourse in intercultural encounters*. Harlow: Longman.

Brindley, G. (1998) Assessing listening abilities. In W. Grabe (ed.), 'Foundations of second language teaching', *Annual Review of Applied Linguistics*, 18: 178–98.

Brinton, D., Snow, M. and Wesche, M. (1989) *Content-based second language instruction*. New York: Newbury.

Brown, George (1978) *Lecturing and explaining*. London: Methuen.

Brown, George and Bakhtar, M. (1983) Styles of lecturing (research report). Loughborough University.

Brown, Gillian (1977) *Listening to spoken English*. Harlow: Longman.

Brown, Gillian (1994) Dimensions of difficulty in listening comprehension. In D. Mendelsohn and J. Rubin (eds), *A guide for the teaching of second language listening*. San Diego: Dominie Press.

Brown, Gillian (1995) *Speakers, listeners and communication: explorations in discourse analysis*. Cambridge: Cambridge University Press.

Brown, Gillian, Anderson, A., Shillcoch, R. and Yule, G. (1984) *Teaching talk*. Cambridge: Cambridge University Press.

Brown, J. and Palmer, A. (1987) *The listening approach: methods and materials for applying Krashen's input hypothesis*. New York: Longman.

Brownell, J. (1996) *Listening: attitudes, principles and skills*. New York: Allyn & Bacon.

Bruner, J. (1983) *Child's talk: learning to use language*. New York: Norton.

Bruner, J. (1986) *Actual minds, possible worlds*. Cambridge, MA: Harvard University Press.

Bruner, J. (1990) *Acts of meaning*. Cambridge, MA: Harvard University Press.

Buck, G. (1992) Listening comprehension: construct validity and trait characteristics. *Language Learning*, 42(3): 313–57.

Buck, G. (2000) *Assessing listening*. Cambridge: Cambridge University Press.

Buck, G., Tatsuoka, K., Kostin, I. and Phelps, M. (1997) The sub-skills of listening: Rule-space analysis of a multiple-choice test of second language listening comprehension. In A. Huhta, V. Kohonen, L. Kurki-Sonio and S. Luoma (eds), *Current developments and alternatives in language assessment. Proceedings of LTRC*, 96: 599–624.

Burgoon, J. and White, C. (1997) Researching non-verbal message production: a view from interaction-adaptation theory. In J. Greene (ed.), *Message production: advances in communication theory*. Mahwah, NJ: Erlbaum.

Burley-Allen, M. (1995) *Listening: the forgotten skill*. New York: Wiley.

Burns, A. (1999) *Collaborative research*. Cambridge: Cambridge University Press

Cairo, J. (1989) *The power of effective listening*. New York: Simon & Schuster.

Campbell, D. (1997) *The Mozart Effect: tapping the power of music to heal the body, strengthen the mind, and unlock the creative spirit*. St Louis, MO: MMB Music.

Canary, D. and Spitzberg, B. (1987) Appropriateness and effectiveness perceptions of conflict strategies. *Human Communication Research*, 14: 93–118.

Canary, D. and Spitzberg, B. (1990) Attribution biases and associations between conflict strategies and competence outcomes. *Communication Monographs*, 15: 139–51.

Candlin, C. (1987) Discourse patterning. In English for cross-cultural communication, in Larry Smith's *Discourse across culture*. New York: Prentice Hall.

Candlin, C. and Mercer, N. (2000) English language teaching in its social context. *Course materials for LING 937*. Open University and Macquarie University.

Carpenter, P., Miyake, A. and Just, M. (1994) Working memory constraints in comprehension: Evidence from individual differences, aphasia and aging. In *Handbook of psycholinguistics*. New York: Academic Press.

Carr, T. and Curran, T. (1994) Cognitive processes in learning about structure: applications to syntax in second language acquisition. *Studies in Second Language Acquisition*, 16: 221–35.

Carrier, K. (1999) The social environment of second language listening: does status play a role in comprehension? *Modern Language Journal*, 83: 65–79.

Carter, R. (1998) *Mapping the mind*. Berkeley, CA: University of California Press.

Carter, R. and McCarthy, M. (1997) *Exploring spoken English*. Cambridge: Cambridge University Press.

Chafe, W. (1979) The flow of thought and the flow of language. In T. Givon (ed.), *Discourse and syntax*. New York: Academic Press.

Chafe, W. (1992) Intonation units and prominences in natural English discourse. In *Proceedings of the IRCS workshop on porsoday in natural speech*. Philadelphia, PEN: University of Pennsylvania Press.

Chafe, W. (1994) *Discourse, consciousness, and time: the flow and displacement of consciousness in speaking and writing*. Chicago, IL: University of Chicago Press.

Chamot, A., Barnhardt, S., Beard, El-Dinary, P. and Robbins, J. (1999) *The learning strategy Handbook*. White Plains, NY: Longman.

Changeues, J., Heidmann, T. and Patte. P. (1984) Learning by selection. In P. Marler and H. Terrace (eds), *The biology of learning*. Berlin: Springer-Verlag.

Charles, C. (1989) *Introduction to educational research*. New York: Longman.

Chaudron, C. (1988) *Second language classrooms*. Cambridge: Cambridge University Press.

Chaudron, C. (1995) Academic listening. In D. Mendelsohn and J. Rubin (eds), *A guide for the teaching of second language listening*. San Diego, CA: Dominie Press.

Chaudron, C., Loschky, L. and Cook, J. (1994) Second language listening comprehension. In J. Flowerdew (ed.), *Academic listening: research perspectives*. Cambridge: Cambridge University Press.

Chen, H. (1999) Guidelines for evaluating ESL listening resources on the WWW. In B. Morrison, D. Cruikshank, D. Gardner, J. James and K. Keobke (eds), *Information technology and multimedia in English Language Teaching*.

Chiang, C. and Dunkel, P. (1992) The effect of speech modification, prior knowledge, and listening proficiency on EFL learning. *TESOL Quarterly*, 26: 345–74.

Churchland, P. (1999) Learning and conceptual change: the view from the neurons. In A. Clark and P. Millican, *Connectionism, concepts and folk psychology*. Oxford: Oxford University Press.

Clark, A. (1993) *Associative engines: connectionism, concepts, and representational changes*. Cambridge, MA: MIT Press.

Clark, A. and Millican, P. (1999) *Connectionism, concepts and folk psychology*. Oxford: Oxford University Press.

Clark, J.M. and Paivio, A. (1991) Dual coding theory and education. *Educational Psychology Review*, 3(3): 149–70.

Cohen, A. (1994) *Assessing language ability in the classroom*. Boston, NJ: Heinle & Heinle.

Cohen, A. (1998) *Strategies in learning and using a second language*. Harlow: Longman.

Cole, R. and Jakimik, J. (1978) Perceptibility of phonetic features in fluent speech. *Journal of the Acoustical Society of America*, 64: 44–56.

Combs, A.W. (1982) Affective education or none at all. *Educational Leadership*, 39: 494–7.

Cook, V. (1988) *Chomsky's universal grammar*. Oxford: Basil Blackwell.

Corder, S. (1967) The significance of learners' errors. *International Review of Applied Linguistics*, 5: 161–69.

Cowan, N. (1993) Activation, attention and short-term memory. *Memory and Cognition*, 21(2): 162–7.

Cowan, N. (1997) *Attention and memory: an integrated framework*. New York: Oxford University Press.

Cresswell, J. (1994) *Research design: qualitative and quantitative approaches*. Thousand Oaks, CA: Sage.

Crystal, D. (ed.) (1995) *The Cambridge encyclopedia of the English language*. Cambridge: Cambridge University Press.

Cutler, A. (1997) The comparative perspective on spoken language processing. *Speech Communication*, 21: 3–15.

Cutler, A. and Butterfield, S. (1992) Rhythmic cues to speech segmentation: evidence from juncture misperception. *Journal of Memory and Language*, 31: 218–36.

Day, R. and Yamanaka, J. (1998) *Impact issues*. Hong Kong: Longman.

DeCarrico, J. and Nattinger, J. (1988) Lexical phrases for the comprehension of academic lectures. *English for Specific Purposes*, 7: 91–102.

Denes, P. and Pinson, E. (1993) *The speech chain: the physics and biology of spoken language*, (2nd edn). New York: Freeman.

Dornyei, Z. (2001) *Applied linguistics in action: teaching and researching motivation*. Harlow: Longman.

Dowling, R. and Flint, L. (1990) The argumentativeness scale: problems and promises. *Communication Studies*, 41: 183–98.

Dulay, J. and Burt, M. (1975) Creative construction in second language learning and teaching. In M. Burt and H. Dulay (eds), *New directions in second language learning, teaching, and bilingual education*. Washington DC: TESOL.

Dulay, J., Burt, M. and Krashen, S., (1982) *Language two*. Oxford: Oxford University Press.

Dunkel, P. (1988) The content of L1 and L2 students' lecture notes and its relation to test performance, *TESOL Quarterly*, 22: 259–82.

Dunn, W. and Lantolf, J. (1998) Vygotsky's Zone of proximal development and Krashen's i+1: immeasurable constructs, inconmeasurable theories. *Language Learning*, 48: 411–42.

Duranti, A. and Goodwin, C. (eds) (1992) *Rethinking context: language as an interactive phenomenon*. Cambridge: Cambridge University Press.

Elgin, S. (1985) *The last word on the gentle art of verbal self-defense*. Englewood Cliffs, NJ: Prentice Hall.

Elgin, S. (1989) *Success with the gentle art of verbal self-defense*. Englewood Cliffs, NJ: Prentice Hall.

Elgin, S. (1993) *Genderspeak: men, women, and the gentle art of verbal self-defense*. New York: Wiley.

Ellis, R. (1994) *The study of second language acquisition*. Oxford: Oxford University Press.

Ellis, R. (1999) Grammar through listening. Presentation at TESOL Conference. New York, March, 1999.

Ellis, R. and Gaies, S. (1999) *Impact grammar*. Hong Kong: Longman.

Ellis, R., Loewen, S. and Basturkmen, H. (1999) Focusing on form in the classroom. Occasional Paper 13, Institute of Language Teaching and Learning, University of Auckland.

Erman, L.D., Hayes-Roth, F., Less, V. and Reddy, D. (1980) The HEARSAY-II speech understanding system: integrating knowledge to resolve uncertainty. *Computing Surveys*, 12(2): 213–53.

Ervin, S. and Osgood, C. (1954) Second language learning and bilingualism. *Journal of Abnormal and Social Psychology*, 49: 139–46.

Esch, E. (1992) Native/non-native interaction (PhD thesis, Open University, Milton Keynes).

Eykyn, L.G. (1993) The effects of listening guides on the comprehension of authentic texts by novice learners of French as a second language (PhD thesis, University of South Carolina). *Dissertation Abstracts International*, 53: 3863A.

Faerch, K. (1984) Strategies in production and reception: some empirical evidence. In A. Davies, C. Criper and A. Howatt (eds), *Interlanguage*. Edinburgh: Edinburgh University Press.

Fahmy, J. and Bilton, L. (1989) *Using authentic texts: a study skills module*. Singapore: Regional English Language Centre.

Ferreira, F. and Anes, M. (1994). Why study spoken language? *Handbook of psycholinguistics*. New York: Academic Press.

Fillmore, C. (1968) The case for case. In E. Bach and T. Harms (eds), *Universals of linguistic theory*. New York: Holt.

Fish, S. (1994) *There's no such thing as free speech and it's a good thing, too*. New York: Oxford University Press.

Fishman, P. (1983) Interaction: the work women do. In B. Thorne, C. Kramare and N. Henley (eds), *Language, gender, and society*. Boston: Newbury House.

Flowerdew, J. (1992) Definitions in science lectures. *Applied Linguistics*, 13: 202–21.

Flowerdew, J. (1994a) Research related to second language lecture comprehension – an overview. In J. Flowerdew (ed.), *Academic listening: research perspectives*. Cambridge: Cambridge University Press.

Flowerdew, J. (1994b) *Academic listening: research perspectives*. Cambridge: Cambridge University Press.

Fodor, J., Bever, T. and Garrett, M. (1975) The psychological reality of semantic representations. *Linguistic Inquiry*, 6: 515–31.

Freedle, R. and Kostin, I. (1996) The prediction of TOEFL listening comprehension item difficulty for minitalk passages: implications for construct validity. TOEFL Research Report No. RR-96-20. Princeton, NJ: ETS.

Freeman, D. and Johnson, K.E. (1998) Reconceptualizing the knowledge base of language teacher education. *TESOL Quarterly*, 32: 397–417.

Frost, A. (1997) *Researchers hooked on teaching: noted scholars discuss the synergies of teaching and research*. Thousand Oaks, CA: Sage.

Fujiwara, B. (1989) Helping students become self-directed listening learners. MA thesis, School for International Training. Brattleboro, VT.

Gagne, R., Briggs, L. and Wager, W. (1992) *Principles of instructional design* (4th edn). Fort Worth, TX: HBJ College Publishers.

Gagne, R. and Driscoll, M. (1988) *Essentials of learning for instruction* (2nd edn). Englewood Cliffs, NJ: Prentice Hall.

Gallaway, C. and Richards, B. (eds) (1994) *Input and interaction in language acquisition*. Cambridge: Cambridge University Press.

Gamble, T. and Gamble, M. (1998) *Contacts: communicating interpersonally*. Boston: Allyn & Bacon.

Gardner, D. and Miller, L. (eds) (1999) *Establishing self-access: from theory to practice.* Cambridge: Cambridge University Press.

Gardner, H. (1993) *Multiple intelligences: the theory in practice.* NY: Basic Books.

Gardner, K. (1990) *Sounding the inner landscape.* Rockport, MA: Element Books.

Gardner, R. and Macintyre, P. (1992) A student's contribution to second language learning. Part II: Affective variables. *Language Teaching,* 26: 1–11.

Garis, E. (1997) Movies in the language classroom: dealing with problematic content. *TESOL Quarterly,* 6: 20–23.

Garner, A. (1997) *Conversationally speaking* (3rd edn). Los Angeles, CA: Lowell House.

Gass, S. (1996) Second language acquisition and second language theory: the role of language transfer. In W. Ritchine and T. Bhatia (eds), *Handbook of second language acquisition.* San Diego: Academic Press

Gernsbacher, M. and Shroyer, S. (1989) The cataphoric use of the indefinite 'this' in spoken narratives. *Memory and Cognition,* 17: 536–40.

Giles, H. (1979) Accommodation theory: optimal levels of convergence. In H. Giles and R. St Clair (eds), *Language and social psychology.* Oxford: Basil Blackwell.

Genesse, F. (1987) *Learning through two languages.* New York: Newbury House.

Glickstein, L. (1998) *Be heard now.* New York: Dell.

Goetz, E., Anderson, R. and Schallert, D. (1981) The representation of sentences in memory. *Journal of Verbal Learning and Verbal Behaviour,* 20: 369–81.

Goffman, E. (1974) *Frame analysis.* New York: Harper & Row.

Goh, C. (1997) Metacognitive awareness and second language listeners. *ELT Journal,* 51(4): 361–9.

Golding, J., Graesser, A. and Hauselt, J. (1996) The process of answering direction-giving questions when someone is lost on a university campus: the role of pragmatics. *Applied Cognitive Psychology,* 10: 23–39.

Goodman, S. and Graddol, D. (1996) *Redesigning English: new texts, new identities.* London: Routledge.

Goodwin, C and Duranti, A. (1992) Rethinking context: an introduction. In A. Duranti and C. Goodwin (eds), *Rethinking context: language as an interactive phenomenon.* Cambridge: Cambridge University Press.

Gregg, K. (1984) Krashen's monitor and Occam's razor. *Applied Linguistics,* 5: 79–100.

Grice, P. (1969) Utterer's meaning and intentions. *Philosophical Review,* 78: 147–77.

Griffiths, R. (1992) Speech rate and listening comprehension: further evidence of the relationship. *TESOL Quarterly,* 26: 385–90.

Grosjean, F. (1982) *Life with two languages: an introduction to bilingualism.* Cambridge, MA: Harvard University Press.

Gudykunst, W. (1995) The uncertainty reduction and anxiety–uncertainty reduction theories of Berger, Gudykunst, and associates. In D. Cushman and Kovacic (eds), *Watershed research traditional in human communication theory.* New York: NYU Press.

Gumperz, J. (1983) *Discourse strategies.* Cambridge: Cambridge University Press.

Gumperz, J. (1990) The conversational analysis of interethnic communication. In R. Scarcella, E. Anderson and S. Krashen (eds), *Developing communicative competence in a second language.* New York: Heinle & Heinle.

Gunderson, H. (1994) *Interview surveys for ESL students.* Santa Barbara, CA: University of California.

Hale, G. and Courtney, R. (1991) Note-taking and listening comprehension on the test of English as a foreign language, ETS report, No. 34. *www.ets.org*

Hall, E. (1980) Giving away psychology in the 80s: George Miller interview. *Psychology Today*, 14, 82.

Halliday, M. and Hasan, R. (1983) *Cohesion in English*. Harlow: Longman.

Handel, S. (1993) *Listening: an introduction to the perception of auditory events*. Cambridge, MA: MIT Press.

Harrigan, J. (1985) Listeners' body movements and speaking turns. *Communication Research*, 12: 233–50.

Harsch, K., Wolfe-Quintero, K., Robbins, J., McNeill, A. and Kisslinger, E. (2000) *Impact Listening 1, 2, 3*. Hong Kong: Longman.

Hatch, E. (1992) *Discourse and language education*. Cambridge: Cambridge University Press.

Helgesen, M. and Brown, S. (1995) *Active listening*. Cambridge: Cambridge University Press.

Henning, G. (1991) A study of the effects of variation of short-term memory load, reading response length, and processing hierarchy on TOEFL. Listening Comprehension Item Performance, ETS report (9).

Hernandez, A., Bates, E. and Avila, L. (1994) On-line sentence interpretation in Spanish–English bilinguals: what does it mean to be in between? *Applied Psycholinguistics*, 15: 417–46.

Hinds, J. (1985) Misinterpretations and common knowledge in Japanese. *Journal of Pragmatics*, 9: 7–19.

Holobow, N., Lambert, W. and Sayegh, L. (1984) Pairing script and dialogue: combinations that show promise for second or foreign language learning. *Language Learning*, 34: 59–76.

Hymes, D. (1964) Toward ethnographies of communicative events. In P. Giglioli (ed.), *Language and social context*. Harmondsworth: Penguin.

Hymes, D. (1972) *Towards communicative competence*. Philadelphia, PA: University of Pennsylvania Press.

International Communication Association *www.icahdg.com*

James, M. (1985) *Classification algorithms*. London: Collins.

James, W. (1890) *The principles of psychology*. New York: Holt. (Reprinted 1950 by Dover Publications, New York.)

Jamieson, J., Jones, S., Kirsch, I., Mosenthal, P. and Taylor, C. (2000) TOEFL 2000 framework: a working paper (TOEFL Monograph Series Report No. 16). Princeton, NJ: ETS.

Johnson-Laird, P. (1984) *Mental models*. Cambridge: Cambridge University Press.

Jusczyk, P. (1997) *The discovery of spoken language*. Cambridge, MA: MIT Press.

Kasper, G. (1984) Pragmatic comprehension in learner–native speaker discourse. *Language Learning*, 34: 1–20.

Kasper, G. and Kellerman, E. (eds) (1997) *Communication strategies: Psycholinguistic and sociolinguistic perspectives*, Harlow: Longman.

Kearsly, G. (2001) Media and learning. *hagar.up.ac.za/catts/learner/2001*

Kemmis, S. and McTaggart., R. (1988) *The action research planner*. Victoria: Deakin University. ECT 432/732 Action Research in Curriculum.

Key, M. (1975) *Paralanguage and kinesics*. Metuchen, NJ: Scarecrow Press.

Kim, H.-Y. (1995) Intake from the speech stream: speech elements that L2 learners attend to. In R. Schmidt (ed.), *Attention and awareness in foreign language learning*. Honolulu: University of Hawaii Press.

Kintsch, W. (1998) *Comprehension*. Cambridge: Cambridge University Press.

Kim, Hae-Young. (1995) Intake from the speech stream: speech elements that learners attend to. In R. Schmidt (ed.), *Attention and awareness in foreign language learning.* Honolulu: University of Hawaii Press.

Kothoff, H. and Wodak, R. (eds) (1998) *Communicating gender in context.* (Pragmatics and Beyond, 42.) Amsterdam: Johns Benjamin.

Kramsch, C. (1997) Rhetorical models of understanding. In T. Miller (ed.), *Functional approaches to written text: classroom applications.* Washington, NY: USIA.

Krashen, S. (1982) *Principles and practice in second language acquisition.* New York: Pergamon Press.

Krashen, S. (1985) *The input hypothesis: issues and implications.* Harlow: Longman.

Kuhl, P. (1991) Human adults and human infants show a 'perceptual magnet effect' for the prototypes of speech categories, monkeys do not. *Perception and psychophysics,* 50: 93–7.

Kuhl, P. and Iverson, P. (1995) Linguistic experience and the perceptual magnet effect. In W. Strange (ed.), *Speech perception and linguistic experience.* Timonium, MD: York Press.

Kuiken, F. and Vedder, I. (2001) Focus on form and the role of interaction in promoting language learning. (Handout) St Louis, American Association of Applied Linguistics.

Kumaravadivelu, B. (1994) The postmethod condition. *TESOL Quarterly,* 28: 27–48.

Lakoff, R. (2000) *The language war.* Berkeley, CA: University of California Press.

Lambert, W., Havelka, J. and Crosby, C. (1958) The influence of language acquisition contexts or bilingualism. *Journal of Abnormal and Social Psychology,* 56: 239–44.

Lambert, W. and Tucker, G. (1972) *Bilingual education of children: the St Lambert experiment.* New York: Newbury House.

Lantolf, J. (ed.) (2000) *Sociocultural theory and second language learning.* Oxford: Oxford University Press.

Lebauer R. (1999) *Learn to listen: listen to learn.* New York: Prentice Hall.

Lehnert, W., Dyer, M., Johnson, P. and Yang, C. (1983) BORIS: An experiment in in-depth understanding of narratives. *Artificial Intelligence,* 20: 15–62.

Lenneberg, E. (1967) *Biological foundations of language.* New York: Wiley.

Levelt, W. (1989) *Speaking: from intention to articulation.* Cambridge, MA: MIT Press.

Levinson, S. (1983) *Pragmatics.* Cambridge: Cambridge University Press.

Lewis, D. (1972) General semantics. In D. Davidson and G. Harman, *Semantics of natural language.* Dordrecht: Reidel.

Lieven, E. (1994) Crosslinguistic and crosscultural aspects of language addressed to children. In C. Gallway and B. Richards (eds), *Input and interaction in language acquisition.* Cambridge: Cambridge University Press.

Linde, C. and Labov, W. (1975) Spatial networks as a site for study of language and thought. *Language,* 51: 924–39.

Liu, H., Bates, E. and Li, P. (1992) Sentence interpretation in bilingual speakers of English and Chinese. *Applied Psycholinguistics,* 133: 451–84.

Long, D. (1990) What you don't know can't help you: an exploratory study of background knowledge and second language listening comprehension. *Studies in Second Language Listening,* 12: 65–80.

Long, M. (1985) A role for instruction in second language learning. In N. Hyltemstam and M. Pienemann (eds), *Modeling and assessing second language acquisition.* London: Multilingual Matters.

Long, M. (1988) Instructed interlanguage development. In L. Beebe (ed.), *Issues in second language acquisition: multiple perspectives*. New York: Newbury House.

Long, M. and Larsen-Freeman, D. (1991) *An introduction to second language acquisition research*. Harlow: Longman.

Long, M. and Robinson, P. (1998) Focus on form: theory, research, and practice. In C. Doughty and J. Williams (eds), *Focus on form in classroom second language acquisition*. Cambridge: Cambridge University Press.

Lowerre, B. and Reddy, R. (1980) The HARPY speech understanding system. in W. Lea (ed.), *Trends in speech recognition*. Voice I/O Applications Conference Proceedings. Palo Alto, CA: AVIOS.

Lund., R. (1991) A comparison of second language listening and reading comprehension. *Modern Language Journal*, 75(2): 197–204.

Lynch, T. (1996) *Communication in the language classroom*. Oxford: Oxford University Press.

Lynch, T. (1997) Tracking learners' progress in one-way and two-way listening tasks. Paper presented at research SIG conference on listening skills, Cambridge, 1997.

MacWhinney, B. (1994) Implicit and explicit processes. *Studies in Second Language Acquisition*, 19: 277–81.

Mager, R. (1988) *Making instruction work*. Belmont, CA: Lake.

Mager, R. and Pipe, P. (1984) *Analyzing performance problems, or you really oughta wanna* (2nd edn). Belmont, CA: Lake.

Magiste, E., (1985) Development of intra- and interlingual inference in bilinguals. *Journal of Psycholinguistic Research*, 14: 137–54.

Mahoney, T. (1997) Scholarship as a career of learning through research and teaching. In R. Andre and P. Frost (eds), *Researchers hooked on teaching*. London: Sage.

Malinowski, B. (1923) The problem of meaning in primitive languages. In C. Ogden and I. Richards, *The meaning of meaning*. London: Routledge.

Mandler, J. and Johnson, N. (1977) Remembrance of things parsed: story structure and recall. *Cognitive Psychology*, 9: 111–51.

Marslen-Wilson, W. (1984) Function and process in spoken word recognition. In H. Bouma and D. Bouwhis (eds) *Attention and performance*, X. Hillsdale, NJ: Erlbaum.

Mason, A. (1994) By dint of: student and lecturer perceptions of lecture comprehension strategies in first-term graduate study. In J. Flowerdew (ed.), *Academic listening: research perspectives*. Cambridge: Cambridge University Press.

Massaro, D. (1994) Psychological aspects of speech perception. *Handbook of psycholinguistics*. New York: Academic Press.

Maynard, S. (1997) *Japanese communication: language and thought in context*. Honolulu: University of Hawaii Press.

McClelland, J. and Ellman, J. (1986) The TRACE model of speech perception. *Cognitive Psychology*, 18: 1–86.

McCornack, S. (1997) The generation of deceptive messages: laying the groundwork for a viable theory of interpersonal deception. In J. Greene (ed.), *Message production: advances in communication theory*. Mahwah, NJ: Lawrence Erlbaum Associates.

McGregor, G. (1986) Listening outside the participation framework In G. McGregor and R. White (eds), *The art of listening*. Kent: Croom Helm.

McLauglin, B. (1992) Myths and misconceptions about second language learning: what every teacher needs to unlearn. Educational practice report #5. University of California, Santa Cruz.

McLaughlin, R. (1987) *Theories of second language learning.* London: Arnold.

McNamara, T. (1998) *Measuring second language performance.* Harlow: Longman.

McNeill, Arthur (1998) *Multi-modal captioning and learning of vocabulary from a/v presentations.* Honolulu: SLRF.

Mendelsohn, D. (1998) Teaching listening. In W. Grabe (ed.), *Foundations of second language teaching. Annual review of applied linguistics*, 18. Cambridge: Cambridge University Press.

Mendelsohn, D. and Rubin. J. (1995) *A guide for the teaching of second language listening.* San Diego, CA: Dominie Press.

Mercer, N. (2000) *Words and minds.* London: Routledge.

Merrill, M.D. (1994) *Instructional design theory.* Englewood Cliffs, NJ: Educational Technology Publications.

Mitchell, R. and Myles, R. (1998) *Second language learning theories.* London: Arnold.

Morley, J. (1972) *Improving aural comprehension.* Ann Arbor, MI: University of Michigan Press.

Morley, J. (1984) *Listening and language learning in ESL: developing self-study activities for listening comprehension.* Orlando: HBJ.

Morton, J. (1969) Interaction of information in word recognition. *Psychological Review*, 76: 165–78.

Munby, J. (1978) *Communicative syllabus design.* Cambridge: Cambridge University Press.

Nattinger, J. and DeCarrico, J. (1992) *Lexical phrases and language teaching.* Oxford: Oxford University Press.

Nichols, M. (1995) *The lost art of listening: how learning to listen can improve relationships.* New York: Guilford Press.

Nissan, S., de Vincenzi, F. and Tang, K. (1996) *Analysis of factors affecting the difficulty of dialogue items in TOEFL listening comprehension* (TOEFL Research Report No. RR-95–37). Princeton, NJ: Educational Testing Service.

Nix, D. (1983) Links: a teaching approach to developmental progress in children's reading comprehension and meta-comprehension. In J. Fine, R. Freedle (eds), *Developmental issues in discourse.* Norwood, NJ: Ablex.

Norman, D. (1982) *Learning and memory.* San Francisco, CA: Freeman.

Nunan, D. (1999) *Second language teaching and learning.* Boston: Heinle & Heinle.

Nunan, D. and Miller, L. (eds) (1995) *New ways in teaching listening.* Alexandria, VA: TESOL, 1995.

Ochs, E. (1986) Introduction, in B. Schieffelin and E. Ochs (eds), *Language socialization across cultures.* Cambridge: Cambridge University Press.

Ohta, A. (2000) *Second language acquisition processes in the classroom.* Mahwah, NJ: Erlbaum.

Oller, J. (1987) Testing in a communicative curriculum, *Forum*, 25: 42–6.

Olsen, L. and Huckin, T. (1990) Point-driven understanding in engineering lecture comprehension. *English for Specific Purposes*, 9: 33–47.

O'Malley, J.M. and Chamot, A. (1990) *Learning strategies in second language acquisition.* Cambridge: Cambridge University Press.

O'Malley, J.M., Chamot, A. and Kupper, L. (1989) Listening comprehension strategies in second language acquisition. *Applied Linguistics*, 10(4): 418–37.

Owens, R. (1992) *Language development* (4th edn). Boston, MA: Allyn & Bacon.

Oxford, R. (1990) *Language-learning strategies: what every language teacher should know.* Boston, MA: Heinle & Heinle.

Oxford, R. (2001) *Applied linguistics in action: teaching and researching learning strategies.* Harlow: Longman.

Oxford, R. and Leaver, B. (1996) A synthesis of strategy instruction for language learners. In R. Oxford (ed.), Language-learning strategies around the world: cross-cultural perspectives (Technical Report 13). Department of Second Language Studies: University of Hawaii at Manoa.

Parker, K. and. Chaudron, C. (1987) The effects of linguistic simplification and elaborative modifications on L2 comprehension. *University of Hawaii Working Papers on ESL*, 6(2): 107–33.

Peters, A. and Boggs, S. (1986) Interactional routines as cultural influences on language acquisition. In B. Schieffelin and E. Ochs (eds), *Language socialization across cultures.* Cambridge: Cambridge University Press.

Pica, T. (1992) The textual outcomes of native speaker–non-native speaker negotiation: what do they reveal about second language learning? In C. Kramsch and S. McConnell-Ginet (eds), *Text and context: cross-disciplinary perspectives on language study.* Lexington, MA: D.C. Heath.

Pica, T. (1994) Research on negotiation: what does it reveal about second language learning conditions, processes, and outcomes. *Language Learning*, 44: 493–527.

Pica, T., Lincoln-Porter, F., Paninos, D. and Linnell, J. (1996) Language learners' interaction: How does it address the input, output and feedback needs of language learners? *TESOL Quarterly*, 31: 95–120.

Pica, T., Young, R. and Doughty, C. (1987) The impact of interaction on comprehension. *TESOL Quarterly*, 21: 737–58.

Pienemann, M. (1999) Language processing and second language development processes: processability theory. Amsterdam: Johns Benjamin.

Reiguth, C. (1987) Lesson blueprints based on elaboration theory of instruction. In C. Reiguth (ed.), *Instructional theories in action.* Hillsdale, NJ: Erlbaum.

Reiguth, C. and Stein, F. (1983) The elaboration theory of instruction. In C. Reiguth (ed.), *Instructional design: theories and models.* Hillsdale, NJ: Erlbaum.

Resnick, L. (1984) Comprehending and learning: implications for a cognitive theory of instruction. In H. Mandl (ed.), *Learning and comprehension of text.* Hillsdale, NJ: Lawrence Erlbaum.

Rhodes, S. (1987) A study of effective and ineffective listening dyads using the systems theory principle of entropy. *Journal of the International Listening Association*, 1: 32–53.

Richards, J. (1990) *The language-teaching matrix.* Oxford: Oxford University Press.

Riley, P. and Zoppis, C. (1985) The sound and video library. In P. Riley (ed.), *Discourse and learning.* Harlow: Longman.

Rinvolucri, M. (1981) Empathic listening. In *The Teaching of Listening comprehension.* London: The British Council.

Robbins, J. (1996) Between 'hello' and 'see you later': development strategies for interpersonal communication. PhD dissertation: Georgetown University. (UMI 9634593).

Roberts, C., Davies, E. and Jupp, T. (1992) *Language and discrimination: a study of communication in multiethnic workplaces.* Harlow: Longman.

Rodman, R. (1988) Linguistics and computer speech recognition. In L. Hyman and T. Li (eds), *Language, speech and mind.* London: Routledge.

Rogers, C.R. and Freiberg, H.J. (1994) *Freedom to learn* (3rd edn). Columbus, OH: Merrill/Macmillan.

Rosch, E. (1975) Cognitive representations of semantic categories. *Journal of Experimental Psychology*, 104: 192–233.

Ross, S. (1997a) Listener inference on a second language test. In Kasper and Kellerman (eds), *Advances in communication strategies research*. Harlow: Longman.

Ross. S. (1997b) Divergent frame orientations in oral interview discourse. In Young and He (eds) *Talking and testing: discourse approaches to oral proficiency assessment*. Amsterdam: John Benjamins.

Rost, M. (1987) The interaction of listener, text and task. PhD thesis, University of Lancaster.

Rost, M. (1990) *Listening in language learning*. Harlow: Longman.

Rost, M. (1991) *Listening in action*. New York: Prentice Hall.

Rost, M. (1994) *Introducing listening*. Harmondsworth: Penguin.

Rost, M. (1999) Developing listening tasks for language learning. *Odense Working Papers in Linguistics*, University of Odense, Denmark.

Rost, M. and Ross, S. (1991) Learner use of strategies in interaction: typology and teachability. *Language Learning*, 41: 235–73.

Rothkopf, E. (1970) The concept of mathemagenic behaviour. *Review of Educational Research*, 40: 325–36.

Rubin, R., Palmgreen, P. and Sypher, H. (eds) (1994) *Communication research measures: a sourcebook*. New York: Guilford Press.

Rubin, J. and Thompson, I. (1998) The communication process. In J. Rubin and I. Thompson (eds), *How to be a more successful language learner* (2nd edn). Boston, MA: Heinle & Heinle.

Ruesch, J. and Kees, W. (1969) *Nonverbal communication*. Berkeley, CA: University of California Press.

Rumelhart, D. and Norman, D. (1981) Analogical processes in learning. In J. Anderson (ed.), *Cognitive skills and their acquisition*. Hillsdale, NJ: Erlbaum.

Sajavaara, K., (1986) Transfer and second language speech-processing. In E. Kellerman and M. Sharwood Smith, *Crosslinguistic influence in second language acquisition*. New York: Pergamon.

Sarangi, S. (1994) Accounting for mismatches in intercultural selection interviews. *Multilingua*, 13(1/2): 16394.

Sarangi, S. and Roberts, C. (2001) Discoursal (mis)alignments in professional gate-keeping encounters. In C. Kramsch (ed.), *Language acquisition and language socialization: ecological perspectives*. London: Continuum.

Schacter, J. and Gass. S. (1996) *Second language classroom research: issues and opportunities*. Mahwah, NJ: Erlbaum.

Schank, R. (1982) Reminding and memory organization. In W. Lenhert, and M. Ringle (eds), *Strategies for natural language processing*. Hillsdale, NJ: Erlbaum.

Schank, R. (1986) What is AI anyway? *AI Magazine*, 8: 59–65.

Schank, R. (1991) Where's the AI? *AI Magazine*, 12: 38–48.

Schank, R. and Fano, A. (1995) Ongoing research projects at the Institute for the Learning Sciences. *Artificial Intelligence Review*, 9: 251–4.

Schmidt, R. (1990) The role of consciousness in second language learning. *Applied Linguistics*, 11: 129–58.

Schmidt, R. (1995a) *Attention and awareness in foreign language learning.* Honolulu: University of Hawaii Press.

Schmidt, R. (1995b) Consciousness and foreign language learning: a tutorial on the role of attention and awareness in learning. In R. Schmidt (ed.), *Attention and awareness in language learning.* Honolulu: University of Hawaii Press.

Schmidt-Rinehart, B. (1992) The effects of topics familiarity on the listening comprehension of university students of Spanish. PhD thesis, Ohio State University (DAI, 5305A, DIALOG, 01238288).

Schmidt-Rinehart, B. (1994) The effects of topic familiarity on second language listening comprehension. *Modern Language Journal*, 18: 179–89.

Schumann, J. (1978) Social and psychological factors in second language acquisition. In J. Richards, (ed.), *Understanding second and foreign langauge learning: issues and approaches.* Boston: Heinle & Heinle.

Scollon, R. and Scollon, S. (1995) *Intercultural communication: a discourse approach.* Oxford: Basil Blackwell.

Searle, J. (1969) *Speech acts: an essay on the philosophy of language.* Cambridge: Cambridge University Press.

Searle, J. (1975) A taxonomy of illocutionary acts. *Language and Society*, 5: 1–23.

Seliger, H. and Shohamy, E. (1989) *Second language research methods.* Oxford: Oxford University Press.

Shea, D. (1995) Perspective and production: structuring conversational participation across cultural borders. *Journal of Pragmatics*, 4(3): 357–89.

Sheerin, S. (1989) *Self-access.* Oxford: Oxford University Press.

Sheerin, S. (1997) An exploration of the relationship between self-access and independent learning. In P. Benson and P. Voller (eds), *Autonomy and independence in language learning.* Harlow: Longman.

Shiffrin, R. (1988) Attention. In R. Atkinson, G. Herrnstein, G. Liddzey and R. Luce (eds), *Stevens' handbook of experimental psychology* (2nd edn, Vol. 2). New York: Wiley.

Shohamy, E. and Inbar, O. (1991) Validation of listening comprehension tests: the effect of text and question type. *Language Testing*, 8(1): 23–40.

Singleton, D. (1995) A critical look at the critical period hypothesis in second language acquisition research. In D. Singleton and Z. Lengyel (eds), *The age factor in second language acquisition.* Clevedon: Multilingual Matters.

Skierso, A. (1998) Textbook selection and evaluation. In M. Celce-Murcia (ed.), *Teaching English as a second or foreign language.* Boston: Heinle & Heinle.

Slobin, D. (1985) Crosslinguistic evidence for the language-making capacity. In D. Slobin (ed.), *The crosslinguistic study of language acquisition* (2 vols). Hillsdale, NJ: Erlbaum.

Snow, C. (1994) Beginning from baby talk: twenty years of research on input and interaction. In C. Gallaway and B. Richards (eds), *Input and interaction in language acquisition.* Cambridge: Cambridge University Press.

Soaves, C. and Grosjean, F. (1984) Bilingual in a monolingual and bilingual speech mode: The effect on lexical access. *Memory and Cognition*, 12, 380–6.

Solorzano, H., Frazier, L., Kisslinger, E., Beglar, D. and Murray, N. (2001) *Contemporary Topics, 1, 2, 3* (2nd edn). White Plains, NY: Longman.

Sperber, D., and Wilson, D. (1986) *Relevance: communication and cognition.* Oxford: Basil Blackwell.

Spiro, R.J., Coulson, R.L., Feltovich, P.J. and Anderson, D. (1988). Cognitive flexibility theory: advanced knowledge acquisition in ill-structured domains. In V. Patel (ed.), *Proceedings of the 10th Annual Conference of the Cognitive Science Society*. Hillsdale, NJ: Erlbaum.

Spiro, R.J., Feltovich, P.J., Jacobson, M.J. and Coulson, R.L. (1992). Cognitive flexibility, constructivism and hypertext: random access instruction for advanced knowledge acquisition in ill-structured domains. In T. Duffy and D. Jonassen (eds), *Constructivism and the technology of instruction*. Hillsdale, NJ: Erlbaum.

Sproston, C. and Sutcliffe, G. (1990) *20 training workshops for listening skills*. Philadelphia, PA: Ashgate.

Steil, L., Barker, L. and Watson, K. (1983) *Effective listening*. Reading, MA: Addison-Wesley.

Stempleski, S. and Tomalin, B. (1990) *Video in action: Recipes for using video in language teaching*. New York: Prentice Hall.

Stone, D., Patton, B. and Heen, S. (1999) *Difficult conversations*. New York: Viking Penguin.

Sturtridge, G. (1997) Teaching and language learning in self-access centres: changing roles? P. Benson and P. Voller (eds), *Autonomy and independence in language learning*. Harlow: Longman.

Swain, M. (1995) Three functions of output in second language learning. In G. Cook and B. Seidlhofer (eds), *Principles and practice in applied linguistics*. Oxford: Oxford University Press.

Swain, M. (2000) The output hypothesis and beyond: mediating acquisition through collaborative dialogue. In J. Lantolf (ed.), *Sociocultural theory and second language learning*. Oxford: Oxford University Press.

Swain, M. and Lapkin, S. (1999) *Sociocultural theory and second language learning*. Oxford: Oxford University Press.

Swain, M. (1985) Communicative competence: Some roles of comprehensible input and comprehensible output in its development. In S. Gass and C. Madden, *Input in second language acquisition*. Boston: Newbury House.

Swales, J. (1990) *Genre analysis*. Cambridge: Cambridge University Press.

Szymanski, M. (1999) Re-engaging and dis-engaging talk in activity. *Language in Society*, 28: 1–23.

Tannen, D. (1984) The pragmatics of cross-cultural communication. *Applied Linguistics*, 5(3): 47–54.

Tannen, D. (1990) *You just don't understand*. New York: Ballantine Books.

Tatsuki, D. (1999) Motivating movies. Internet TESL Journal (November) *www.aitech.ac.jp/~iteslj/index.html*

Tauroza, S. and Allison, D. (1994) Expectation-driven understanding in information systems lecture comprehension. In J. Flowerdew (ed.), *Academic listening: research perspectives*. Cambridge: Cambridge University Press.

Thomas, J. (1995) *Meaning in interaction: an introduction to pragmatics*. Harlow: Longman.

Tomatis, A. (1991) *The conscious ear: my life of transformation through listening*. Barrytown, NY: Station Hill Press.

Tomlinson, B. (1998) *Materials development in language education*. Cambridge: Cambridge University Press.

Toulmin, S. (1987) *An introduction to reasoning* (2nd edn). New York: Macmillan.

Trabasso, T. and Magliano, J. (1996) Conscious understanding during comprehension. *Discourse Processes*, 21: 255–87.

Tsui, A. (1994) *English conversation*. Oxford: Oxford University Press.

Tyler, A. (1995) The co-construction of cross-cultural miscommunication: conflicts in perception, negotiation, and enhancement of participant role and status. *Studies in Second Language Acquisition*, 17: 129–52.

Underwood, M. (1989) *Teaching listening*. Harlow: Longman.

Ur, P. (1984) *Teaching listening comprehension*. Cambridge: Cambridge University Press.

Ury, W. (1991) *Getting past no*. New York: Bantam Books.

Valett, R. (1977) *Humanistic education*. St Louis, MO: Mosby.

van Ek, J.A. (1973) The 'threshold level' in a unit/credit system. In *Development in adult language learning*. Strasbourg: Council of Europe.

Vandergrift, L. (1996) The listening comprehension strategies of core French high school students. *Canadian Modern Language Review*, 52: 200–23.

Vandergrift, L. (1998) Successful and less successful listeners in French: what are the differences? In *French Review*, 71(3).

Vandergrift, L. (1999) Facilitating second language listening comprehension: acquiring successful strategies. *ELT Journal*, 53(4): 73–8.

van Lier, L. (1995) *Introducing language awareness*. Harmondsworth: Penguin.

van Patten, B. (1990) Attending to form and content in input: an experiment in consciousness; *Studies in Second Language Acquisition*, 12: 287–301.

van Patten, B. (1996) *Input processing and grammar instruction in second language acquisition*. Norwood, NJ: Ablex.

Verschueren, J. (1999) *Understanding pragmatics*. London: Arnold.

Vogely, A. (1995) Perceived strategy use during performance on three authentic listening comprehension tasks. *Modern Language Journal*, 79(1): 41–56.

Volet, S. (1991) Modeling and coaching of relevant metacognitive strategies for enhancing university students' learning. *Learning and Interaction*, 1: 319–36.

Vygotsky, L. (1978) *Mind in society: the development of higher psychological processes*. Cambridge, MA: Harvard University Press.

Wallace, M. (1998) *Action research for language teachers*. Cambridge: Cambridge University Press.

Wanryb, R. (1990) *Grammar dictation*. Oxford: Oxford University Press.

Weir, C. (1993) *Understanding and designing language tests*. Harlow: Longman.

Weizenbaum, J. (1966) ELIZA- A computer program for the study of natural language. *Communication of the Association for Computing Machinery*, 9: 36–45.

Wells, G. (1981) Learning through interaction: the study of language development. Cambridge: Cambridge University Press.

Werker, J.F. (1991) The ontogeny of speech perception. In Mattingly, G. and Studdert-Kennedy, M. (eds.), *Modularity and the motor theory of speech perception*. Hillsdale, NJ: Erlbaum.

Wheeless, L. (1976) Self-disclosure and interpersonal solidarity. *Human Communication Research*, 3, 47–61.

White, G. (1998) *Listening*, Oxford: Oxford University Press.

Wilenski, R. (1981) Understanding goal-based stories. (Department of computer science research #140) New Haven: Yale University.

Wilmot, W. (1979) *Dyadic communication*. Reading, MA: Addison Wesley.

Wodak, R. (ed.) (1997) *Gender and discourse*. (Sage studies in discourse.) London (UK) & Thousand Oaks (CA): Sage.

Wodak, R. (1996) *Disorders of discourse*. London: Longman.

Wolvin, A. and Coakley, C. (1992) *Listening*, 4th edition. Dubuque: IA: Brown.

Wolvin, A. and Coakley, C. (eds) (1993) *Perspectives on Listening*. Norwood: Ablex.

Wong-Fillmore, L. (1991) Second language learning in children: a model of language learning in social context. In Bialystok, E. (ed.), *Language processing in bilingual children*. Cambridge: Cambridge University Press.

Yang, R.-L. (1993) A study of the communicative anxiety and self-esteem of Chinese students in relation to their oral and listening proficiency in English. Doctoral dissertation, University of Georgia, USA. Dissertation Abstracts International, 54. 2132A.

Yepes, J. (2001) Using analysis of retrospective interviews following a TOEFL listening task to refine a model of L2 listening comprehension. Paper presented at AAAL conference, St. Louis, USA.

Yule, G. and Powers, M. (1994) Investigating the communicative outcomes of task based interaction. *System*, 22, (1) 81–91.

Index

academic listening, 37, 38, 134, 162–3, 179, 233–5, 263
accent, 31, 76, 171, 260
accentuated input, 91 *see also* amplified input
accommodation (social) 89, 91, 134–6, 181
acculturation, 113
acoustic variability, 85
activation spaces in memory, 63 *see also* short-term memory
active information *see* short-term memory
active listening, 158, 267–9
activity frames, 216 *see also* participation frame
advance organizers, 164, 235, 238
Affective Filter Hypothesis, 108
affective involvement, 48
allophonic variations, 21
ambiguity, 66, 119, 129, 232 *see also* confusion
amplified input, 146
anaphoric reference, 65 *see also* reference
anchored instruction, 106–7
Andre, R. and Frost, P.
    on research, 201
anxiety, 48–9, 57, 99, 108, 178, 238, 272, 282
appreciative listening, 158 *see also* listening styles
aptitude specific instruction, 105
assessment, 144, 161, 169–90, 228–9, 234–5, 262–3 *see also* tests
assimilation, 24–5, 89, 96, 119, 124
attention
    as part of consciousness, 12–16
    in perception, 17–35
    as focus of active memory, 70
    in L1 development, 84–8
    in L2 development, 90–2
    in input processing, 97–8
    in learner training, 111–13

audition, 7–10
Ausubel, D.
    on strategies, 111
authenticity, 123–5 *see also* materials for teaching listening
automatized processes, 110
autonomous learning, 165 *See also* self-access
awareness, *see* attention, consciousness

backchanneling, 52–4, 125, 209, 217, 227
background knowledge, 45, 48, 64, 72, 95, 110, 131, 163, 174–8, 213, 224, 232, 245 *see also* memory, schema
Baddeley, A.
    on memory, 20
Bartlett, C.
    on constructive memory, 64
BBC, 257
Beebe, L.
    on input, 123
Behind the News, 257
benchmarking, 57, 228
Benson, M.
    on academic listening, 163
Benson, P.
    on self-access, 165, 166
Berwick, R. and Ross, S.
    on accommodation, 180
bilingualism, 94–6
Bisanz, G. et al.
    on new information, 66
bottom-up processing, 96, 221, 264
Bremer, K. et al.
    on discourse modifications, 132
    on understanding, 217, 227
    on learnig to listen, 233
bridging inferences, 67 *see also* inferences